A PLUME BOOK

RUSH

TODD G. BUCHHOLZ is an internationally accl...
NPR, PBS, the BBC, and other major networ...
Times, *Wall Street Journal*, and *Washington*...
nomic policy at the White House and a manag........ ...e legendary Tiger investment fund. Buchholz holds advanced degrees from Cambridge University and Harvard
Law School, served as a Fellow at Cambridge, and was awarded the Allyn Young Teaching Prize by Harvard University's Department of Economics.

Praise for *Rush*

"I found myself nodding so hard as I read all this, full of awe at the bravery of extolling
these virtues of capitalism, that I almost cricked my neck." —*Financial Times*

"In his amusingly over-caffeinated book, Buchholz sprints back and forth from Socrates
to Sudoku, Chris Rock to Rousseau. He assembles anecdotes and psychological case
studies to back his point that what we really need and want is to keep our neurons
firing. . . . Buchholz can be a rip-roaring companion." —*New York Post*

"Wicked smart."
—Neil Cavuto, host of FOX's *Your World* and author of *Your Money or Your Life*

"Offers a valuable corrective to many accounts of zero- and negative-sum games."
—Tyler Cowen, author of *Create Your Own Economy*

"*Rush* breaks new ground in explaining the competitive and neuroscientific drives that
underlie our civilization. It is loaded with powerful insights and penetrating ideas. If
you want to better understand how our past will shape our future, read this book."
—Dr. James Canton, author of *The Extreme Future*

"A brilliant synthesis of economic and neurobiological forces, put together into a
witty and persuasive story of why human beings can't stop rushing around to improve
their lives."
—Dr. Denis Burdakov, laboratory director,
Cambridge Neuroscience, Cambridge University

"Buchholz projects a communicable affection for the loud business of life, of risk-taking
and devoted engagement in the pursuit of happiness." —*Kirkus Reviews*

"*Rush* is an outstanding business book, but it should inspire us on many levels."
—*Huntington News*

"Buchholz is a formidable opponent. He writes with flair. He argues with good humor
and intellectual depth." —*Seattle Post Intelligencer*

Also by Todd G. Buchholz

NONFICTION

New Ideas from Dead Economists

New Ideas from Dead CEOs

Lasting Lessons from the Corner Office

From Here to Economy

Market Shock

Bringing the Jobs Home

FICTION

The Castro Gene

RUSH

Why We Thrive in the Rat Race

Todd G. Buchholz

A PLUME BOOK

PLUME
Published by the Penguin Group
Penguin Group (USA) Inc., 375 Hudson Street, New York, New York 10014, U.S.A. • Penguin Group (Canada), 90 Eglinton Avenue East, Suite 700, Toronto, Ontario, Canada M4P 2Y3 (a division of Pearson Penguin Canada Inc.) • Penguin Books Ltd., 80 Strand, London WC2R 0RL, England • Penguin Ireland, 25 St. Stephen's Green, Dublin 2, Ireland (a division of Penguin Books Ltd.) • Penguin Group (Australia), 250 Camberwell Road, Camberwell, Victoria 3124, Australia (a division of Pearson Australia Group Pty. Ltd.) • Penguin Books India Pvt. Ltd., 11 Community Centre, Panchsheel Park, New Delhi – 110 017, India • Penguin Group (NZ), 67 Apollo Drive, Rosedale, Auckland 0632, New Zealand (a division of Pearson New Zealand Ltd.) • Penguin Books (South Africa) (Pty.) Ltd., 24 Sturdee Avenue, Rosebank, Johannesburg 2196, South Africa

Penguin Books Ltd., Registered Offices: 80 Strand, London WC2R 0RL, England

Published by Plume, a member of Penguin Group (USA) Inc. Previously published in a Hudson Street Press edition.

First Plume Printing, August 2012

10 9 8 7 6 5 4 3 2 1

Ⓟ REGISTERED TRADEMARK—MARCA REGISTRADA

The Library of Congress has catalogued the Hudson Street Press edition as follows:
Buchholz, Todd G.
    Rush : why you need and love the rat race / Todd G. Buchholz.
        p.   cm.
    Includes bibliographical references and index.
    ISBN 978-1-59463-077-4 (hc.)
    ISBN 978-0-452-29795-1 (pbk.)
    1. Competition—Social aspects.   2. Movement, Psychology of.   3. Happiness.   I. Title.
    HD41.B83   2011
    650.1—dc22   2010047028

Printed in the United States of America
Original hardcover design by Catherine Leonardo

PUBLISHER'S NOTE
While the author has made every effort to provide accurate telephone numbers and Internet addresses at the time of publication, neither the publisher nor the author assumes any responsibility for errors, or for changes that occur after publication. Further, the publisher does not have any control over and does not assume any responsibility for author or third-party websites or their content.

BOOKS ARE AVAILABLE AT QUANTITY DISCOUNTS WHEN USED TO PROMOTE PRODUCTS OR SERVICES. FOR INFORMATION PLEASE WRITE TO PREMIUM MARKETING DIVISION, PENGUIN GROUP (USA) INC., 375 HUDSON STREET, NEW YORK, NEW YORK 10014.

To my ancestors, who managed to avoid getting eaten by saber-toothed tigers, trampled by woolly mammoths, or lost at shipping docks in the 1800s on their way to America.

CONTENTS

PREFACE

"I Made a Mistake"

This is not the book you were supposed to read. I changed my mind. Several years ago I began to write a book about happiness and the economy. It was to be called *Tail Hunters: How Americans Are Chasing Success and Losing Their Souls.* I was distressed to see so many people racing after money, paying plastic surgeons to redo their faces, and goading their children to kick soccer goals every Saturday morning. They all were chasing the "tail end" of the bell curve. Everyone wanted to be richer, skinnier, and, well, more outstanding. Of course, not everyone can reach the tail. In my career as a White House adviser, hedge fund manager, and economics teacher at Harvard, I've had plenty of dinners with billionaires and bon vivants whose faces were so stretched by plastic surgery they looked like they were reentering the earth's atmosphere. But most of us are stuck in the middle of the bulging bell curve and can't climb out. I was convinced that bad parenting and misleading media images tricked people into wasting their lives pursuing a tiny sliver of possibility. I wasn't alone in this view. Bookstore shelves are nearly collapsing under the "tsk-tsks" of philosophers, psychologists, political scientists, and economists sounding a similar alarm. Happiness studies have "proved" that even a strong economy makes us miserable. The financial meltdowns of 2008 and 2009 spilled enough red ink that I could have written that scolding book in bold-faced, bloodred letters.

But I was wrong. Those jeremiads condemning us for rushing around and competing too much are too easy to spout and too shallow to hold water. There is no proof that cutting out the frenzy would make us happier. The claims reflect an enduring yearning to return to Eden. Now, Eden was apparently a sunny, peaceful place, and the very name means pleasure. But there's no going back. We have no map, no entry ticket, and no idea how to behave in a garden of bliss.

I took the tail-hunting idea and began to spin it around like a Rubik's Cube, researching and thinking about Adam Smith, Michelangelo, Darwin, Freud, the history of civilizations, the history of art, and the behavior of modern economies. How does happiness really fit into the economy? What would happen to the economy if we took happiness studies seriously? I began to tear apart my old book manuscript and develop a new and controversial idea: that happiness comes from the rushing around. We feel better chasing the tails, even if we never catch them. The hunt makes us happier. I began to write at a furious pace, feeling that I was knocking down false prophets who speak from pulpits, classrooms, and yoga mats and make their followers feel guilty about trying to eke out some success in a chaotic world.

Along the way, a close friend became annoyed with me because I was more limber than she. She was taking a yoga class and explained that she was frustrated. She was struggling, trying to balance her body in the Crow Pose (bakasana). I hopped onto the floor. "You mean this?" I asked, putting my palms down on the floor in front of me, resting my elbows on my knees, and raising my head and feet off the floor. "Yes," she sneered, stamping her toe-ringed foot. "How did *you*? This is ridiculous. You know nothing about yoga!" she shouted indignantly. It was true. I had simply learned to do this in third-grade gym class and never forgot.

But it made me think. Then I turned indignant. Why was she mad at *me*? Since when is yoga about keeping up with the Joneses and trying to out-Zen your neighbor?

Then I saw it. I was almost finished writing this book when the *New York Times* featured a story about yoga. But this was not your old yogi's yoga. It was avowedly competitive yoga. Men and women in Lululemon tights trying to prove that they are the most limber in the room. Who could tuck their heads under their butts and lower their blood pressure furthest? It reminded me of a news report about meditating yogis trying to levitate themselves and sail over a stack of gym mats. In fact, the yogis merely hopped. Grimacing. Who knows how many tubes of Bengay they squeezed out afterward to salve their aching muscles.

What does this tell us? That the spirit of competition and the rush of life is mighty. It is integral to our beings. Blame it on evolution, blame it on God, blame it on Dan Brown and *The Da Vinci Code* conspiracy. But the twisted strands of DNA that make us human cannot be unfurled and examined without finding competition. And the happiness we seek cannot be found if we foolishly try to run away from who we are.

WHERE THE WILD THINGS ARE

Fasten your seat belts; this is going to be a bumpy ride into unknown territory. Medieval maps marked such terrain with stark and arresting warnings: "Here Be Dragons." The mapmakers worried that beyond England and Spain awaited beasts from hell. This isn't a journey to hell, but many of the places we end up are going to seem pretty unlikely. To follow the story of competition and the human race for happiness, we will delve into our Darwinian past, the people of the Stone Age, and foragers in South America today. We must also don pith helmets and

explore the history of the world economy to see how agricultural villages turned to trade, then turned to industry, and then to the technological revolution that ignites diodes across the planet today. Many
people condemn our fast-paced lives for creating a dog-eat-dog world.
But that ignores thousands of years of human history. Just think about
life expectancy. As recently as 1900, Americans could expect to live only
to age forty-seven. In the laid-back days of Native Americans before the
settlers trampled, perhaps thirty. Today, despite the grumblings and
stress of office buildings, credit card debt, and crowded schools, life
expectancy in the developed world is closing in on eighty. It will go
higher. Could it be that competition extends life?

To make the connection between competition and happiness, we
will deploy fMRI and PET scanners so we can uncover the secrets that
lie behind our frontal lobes and our reptilian brains. We will look at
Darwin's notes and see how the unavoidable race among species helps
shape the economy. We will look at the workplace and the home and
find all sorts of surprises: Stress is good for you; retiring makes you
stupid; and the hardest-working people are not the downtrodden, but
those who can afford more vacations.

Come along, you don't have time to waste.

PART 1

THE RUSH OF LIFE
Our Brains, Our Bodies, Our Economy

CHAPTER 1

Bye-Bye, Eden, Forever

What's the Big Idea?
We compete to survive and feel better about
ourselves.

I was a young man living in Manhattan, earning a big salary and eating at restaurants most nights. Though I had just married and was happy with my bride and my social life, work was miserable. It was boring. Merger documents and dry economic analyses. And there was not enough work to keep me busy. I felt like the old ladies in the oxymoronic Catskill joke who complain, "The food is terrible, inedible—and the portions are so small!" So I took a huge pay cut and joined the public sector. Well, that last sentence was honest but misleading. I took a pay cut and took a job at the White House as an economic adviser to the president of the United States. We moved to Washington, D.C., and I was thrilled to have one of those White House offices that lobbyists would line up to visit. Since third grade I had dreamed of working in the White House. I started on a Monday, and by the following Monday afternoon I felt depressed. Why? Because at the Monday-morning staff meeting I learned that many of my colleagues had been in their offices over the weekend. But my boss had not called me to ask me to work on Saturday or Sunday. Now, I am not a compulsive fiend who needs to work seven days a week. Nonetheless, I *wanted* my weekend imposed upon. I wanted to be wanted. My happiness was not going to be a function of my White House salary; my happiness was going to be a function of how much respect and self-respect I would gain. This was not about bank accounts, shopping binges, or even power. This was about waking up in the morning and trying to contribute, to create, and to possibly receive that coveted "atta boy." All the rest was dross. Well, a few weeks passed, and I soon found myself in the office on weekends. Just what I wanted. Oh, you should know, I didn't get overtime, only the psychic compensation that human beings have craved for ten thousand years.

I found happiness in a job, in a mission, in a situation where I had to shoulder some responsibility. I'm afraid, though, that it has become fashionable to look down on such things, to sneer at job seekers and job doers as unthinking rodents trapped in a rat race. A trunk load of books will tell you that happiness is found away from the job and away from any stress. Here's the enlightened recipe: Retreat, withdraw, and exhale while chanting mantras. Henry David Thoreau set the example by stomping his way into the woods at Walden Pond.

No doubt, the quest for bliss has launched a big industry. Journals and articles have been dumped on the public, all devoted to helping us find happiness. Statistical studies compare happiness across the globe, from Inuit communities chewing on blubber to monks living in cells in Tibet to bottle-nosed dolphins penned up in SeaWorld. A *Journal of Happiness Studies* compiles empirical and philosophical research, while one happiness "authority" bills himself as the "Indiana Jones of happiness." Charismatic crazies lead perfectly normal people to die in sweat lodges. Popular yoga and meditation classes introduce physical contortion and deep breathing. Of course, it would be easy to mock the happiness gurus and their followers, who devote so much of their time and money trying to avoid desperation. Thoreau famously wrote that most of us lead lives of "quiet desperation." In fact, I think Thoreau was wrong. Most people can find enough happiness to avoid drugs and avoid wasting their days in a vicarious world, watching washed-up "stars" on reality television. But it is not easy. And it has little to do with the popular nostrums tossed about by happiness gurus.

In this book I will argue that much of the common happiness advice is feckless, and sometimes dangerous. It starts with harmless prescriptions like meditation for adults and timeouts for children. If fifteen minutes of meditation is good, thirty minutes must be better. Sitting cross-legged in a room trying to lose one's sense of self strikes me as a reckless state of mind, if you give a darn about other people. The Buddha (who does share much good advice) did in fact abandon his wife and child in order to go on a quest to find himself. That's hardly a heroic example. Buddhist male-only monasteries may reflect a high pursuit of spirituality, but unless you are ready to trade in your car for an orange-colored monk's robe, you will have to grapple with the complex world we actually happen to live in, packed with stress, hatred, love, affection, traffic, caffeine, and cotton candy. I happen to think we are better people for facing this world head-on than chasing after a monastic Shangri-la.

THE NEW ORIGINAL SIN: CAPITALISM

In my view, during the twentieth century capitalism became the new original sin. Just as original sin expels human beings from Eden, capitalism becomes the new sin that prevents us from returning to Eden. If we could just expunge the drive to compete, and the desire to acquire, we could finally claw our way back to that noble, leafy, and peaceful place we left behind in Genesis, where we never wanted anything, let alone tried to get it. I will call such believers *Edenists*. (Note that even atheists can adopt an Edenist mind-set).

When happiness gurus get on a roll, they take individual advice and extend it to all of society: Not only should you take a timeout, but the entire economy should be given a timeout, or the economic equivalent of Ambien. Shut down capitalism and replace it with a kibbutz for three hundred million people. Why? To prevent envy and to drain our competitive juices. The happiness gurus believe that competition is cancerous, eating away at our souls and our chances for happiness. If we could just stomp out competition, we could achieve self-realization and bliss. Rather than relying on policy non sequiturs to achieve happiness, we would be better off dressing up like Druids and prancing around the rocks of Stonehenge hoping that it will help us pay our mortgage bills. (Yes, such tours are available.)

In fact, if you would like to visit an ancient economy stuck in Stone Age splendor, plan a trip to Bhutan. This little nation, with a per capita GDP about equal to the summer take-home pay of a kid's lemonade stand in Des Moines ($1,400), is tucked in the Himalayas and has swallowed almost all the happiness potions. The king has forsworn gross national product, and instead requires his country to pursue "gross national happiness." The king banned Coke and Pepsi (so smugglers sneak in the contraband). There is a national uniform for professionals, most buildings look the same, and "tourists are taken to all the same places and served the same food," wrote one visitor, who couldn't find Starbucks or espresso but did discover a valuable cache of Nescafe instant packets. Bhutan also mandates Buddhism as a state religion, so no one can be envious of anyone else's creed. It appears that gross national happiness requires a lot of uniformity and government control in order to beat out the urge to compete.

I admit that now is not a popular time to link happiness with competition. I understand the rage in Western countries against the failings of modern life, especially following the financial market meltdowns of 2008 and 2009. Didn't hypercompetitive bankers lead to the ruin of Lehman Brothers and Bear Stearns? Didn't supercompetitive brokers baying for bucks in trading rooms nearly bankrupt the world? Didn't reckless oil drillers lead to a devastating spill in 2010? So why not join the globalization protestors and hurl rocks into plate-glass windows at Starbucks? Maybe that will bring us joy. After all, as the financial markets thrash us and threaten our jobs, we are tempted to give up on modern life. So long to 401(k)s, ski vacations, and bucking for that salary hike that I wasn't going to get anyway. I sometimes wonder if Sarah Palin boasts of her gun skills because she worries that the only industries left in America will be hunting and gathering.

No doubt, amid the financial wreckage, we all felt cheated, by the CEO crooks, the mortgage broker morons, and the short sellers. And we feel a natural yearning to go back to simpler times, to some Eden that exists in our Jungian memory. Maybe throwing rocks will remind us of how jolly we were during the Stone Age.

But "Kumbayah" does not work. Sitting around a metaphoric campfire, holding hands and singing communal songs does not make human beings happy. Sweaty, yes. Sooty, perhaps. But not happy.

More tourists have trampled on Thoreau's Walden Pond snapping photos than have seriously considered giving up their cell phones to pick berries. We are delighted to try pomegranate juice—in the hope of finding the secret to clear skin and lower blood pressure—but virtually no American will plant his own bush and give up television. We may embrace symbols of a more homemade life, but these are tokens of wishful thinking, not titanic changes of substance.

Are we just selfish hypocrites who have fallen too deeply in love with a synthetic commercial world, with all its gadgets and traffic? Happiness books typically implore us to surrender our raw capitalistic drives, to levy taxes on high earners, and to derail the rat race before the entire world turns into a human-size Habitrail, plastic and pointless. And speaking of a Habitrail, these Edenists claim we are spinning on what has become known as the hedonic treadmill, so that the more we have the more we want. Typical advice: "Don't worry, be frugal." Or reach for the Prozac.

In this book, I will take on a seemingly preposterous task, employing the latest research in neuroscience and behavioral economics to argue the opposite: It is the race itself—sloppy, risky, and tense—that can bring us happiness. It is the very pursuit of love, new knowledge, wealth, and status that literally delivers the rush, lights up our brains, releases dopamine, and ignites our passion. Furthermore, I'm going to argue that the cause and effect between competition and happiness is hardwired into every one of us. Some of the results will surprise you. Competition makes people more fair, and it also makes them taller.

Neuroscientists report that when a person begins to take a risk, whether it's gambling or ginning up the nerve to ask a pretty girl to the prom, his left prefrontal cortex lights up, signaling a natural high. Alpha waves and oxygenated blood surge to the brain. Sitting alone in a pup tent does not yield the same effects. Likewise, our competitive juices cannot be separated from our desire to learn more. Ironically, those who deride competition are often the first to exalt education. They seem to have images of Plato sitting on a log. I exalt education, too, but it is foolish to pretend that desires do not press us forward to learn more, to *gain* more knowledge, and therefore to get smarter. The contented do not grow smarter, they grow moss.

WE DID NOT INHERIT THE GIFT OF GLEE

We shall see that despite Jungian memories of Eden perhaps embedded in our psyches, our evolutionary ancestors did not bestow on us the gift of glee. Glee does not come easily or naturally. Any early *Homo sapiens* who sat in the cave with a silly smile on their faces probably turned out to be lunch for a bear, or for one of its forebears. An old Latin phrase describes man's struggle, *homo homini lupus*, "man is wolf to man." But this is too harsh a judgment on wolves. Wolves do cooperate, in nursing their young and in chasing down an elk. But don't forget: they cooperate *because* they are engaged in a competition against nature. Wolves are not taught that they once lived in Eden. They don't get nostalgic. But they have evolved and developed cooperative mechanisms because they know that the alternative is starvation. Likewise, early man was often running away from some predator, whether beasts, fellow men, or the predatory wallop of blizzards, monsoons, and famine. A competition against predators and an unforgiving planet forced us to cooperate. Competition begat cooperation. Competition is the root of our success, not an anchor dragging us into misery.

Our history is struggle—and so is our future. Now, given this bleak, non-Edenic picture, why would anyone think we would be programmed for happiness and naturally designed or fit for anything but competition? Why would anyone think that sitting in the tent and returning to "nature" would help us find our "true selves" and that this true self would be happy and, well, selfless? Our true self showed up on Earth naked, exposed, hungry, and scheming to make it through a chilly night. Buddhists may tell us to stop struggling, but that is only a good choice if you've got servants to tuck you in a blanket and feed you. "Back to nature" and "back to our true self" has nothing at all to do with peace and paradise. Edenists are trying to crawl back down an evolutionary DNA ladder that never existed.

I am not saying that we are nothing but selfish brutes. True, we have selfish drives, but they do not always dominate, especially when we relate to our children or close family members. Here the hardwiring takes over again. Biology endows us with a nepotistic streak and sometimes an altruistic streak for a reason. Remember the last time you were on an airplane and heard the flight attendant read by rote the required safety notice instructing parents to "first put an oxygen mask on yourself before placing it on your child"? Why did the FAA require this announcement? Because parents would have a protective impulse to first take care of their children. The FAA is trying to block nature's unselfish pathway in the brain. Still, it is impossible to imagine a society where people treat each other as selflessly as they may treat their own children.

STOP APOLOGIZING: LIFE IS NOT AN AA MEETING

You will come no closer to a blithe spirit by apologizing for your complex and contradictory human drives. Life is not an AA meeting where we must confront and confess. Socrates said the unexamined life is not worth living. True, I suppose. *But the overexamined life is not worth living, either.* Neuroscience shows that we make a dreadful mistake when we try to deny our emotional drives in the pursuit of a more pure, objective rationality. I will reveal studies demonstrating that we need our emotional selves, even our selfish and scheming selves, in order to function. We will see that investors perform best not when they shield themselves from emotion, but when they recognize their emotional biases and fears. Victims of brain injuries who lose their ability to feel pity and love cannot decide what to eat for lunch or why they should report for work—even when the cold, rational part of their brains remains vibrant. I recently gave a talk to clients of U.S. Trust, a division of Bank of America. I used an analogy to *Star Trek*. Mr. Spock represents pure reason. He can calculate pi to the millionth decimal place. Captain Kirk is human in every way, inclined to bang his fist on the arm of the command chair, fall in love with a shapely lieutenant, but he is also capable of tough decisions. Which character would you want serving as captain? Which character would you want serving on the Supreme Court? Which character would you want managing your portfolio? Would Mr. Spock have been so bedazzled by the brilliance of the iPhone that he would have bought shares of Apple at one-tenth of their current price? Now, I am not saying that you should invest based on whether your eyes well up with tears at a new advertising campaign, but I am going to prove to you that our best chance of success and happiness in life comes when we respect, not disdain, our better *and* our worse natures.

BLIND FAITH IN THE NOBLE SAVAGE

Nothing makes a happiness guru sadder than seeing someone pull into Walmart in a big SUV and buy a big flat-screen television. Why? Because the height of true happiness, or "authentic happiness," as the psychologist Martin Seligman calls it, is achieved when someone is self-motivated to pursue wholesome activities in order to fulfill his natural gifts. Hard to argue with that goal. It is an excellent prescription for a "good person," though it might not match most people's recipe for a happy person. In contrast, individuals driving SUVs to Walmart to pick up a big hunk of electronics look as if they are showing off, wasting resources, and getting ready to sit on their rear ends watching someone else run around on a screen. What should they do, according to the happiness teachers? Smash the TV, ditch the SUV, and stop buying from big conglomerates. They should pursue a more "natural" life, unspoiled by modern fancies and factories.

This might sound like a politically correct view that emerged among intellectuals sometime in the 1960s. A British economist actually titled an article "The Hippies Were Right All Along About Happiness." But the longing for Eden goes back, well, you would have to ask Adam himself. Intellectuals since Jean-Jacques Rousseau in the 1700s have been harping on the inner goodness that we allow society to spoil. Whereas more than a century earlier Thomas Hobbes had proclaimed that before society, life was "nasty, poor, brutish and short," Rousseau countered that "man is born free, but everywhere we see him in chains." He popularized the notion of the noble savage, the man unspoiled by civilization's greed and garishness, and declared that there is "no perversity in the human heart." Rousseau and his followers imagine men pure of heart swinging from trees and loping with leopards in Africa. In 1912, Edgar Rice Burroughs concocted Tarzan, who appears to possess a soul superior to that of his Victorian visitors. Contrast Tarzan with the ultra-civilized, urban socialite Dorian Gray, who in Oscar Wilde's haunting 1890 story sells his soul just to maintain his superficial youth. Kevin Costner's overly long 1990 movie, *Dances with Wolves*, conveys the same spirit. In the movie, even a white man is able to return to Eden and get along well with fang-bearing predators. But when it comes to noble savage themes, I prefer *George of the Jungle*. In the 1997 comic movie, apes can talk, and when guileless, gorgeous George is asked his family name, he shrugs and says, "Primate. George Primate." Being a primate, associating oneself with apes and a more primitive being, seems far nobler than hobnobbing with socialites on San Francisco's Nob Hill, as he does later in the movie.

A COLLECTIVE MEMORY OF PARADISE?

But maybe this noble savage obsession is more than just nostalgia for something that never was. Perhaps there is something aboriginal about these yearnings for aboriginal life. Perhaps it is natural to long for an imaginary yesteryear. Jung would, of course, chalk it up to an archetype of our collective unconscious. The anthropologist Claude Levi-Strauss found common tales among far-off peoples, mapping out, for example, numerous parallel myths about the birth of twins bringing about cosmic trouble, bad weather, and supernatural acts. Women in some tribes would avoid eating double-yolked chicken eggs for fear of giving birth to twins. In the twentieth century many a soap opera script rested on the sudden appearance of an "evil twin." Like the nearly universal fascination with twins, there appears a deep-rooted focus on a natural paradise.

Is it possible that we have embedded in our genes and brain function a kind of ancient memory or tropism toward the tropics? In his powerful book *The Blank Slate*, Steven Pinker points to surveys of art around the world demonstrating the universal appeal of landscapes, especially those that show panoramic views of meadows, flowers, and trees, which would signal to our brains fecund fields with places to hide from predators. This is, of course, conjecture. We cannot now know whether there is a congenital legacy, or whether pretty flowers just tickle our fancy because the sight of irises stimulates our irises. Moreover, there is danger in introducing Jung's fanciful memories, dreams, and reflections into science before they can be tested. Here is the danger: Flowery conjecture can easily be twisted into an ideology that blocks real scientific inquiry. As Pinker sets forth compellingly, a good part of the twentieth century was dominated by sociologists, psychologists, and anthropologists grafting their biases about noble savages onto their data and survey reports.

PEOPLE ARE NOT CHALKBOARDS

As a student, my first published article reviewed a startling new book that cracked an icon. The book was Derek Freeman's *Margaret Mead and Samoa: The Making and Unmaking of an Anthropological Myth*. Mead, a protégé of the leading anthropologist Franz Boas, had traveled to Samoa in the 1920s to investigate a simpler people, to see whether they avoided the manias and pathologies of modern life. Under the tutelage of Boas and Ruth Benedict, Mead believed that human beings were essentially "plastic," and that they could be shaped by society, by how they are nurtured, and that there was no fundamental human nature that would sneak through. Boas and Mead were in good company, and Boas's influence seemed to grow as the twentieth century wore on. The British scholar Ashley Montagu, another Boas protégé, argued that "Man is man because he has no instincts, because everything he is and has become he has learned, acquired, from his culture, from the man-made part of the environment, from other beings." Now here's the irony regarding Montagu, who died in 1999, a very famous scholar who made numerous appearances spouting his views on *The Tonight Show Starring Johnny Carson*. When his obituary appeared, many of his followers were shocked to discover that, just as he thought man's behavior was thoroughly invented, not natural, Montagu himself had thoroughly invented himself, trading in his ethnic name for a thoroughly British name and concocting a backstory of privilege. As a young man, he had changed his legal name to "Montague Francis Ashley Montagu," which sounds as if he had been nursed by Queen Victoria herself. Turns out he started life as Israel Ehrenberg, a real East Ender. Now, it would be wrong to suggest that Montagu's name change invalidates his work. No, it's his work that invalidates his work, including his claim that chimpanzees were pacifist vegans. And he was not the most glaring in his ideology. The Rousseau-Boas-Mead-Montagu view so captivated academics that it seemed nearly every drive and desire was simply a matter of training and advertising. Even the sex drive was alleged to be a result of clever marketing. A psychologist named Zing-Yang Kuo asserted that the human desire to have sex is merely manufactured by social images. Tell that to a fourteen-year-old boy.

Now back to Mead. She visits Samoa, spends much more time than you would if you were visiting on a Princess Cruise ship (*The Love Boat*), and then returns to the United States with some startling conclusions. Unlike Americans and Europeans, Samoans look after each other and do not exhibit jealousy. Unlike in our crass culture, they do not covet each other's beads or clay pots. And unlike our randy, relentlessly anxious teenagers, Samoan teens have casual sex, without guilt, without jealousy, and without catfights or gang rumbles at the gym. In other words, although Shakespeare resonates in London, Tokyo, and Berlin, somehow the Samoans would not understand the point of *Romeo and Juliet*, even if translated into everyday Samoan.

The problems here are many. First of all, Mead's turned out to be shoddy research. Aside from her inability to speak the language, Mead did not seem to think through the implications of her findings. Let's say that, indeed, humans were as pliable as Play-Doh, easily imprinted and shaped by whatever patterns it rubs against. Would a Play-Doh species survive the battle of evolution? More likely it would become slaves or dinner for another. Rousseau wrote that men are born free yet are everywhere in chains, but how could a Play-Doh species avoid the chains of domination by another species? Let's say that the drive to procreate and impulses to build shelter and gather food were all a matter of nurture and could be reversed, discouraged, or beaten out of human beings by any person or species holding a stronger opinion. In this vision, humans would not know to run away from thunder and lightning, to seek shelter in a storm, or to keep clear of lions, tigers, and bears. A pack of wolves or a clan of chimps could subdue them, subjugate them, and eat them.

Second, the "plasticized" view of mankind inspired megalomaniacs. That wasn't the underlying intention, and many of Mead's followers devoted their lives to trying to help people, even identifying themselves as "peace activists." Nonetheless, just as Wagner unwittingly gave Hitler the melody of the Holocaust, the Boas school gave Stalin a justification for trying to rewire the faulty neural circuiting of the Soviet people. Under the Boas approach, people are just waiting to be shaped. So why should an ambitious dictator like Stalin leave that shaping to chance? Better to mold the people as he sees fit and send them to whatever collectivist fields he feels like. No wonder Stalin called himself a "Constructor of Happiness." Even less monstrous megalomaniacs with artistic pretensions got into the act. George Bernard Shaw, identified as a Fabian socialist, was gung ho for eugenics and even considered gassing people who did not conform to his ways. This is the kind of thinking that led B. F. Skinner to rear his daughter in a box, and then try to tell the world it was a successful experiment!

Third, Mead's convictions reinforced the idea that all of human history was just a big mistake and that what we know as progress was actually retrogress. It also inspired a whole string of snide but sometimes witty quips, such as Gandhi's, who, when asked what he thought of Western civilization, responded, "It would be a good idea."

The noble savage tradition argues that nobility comes from nature and is quickly corroded by modern society. The tradition contends that honor, honesty, and an innocent love of human, animal, and plant life thrive only in those places beyond our colonialist maps. Western society, with its advertising, commercialism, and unstoppable adventurism, looks thoroughly corrupting. Yet all it takes is a little knowledge of history to see the blindness of romantics. I'm sure the Aztecs had a reason to tear beating hearts from the chests of young men strapped down for sacrifice, but they didn't do it because they were "at one with nature." The truth is that nobility does not descend from the jungle, the forests, the deserts, or anyplace else. Nobility comes from harnessing some innate human drives and then teaching people to behave better, and to appreciate the warm feeling in their hearts when they do. Later in this book, we will look at historical civilizations, as well as contemporary cultures that live as hunters and foragers, in order to see this.

EDENISTS AND THE GREAT NON SEQUITURS

I was shocked when I started reading about the Buddha when I was a young man and discovered he was not naïve and may not have been fat. To hear Buddhist therapists today, you would think that happiness comes from deep breathing, Zen-like trances, and being kind to bunny rabbits. It turns out that the Buddha understood less honorable human drives, too, and sometimes recommended we embrace those impulses. For example, any self-respecting Buddhist trying to reach a higher plane of existence today would shun materialism, and perhaps aspire to dress simply like the Tibetan monks who protest China's domination. But it turns out that the Buddha recommended men do more than meditate. They should marry. They should work. And then they should give their wives what? Solace? Succor? Back rubs? No. The Buddha told men to give their wives jewelry. He believed that women host an intrinsic desire for jewelry. It sounds rather sexist to me, but the point is that the impulse for materialism did not start when Macy's opened the world's largest department store in New York. The Buddha was more of a realist than so many of his fans in Western countries.

Happiness scholars love to denounce acquisitions, and such calumnies have a long tradition. We might admire religious leaders who take a vow of poverty because we realize how difficult that would be, perhaps as difficult as a vow of chastity. In the 1920s, R. H. Tawney wrote about the "Acquisitive Society." Thorstein Veblen and John Kenneth Galbraith published screeds on conspicuous consumption that became standard texts in economics courses. "Once a country has filled its larders, there is no point in that nation becoming richer," wrote a "happiness economist" a few years ago. The University of Warwick professor Andrew Oswald further argues that the hippies, "the road protesters, the down-shifters, the slow-food movement—all are having their quiet revenge . . . being confirmed by new statistical work by psychologists and economists."

Under the guise of "happiness," some prominent economists and psychologists argue for squeezing people with high taxes and strangling businesses deemed too successful. Daniel Gilbert summarized these findings in an academic paper, writing, "Windfalls are better than pratfalls, A's are better than C's, and everything is better than a Republican administration." A well-published behavioral economist opined that he doesn't see how "anybody could study happiness and not find himself leaning left politically." Why would happiness scholars urge governments to jack up taxes or exert tighter controls on private people? To stomp on the corrupting influence of competition. Another happiness psychologist urges "increas[ing] national control of labor relations." Huh? Should the president set the wages for the guy who cuts your hair? How about a national vote on next year's take-home pay? Is there any evidence that more "national control" of labor makes workers happier? Through the work of Mead, Galbraith, and their progeny, "experts" on happiness are now misunderstanding human drives, misdiagnosing psychological problems, and prescribing dangerous antidotes to perceived problems. Let me trace the argument.

First, psychologists and some economists bemoan the hedonic treadmill I alluded to earlier. Coined by Philip Brickman and Donald T. Campbell, this dangerous piece of exercise equipment conjures a striking image of consumers constantly trying to acquire material things, but never getting closer to the delight they seek. Even after hopping into the Jacuzzi or speeding down the freeway in a bright red Corvette, the consumer soon loses his enthusiasm and reverts to his prior mood. There is certainly evidence that buying things does not by itself make us happier. And if we buy with debt, we could find ourselves buried in bills and guilt. Brickman and Campbell produced the landmark 1971 study showing that lottery winners do not get a permanent high from their loot. Even Adam Smith, the father of economics, observed that while the desire for more food is restrained by a full belly, the desire for "precious metals and the precious stones, as well as for every other convenience and ornaments of dress, lodging, household furniture" seems without limit. Richard Easterlin surveyed Americans, asking how many goods and luxuries—home, car, television, swimming pool—they needed in order to live the "good life." Over the course of a sixteen-year survey, participants obtained more goods, but somehow they always stayed several items short of "enough." Enough is a moving target.

After depicting the hedonic treadmill, Edenists go on to array data seeming to show that earning more income does not make people any happier, and it is not just an American phenomenon (known as the Easterlin Paradox). Japanese incomes soared from the 1950s to 1980s, lifting the country from poverty to roaring prosperity. And yet it did not lift spirits. A measure of happiness did not budge, staying at 2.75 on a scale of 1 to 4 (a higher number being happier). Likewise, Mexicans are happier than the French, and wealthy San Franciscans are more dour than Chattanoogans.

Then the Edenists denounce the sin of envy. H. L. Mencken had quipped that a wealthy man was one who earned $100 more than his wife's sister's husband. Take this quiz. Would you rather earn $100,000 in an office where everyone gets paid $100,000, or $80,000 in an office where everyone earns $60,000? Most people choose the latter, preferring an advantage over their peers. For this they are condemned as moral dwarves. The Cornell economist Robert Frank devised a clever metaphor of trees in the forest. If each tree needs to be higher than the next, each tree ends up using more resources in order to peek above its neighbors. Why couldn't the trees just call a truce on the senseless competition?

But is this a fair way to characterize how people perceive their incomes and wealth, all a matter of not just keeping up with the Joneses but actually trying to beat them over the head? Does the data unequivocally show that a higher income does no good for happiness? The answers to these two questions are "no," and "not really." Surveys on happiness show that poor people are less likely to be happy than middle-class or rich people. Poor people have trouble affording lunch, health care, and homes free of burglars. Now, it may be true that earning $70,000 instead of $50,000 does not change happiness, but it is a groundless leap to say that $50,000 is no different from $15,000. Money does matter. And there is nothing noble in not having any, unless perhaps you are following the precepts of your church. As Tevye in *Fiddler on the Roof* says, "It's no shame to be poor—but it's no great honor either."

Nor would it be an honor to make everyone equal and everyone poor. The rock band called Rush recorded a song back in 1978 called "The Trees," which would preemptively rebut Robert Frank's metaphor. In the song, there's unrest in the forest, because the oaks want more sunlight and are leaving the maples in the shade. The maples cry "oppression" and form a union. Then the government passes a "noble law" to keep all the trees equal in height—by "hatchet, axe and saw." The moral: Chopping down competition can be dangerous and counterproductive work.

What of the assertion that we are engaged in a rat race simply to beat the Joneses to more stuff, like a furious scrum at Filene's Basement? This, too, fails. Whether we call it a rat race or not, most human beings are engaged in work. Once Adam and Eve left Eden, the apples stopped falling to our feet. We had to plant and reap. Or take the six a.m. train from Secaucus to Penn Station. We seek success in our work not so much to boast or clobber the Joneses into psychological submission. We seek success because it validates our lives, and gives us a feeling that we are worth loving, and that we were worth the love and effort our parents lavished on us. Yes, money is involved, but money is simply a convenient way for society to arrange economic relations, to avoid the clumsiness of a barter system. What about the embarrassing admission that we prefer to earn more than our colleagues? How can this be defended? We prefer to earn more than our colleagues at work not because we are nasty and want to be envied, but because that is a signal that we have earned our keep. If everyone were paid the same, if everyone lived in the same house, our minds would receive no signal that we are expending our energy in a prudent or productive way. The dollars, the baubles, and the bangles we gain from work spark an aboriginal sentiment that excites the vital juices that keep our hearts beating and the oxygen flowing to our brains. They signal to us that we will not be ground down to dust in the evolutionary cycle.

Furthermore, success is not always defined by money. Many talented people deliberately choose careers that do not yield bulging paychecks—for example, professors, ministers, chefs, and playwrights. Yet they may consider themselves enormously successful. If they feel successful, studies show that their happiness quotient will likely exceed that of someone who earns more money but considers himself unsuccessful. So what really is the connection between money, happiness, and the so-called hedonic treadmill? The truth is, most people have a deep need to work and to create. While this need can be quashed by bad habits and bad government policies, most people wake up in the morning and step onto a train, into a car, or even into their home office wearing fluffy bedroom slippers in order to *earn something*. At the end of the day, on the surface they may have earned dollars, euros, or wampum. But what they are really trying to earn is self-respect and the respect of others. Some will spend their monetary earnings on trinkets and useless electronics. Others will count their pennies and spend frugally. Regardless, our competitive drive is not ultimately about showing off to others. It is about showing ourselves that we deserve to live and then to live on through our progeny.

BOWLING WITH OTHERS

We should not be so quick to judge the trinkets of another. Robert Putnam, a Harvard political scientist, hit the best-seller list in 2000 with a depressing book called *Bowling Alone*. Putnam charted the decline in bowling leagues and other civic and social activities. His findings have been scrutinized, criticized, and amended—after all, the "soccer mom" and "soccer dad" phenomenon of the past twenty years brings parents and children together every weekend. Nonetheless, Putnam was onto something, for men today do report fewer friends than in prior eras. Between telecommuting, virtual offices, and lean manufacturing, the image of camaraderie on the assembly line has faded into a blurry 1960s ad for Pabst Blue Ribbon beer.

Nonetheless, I would not blame consumerism for splintering friendships and communities. I contend that certain consumer goods might actually help create more communal feelings. For example, American homes are 50 percent larger than they were in the 1970s. But this explosion in square footage does not mean that homes have

50 percent more bedrooms than they did in the 1970s. Instead, people desire larger kitchens and "great rooms." And what do they do in these larger common rooms? They commune with their families and their neighbors. Likewise, Edenists can sneer at ultra-size outdoor granite and stainless steel barbecue units, but what does the owner of this $2,000 barbecue do? He flips burgers and steaks for his family and his neighbors. Finally, Edenists can disdain sixty-five-inch flat-screen televisions. But doesn't this increase the odds that the owner will invite his buddies over to watch *Monday Night Football*, or that Grandma might come over to watch the finale of *American Idol*? The point is, our "acquisitive society" may be acquiring more than greed and more than envy.

After condemning envy, Edenists move on to argue that such vapid competition leads to inequality, which makes people sick, which then makes them unhappy. Or it makes them unhappy, which makes them sick. And what is the solution to all this waste, stress, and abuse? Once again, stomp on competition, regulate businesses and entrepreneurs, and tax people who earn more money than "they should." Baron Richard Layard, a British economist and the author of *Happiness: Lessons from a New Science*, seems to think we all would be better off psychologically if we erased some zeroes from salaries or bank accounts. After all, he says, "extra income has done so little to produce a happier society, there must be something quite wasteful about much of it." Although Layard's views are wrapped in "new science," they also reflect E. F. Schumacher's *Small Is Beautiful*, a book that millions of undergraduates had to read in the 1970s, until roughly the time President Jimmy Carter gave his fireside "malaise" speech in a cardigan sweater and looked so sad the fire went out. Schumacher, the world's first German-born, Buddhist-British economist, and the chief economist for the British Coal Board, argued for "enoughness," a Buddhist view that we should get by with far less. For Schumacher, modern society "requires so much and accomplishes so little." True, until you remember that in 1900 life expectancy was just forty-seven years and polio crippled millions of children.

In fact, small is not necessarily better or more blissful, and there is a difference between the simple life and the life of a simpleton. Let us take a quick look at the flaws in the Edenists, flaws that will be further uncovered in subsequent chapters. First, let me start by admitting I am no fan of conspicuous consumption. I think Rolex watches are too glitzy and I feel proud when my children complain that everybody else has a bigger television than we do. My brother recently asked whether I was still watching TV on that "microwave oven." Further, I would admit that some Americans may be breathlessly running on a hedonic treadmill. But that does not mean you will likely become happier by either trying to step off the treadmill or asking society to quash competitive urges—that is, throw the societal treadmill into a bonfire. Here are the problems lost on these social critics: (1) Any system involving human beings that lasts longer than a few years and involves more than a few people will be competitive; (2) We cannot go back to Eden, because even if Eden existed, human beings have evolved and are no longer suited for paradise; (3) The dastardly desire to acquire is not, in fact, chiefly driven by a crass materialism invented by snarky businessmen with manipulative advertising campaigns. Human beings do not get on the treadmill to pursue stuff; they get on the treadmill because work makes them feel better about themselves, and succeeding at work validates their lives and gives them a bigger chance of perpetuating their genes; and finally, (4) Without the competitive urges, most of you reading this book now would be dead.

These assertions are grounded in neuroscience, anthropology, and economics, and I will unpack and unfurl them in the chapters ahead. Since you are alive—meaning your ancestors managed to brave slings, arrows, and saber-toothed tigers—I invite you to brave the lances of the Edenists and go forward.

CHAPTER 2

What Is Competition? What Is Happiness?

What's the Big Idea? Happiness is about activity, not lolling about, and competition is about systems, not just individuals.

The phone rang in my office at the White House. Now, when you work in that place and the telephone rings, you're always hoping it will be monumental. Was it the president? Gorbachev? Alan Greenspan trying to refinance his mortgage? Not this time. It was a woman from the public liaison office asking whether I would give a speech to a group of visiting industry executives. "Who are they?" I asked. "The Anti-Friction League," she said. "Anti-friction? I'm not sure I'm against friction. Does the president have a policy on this?" It turned out to be the American association of ball bearing manufacturers. Now, in some manufactured products like machine tools, it's good to wipe out friction. But it would be bad to wipe out all friction in society. Though often denounced, friction (like competition) sometimes brings good things to life. The American Revolution and the emancipation of slaves came from friction. The Berlin Wall was sledge-hammered, sending sparks and dusty shrapnel everywhere. Freedom followed. All this from friction.

In everyday life, we see friction. We tend to think about friction as road rage, or an argument with our boss. But friction often emerges from creativity, too. The scientist who quits his job to start a new business. The saxophone player who ad-libs a dissonant riff and ignores the notes written on the treble clef. Friction is often good. Everyone has rough edges, and in intimate physical affairs, some of those edges feel good. Society cannot structure itself like a population of ball bearings, trying to remove all friction. Trying to grind down all friction and stomp on the moving agents in the world that rub up against each other would actually hurt society, not help it. When we examine what competition and happiness really are, we will see that they are interconnected. Happiness is not a peaceful, frictionless bliss. That would be mixing up happiness with dozing off to sleep.

WHAT IS COMPETITION? THE MICRO AND THE MACRO

Historically, competition has not trapped us on a rodent's wheel. It has liberated us both materially and psychologically. What do I mean by competition? I look at it from two dimensions: *micro* and *macro*. *Microcompetition* concerns an individual trying to get ahead, attempting to better himself and improve his lot in life. Picture the guy studying for his CPA exam, or putting in an extra hour at the office, or the saleswoman walking up to greet the customer, rather than waiting for the customer to saunter by. Sometimes people do look over their shoulders to see how they compare to others. There's no shame in peeking over the fence to see what the Joneses are up to, and there's no avoiding it, either. It is part of our biological survival mechanism. In modern economies, we tend to associate competition with amassing money. But microcompetition does not have to be about grabbing more money than everybody else. Yes, we often compete with others. But just as important, competing with ourselves to develop our athletic, musical, or intellectual talents calls on the same primal impulses. Even an exalted rock star–philanthropist like Bono presumably tries to write a better song each time he sits down at a keyboard with his pen. Microcompetition may also focus on an individual firm or business trying to gain profits or market share.

Macrocompetition concerns the larger economic system we live with, not just the individual participant. A free-enterprise system with private property and private profit spurs macrocompetition in obvious ways. But let's not kid ourselves, *all* systems arouse macrocompetition. They just have different methods of doing it. Even under Soviet communism, people competed to gain favor with leaders, to scrape up vouchers for food, and to nab an available apartment in Moscow. But the Soviet system wanted its citizens to feel guilt and shame for doing so. In Maoist China in the early 1980s, "no one talked about what they wanted to do. Students who were trying to enter graduate school overseas kept their plans to themselves, hiding college applications under their mattresses, scurrying to their mailboxes when none of their classmates were looking," writes John Pomfret, who attended college in Nanjing, the sole American in his class. "My classmates snooped on each other, read each other's diaries, feared and suspected one another— an expression of the deep mistrust they perfected during Cultural Revolution." They couldn't wait to outdo and undermine each other.

In contrast, a private-property, free-enterprise system overtly encourages individuals, firms, and structures to compete for time, money, prestige, and attention. When I speak of competition in this book, I will be referring to both the individual micro drives and to the macroeconomic-social system that encourages them.

Together, micro- and macrocompetition create a complex web. Let's take a familiar example. Open up virtually any magazine these days and you'll see pharmaceutical firms vying for erectile dysfunction dollars. Think about all the levels of competition wrapped up in this industry: Men who suffer from the ailment feel a biological and psychological need to regain their potency. Pfizer, Eli Lilly, and others have devoted billions of dollars to develop drugs to fight the problem. Now, these firms engage in widespread advertising campaigns to attract clients. You can see three levels of competition: (1) the men feeling primal urges to demonstrate their potency and spread their seed; (2) the firms and their scientists in laboratories racing to find better and better treatments; (3) the marketing campaigns to attract customers. Each level of competition is needed to produce the end result: millions of men with newfound self-esteem (and many minutes of embarrassing television advertising).

All levity aside, we can thank competition for inspiring new vaccines and extending human life. During the late 1980s, mortality from heart attacks plunged by several percentage points as new cardiac drugs came to market. I performed some of the research for this book while serving as a fellow at St. John's College, Cambridge, in a charming old office just a few blocks from the Eagle pub. This was the pub where, during World War II, Royal Air Force and Yankee pilots drank, bet, and bickered. This was the pub where Watson and Crick interrupted lunch one day in 1953 to announce they had found the "secret of life," the DNA double helix. They were not driven by a campfire, holding hands, or breathing through alternate nostrils. They were driven by beer, moxie, ego, and the competitive juices twisted up in their DNA.

In early 2010, a remarkable man named Arnall Patz died at age eighty-five. He wouldn't take no for an answer and saved thousands of babies from blindness. In the late 1940s, Patz was a young ophthalmology resident in a city hospital in Washington, D.C. He had just finished his service as an army doctor in the war. At the hospital and around the country, there seemed to be an epidemic of blindness among premature babies—over ten thousand cases (including a baby later known as Stevie Wonder). Patz suspected that the incubators were emitting too much pure oxygen for their developing eyes. His bureaucratic superiors thought he was crazy. He applied to the NIH for a study grant and the experts there turned down his "wild idea." Patz could not sit still or leave well enough alone. He borrowed money from his brother Louis to conduct his own experiment. A few nurses tried to undermine the experiment, sneaking into the preemie ward and cranking up the oxygen. By 1952, with good data, Patz was able to unveil stunning results: None of the preemies with lowered oxygen went blind, compared to 25 percent of those undergoing the standard procedure. Patz was competing against a medical establishment and a government bureaucracy. He could not have saved so many babies from blindness had he not been driven, rushing to his lab, and less concerned about hurting the feelings of those who stood in his way.

SO WHAT ABOUT HAPPINESS?

We're busy. We're annoyed. We're the "overworked American," trying to raise the "at-risk child." You know the clichés, the book titles, and the nagging feeling that you are drowning in a society that just tells you to push harder, and push aside anyone who gets in your way. With four-letter words streaming out of television sets, everything around us seems coarser and cruder. Surely it must be someone's fault. Lately, authors, professors, and therapists have taken to blaming competition. They say it robs us of our happiness. I think they've got the wrong prescription for the wrong diagnosis. But before going further, we have to ask: What is happiness, anyway?

Worrying about happiness seems to be a luxury. A starving man, hoping for a meal, does not spend much time thinking about good cheer. A cardiac patient, about to have his chest sawed open by a surgeon, worries about seeing tomorrow, and how his family will manage without him, not about bliss. Likewise, our forefathers who slaved away in fields, or bent over an anvil in a hot blacksmith's shed, could not afford too many thoughts about joy. But today, we can listen to happiness lessons on our smartphones, in our cars, or download them onto electronic book readers. There's nothing wrong with thinking about happiness. But we should start by recognizing that the very study of happiness may itself be a symptom of social success and prosperity. Have you ever asked Grandpa, or your great-aunt who grew up in the 1930s, whether they were poor as children? Unless you are a Rockefeller or Kennedy, the answer is almost always the same: "Well, I guess we were, but we didn't know it at the time." Only as they became more prosperous could they look back and recognize their deprivation. In a similar way, our rising standard of living prods us to ask ourselves whether we are happy. Our ancestors seldom bothered to ask.

The formal study of happiness may be modern (in contrast to philosophizing about happiness, which goes back to the ancients), but it is still important. For one thing, happier people tend to treat other people better. We'll later see that helping others is a reliable route to feeling better about ourselves. In fact, happiness may even be contagious. A remarkable study of social networks concluded that if your friend who lives within a mile becomes happy, it increases the probability that you will become happy by 25 percent. The effect goes beyond one degree of separation. The study suggests that if your friend's friend's friend becomes happy, it has a bigger impact on you being happy than having an extra $5,000 in your pocket. I'm a bit dubious about happiness magically flying through the air from house to house like the tooth fairy, but it does seem that happy people are more willing to help, to nurture, and to lift the spirits of others.

Happy minds seem to think more clearly than depressed minds. Imagine you are faced with a stressful test, whether meeting a future mother-in-law, taking the written portion of the state motor vehicle exam, or trying to solve Fermat's Last Theorem. If you are happy, you will perform better than if you are grouchy. Happy fans of word puzzles solve 20 percent more puzzles than cranky ones. So if you are stumped by Sudoku on a train, do not turn to the girl yelling at her boyfriend on her cell phone.

There is one caveat to the idea that happiness fuels brainpower. I'd call it the "automobile showroom exception." If you are walking into a Chevy showroom and looking to negotiate a deal with the salesman, you are probably better off not giving off gleeful vibes, and not falling in love with that Camaro. An Australian researcher has shown that when he drove people "down in the dumps" by showing them clips from the gloomy movie *Angela's Ashes*, they actually turned out to be better negotiators. If I were looking to sue someone, I'd shy away from a happy-go-lucky lawyer. Clarence Darrow had a great scowl.

Another reason happier people think better is that happier people tend to be healthier. Their arms, legs, and stomachs feel better. Now, this is not as simple as it seems. You may be thinking, C'mon, Buchholz, you are falling for a reverse causation error: Those miserable people are miserable because they are sick. Sickness drains their energy and makes them feel lousy. But I am not so foolish as to fall so quickly (it usually takes a little more time). How could we scientifically test the claim? How about deliberately injecting the flu virus into healthy people and watching their antibodies respond? Richard Davidson, a scientist at the University of Wisconsin, found enough volunteers willing to roll up their sleeves and wince. Then he monitored their brains and the antibody count in their bloodstreams. Sure enough, those volunteers with stronger left brain function (which indicates more positive moods, as we will see in chapter 3) produced and then launched more killer antibodies to attack the virus. Such people also send out more seek-out-and-destroy cells to attack bacteria. So again, if you are struggling with Sudoku on the train, do not ask for help from the guy clutching the handkerchief.

Happiness matters for yet another reason. A simple reason. We want to be happy; at least most of us do.

THREE KINDS OF HAPPINESS

The most famous comment from a Supreme Court Justice has nothing to do with slavery, Abraham Lincoln, or *Bush v. Gore*. It is Potter Stewart's statement that he can't define pornography but "knows it when he sees it." Defining happiness is trickier. And I can't make an argument about competition and happiness without wrestling with the definition. It's a tough wrestling match, I must admit. And I don't have a specially designed description that I will rely on to prove my arguments. But it's helpful to understand the various meanings used in happiness surveys and in the literature. So let me explain those before giving you my best shot at a definition. We can start by traveling to Iceland in search of etymological roots and find that "happ" implies luck, as in happenstance. In Germany, *"Glück"* implies happiness and good luck. But these seem like false starts, for good luck does not guarantee happiness. Lucky lottery winners often end up bitter and broke. Happiness—if it is going to last for more than a few minutes or hours—is not an accident or a lucky number. So let's leave behind Happlanders and Laplanders.

Happiness is not just a quick burst of physical pleasure, an orgasm, or a shot of air-conditioning on a sultry day. These may be thrilling sensations, but when we think of happiness we usually think of some connection between mind, body, and spirit that can energize and lift us for more than a few moments. Besides, we get used to pleasures pretty quickly. Once we register the cool air-conditioning on our sweaty skin, we take it for granted. The Cinnabon company cleverly propels an alluring aroma into a shopping mall, inducing people to drop in and buy a cinnamon bun. But if you worked behind the counter, you would no longer be enticed because your taste buds and sense of smell would have gotten used to it.

Writings on positive psychology, led by Martin Seligman, tend to distinguish a hierarchy of three levels of happiness, beginning with mere pleasure and rising up to a purposeful, fulfilling life. Rather than twisting words to illustrate these definitions, I will ask you to think about people you consider happy. Try to picture their faces. I'm going to ask you to imagine three different sorts of smiles, three different versions of happiness. We'll see that happiness is not just luck, nor is it a passing tingle in our nervous system.

First picture someone *jolly*, who shakes off bad news and laughs at life, like a Santa Claus character. Another might have a beatific smile, rocking his head from side to side *enraptured* by music, like Stevie Wonder. A third might nod his head in an approving manner, and smile with a glow of *fulfillment* that comes from sacrificing, or volunteering, or fighting for justice and finding hints or even hugs of success—picture Nelson Mandela in 1993, still scarred from prison, but knowing the battle was worth all the pain, the victory overwhelming.

Now, of course, I have no idea whether Stevie Wonder really considers himself happy or whether it is simply the case that his neck moves more gracefully than mine. But these images illustrate three different forms of human happiness.

PLEASURE

Now I must tell you that none of these three models of happiness is totally complete or fulfilling. Take your jolly friend who experiences an almost unending spasm of fleeting bursts of glee and belly laughs. You might envy his natural high, but sometimes euphoria can be aroused merely with a bottle of beer, a snort of cocaine, or a prescription pill. Would this state count as happiness? Or is your friend just having a chemical reaction to fleeting bursts of neuro-agents? What if the jolly person is a real ninny, and is simply getting physical pleasure all day from pornography and Hershey's Chocolate Kisses? I suppose he might consider himself happy, but if we are talking about how to structure society and how to handle our natural drives, the jolly ninny does not set an admirable standard that others should aspire to. John Stuart Mill argued with Jeremy Bentham about this concept, with Mill insisting that certain pursuits were intrinsically more appealing than others. In Mill's high-minded view, poetry should beat pick-up sticks and a hurdle race among fleet-footed men should beat a cockfight in an alley. Mill said he would rather be a disgruntled Socrates than a contented pig.

Robert Nozick, who taught at Harvard in the 1970s and 1980s, proposed a thought experiment to make the point that "any old pleasure" is not the same as happiness. You can call it "deal or no deal," if you like. Let us say I could guarantee you a lifetime of pleasure, no matter how you like to get that pleasure, whether from books, sex, or balmy vacations on a palmy beach. And you will no longer feel the frustration of burst water pipes, the oppression of nasty bosses, or the heartbreak of psoriasis. There is one catch, however. No, you don't have to sell your soul to the devil. But you do have to lie down on this comfortable bed, snuggle up against this pillow, and go to sleep. While spending the rest of your life in sleep, your body and brain will feel all the intense pleasures you covet. Moreover, your mind will not even know that the pleasures are fake. Would you do it? Would you choose a lifetime of wet dreams over a life, however dry? Most everyone turns down the theoretical bargain, because we desire more than just tingling, gleeful nerves. Those tingling sensations get interpreted in our brains, and our brains want them to mean something, to signal some purpose.

When we consider a life of mere pleasure, the Greek god of parties and wine, Dionysus, comes to mind, draped in bunches of grapes. Again, I have nothing against jolly people, and they do experience a form of happiness, but is it necessarily complete? Does it set a standard that we'd want to emulate or guide others to?

Before completely trashing pleasure for its own sake, let's not forget that pleasure has always played an awfully important role in keeping human beings and other animals alive. Generally, fetid odors warn us of deadly, spoiled plants and animals, discouraging us from noshing. Sweet tastes invite us to ingest valuable carbohydrates. The pleasures of the flesh encourage us to procreate. If we did not pursue pleasures, mankind today would be just another fossil fuel buried on top of the dinosaurs.

RAPTURE

For a second level of happiness, let's look at our *enraptured* Stevie Wonder, lost in the beat of the music. It certainly is a lovely feeling. Aristotle gave this sensation the melodious name *eudaimonia*, and we feel it when we are lingering over a delicious meal, a scintillating conversation, or strolling through a lush garden. It is the "good life," inspiring us to use our talents, not just our credit cards, to find pleasure. Aristotle, who lauded "activities of the soul," would not have condoned retail shopping therapy. Aristotle taught that each of us is naturally intended to do fulfilling things, but those things may be different from person to person. Stevie Wonder was *meant* to compose and sing. Meryl Streep was *meant* to act. Neither was meant to land an aircraft like the

US Airways pilot Chesley Sullenberger. All of these people get absorbed in their professions. Aristotle liked acorns. To him, an acorn was naturally directed to grow up to become a tree. Anything that stood in the way corrupted nature. Likewise, he would applaud a child with a talent for music, and hope that the child would grow up to express his talent, perhaps becoming a professional lutist or flutist. Virtue came in allowing our inner gifts to open up to the outside world. And for Aristotle, the more complex, the better. A talent for chess would beat a talent for craps. Later we will discuss the concept of "flow," in which we get lost in our work or play, and time zips by. But is eudaimonia complete happiness? How could there be anything wrong with it? With eudaimonia we may get lost in high-minded activities, but the endeavor can be solitary or even selfish. You might get lost in a violin concerto and not notice the homeless child you just stepped on. The German physicist Werner Heisenberg could get lost in beautiful equations and feel good about it, but what if the purpose of those transcendent equations was to design an atomic bomb to help the Nazis defeat the Allies and to exterminate Jews?

FULFILLMENT

And so we are left with a third kind of happiness, *fulfillment*, which the psychologist Martin Seligman calls "the meaningful life." The meaningful life has a moral component and tries to combine eudaimonia with a recognition that using our talents, skills, and energy to help others can bring about an even higher, more lasting kind of bliss. Instead of pursuing base desires and urges, whether symbolized by Dionysus in a toga or Freud wielding a cigar, the meaningful life would follow Viktor Frankl, the Viennese psychotherapist and author of *Man's Search for Meaning*, who found that even in a Nazi death camp he could nourish his soul by trying to comfort the victims. A prisoner himself, who lost his wife and parents to guns and gasses at Bergen-Belsen and Auschwitz, Frankl set up therapeutic units to battle suicidal thoughts. The quest for a meaningful life follows Frankl, Mandela,

Mother Teresa, and maybe even your barista at Starbucks, if she dotes on the elderly. You do not need to be a Nobel Prize winner or a saint. You do need to be feeling a spiritual pleasure in being engaged with others.

Nonetheless, I find that even the meaningful life presents a paradoxical way of describing happiness and raises all sorts of questions. What if meaning and virtue do not necessarily bring about a state of mind that the individual recognizes as happy? Don't we want to feel good about feeling good? What if the individual's friends and family do not perceive him as happy? Can you be happy if everyone who knows you considers you dour and depressed? I suppose happy may not be in the eye of the beholder, but it has to be in someone's eyes. Take the case of Mother Teresa, who confessed, toward the end of her life, that she was not so sure she was doing the right thing, that she wished she had felt the ecstasy of less saintly believers: "Where is my faith? Even deep down . . . there is nothing but emptiness & darkness." Was Mother Teresa in the end hoping for the happiness of someone less virtuous, less committed, less profound?

Make no mistake, when we intertwine definitions of happiness with words like "eudaimonia" and "meaning," we end up making moral judgments. Now, I am not necessarily against moral judgments, but they do make the slope slippery. It seems to me that most of us would describe the ideal life as combining some aspect of each: pure pleasure, losing ourselves in developing our talents, and sparing some time to help others. Tingling nerve endings and pure pleasure do not last a long time. We get used to it. But feeling good about feeling good has more staying power.

The meaningful life fits best with traditional religious and moral teachings. Millions of people who have never set foot in a therapist's office aspire to the meaningful life. But why do positive psychologists impose a morality and a hierarchy on types of happiness, claiming that a meaningful life is superior to a pleasurable life? Well, they have discovered a pragmatic, scientific reason to create this hierarchy of happiness. It can be a depressing reason. Like it or not, you cannot do much about your ability to be a jolly, pleasure-loving person. Studies of identical twins separated at birth tell us that at least 50 percent of the variance among people's happiness is engraved in their genes. Taking a tickly feather to a grouch will not turn him into a teddy bear. In contrast, psychologists exalt eudaimonia because they know it can be nurtured by encouraging people to find and develop their hidden talents. And, of course, the meaningful life can be encouraged by showing people how to use their talents in a way that helps other people. Aristotle did not naively assume that people are born virtuous. He believed in good habits. If you get used to putting money in the church plate or the synagogue *tzedakah* box, it can become "second nature." Ah, listen to the old phrase—"second nature." It admits that we have an encoded behavior, but then holds out hope that we can graft a new code on top of it. When I was a kid, I recall shopping with my mother and her stopping to give money to people standing in front of stores with boxes for Deborah Heart and Lung Center. I did not know much about Deborah, or why my mother always gave. Yet to this day, I will reach into my pocket for that cause. My mother and father gave me not just my "first nature," but tried to inculcate a "second nature." And sure enough, studies show that one of the best ways to feel happier is to give to charity. On the other hand, if I'd spent more time with my friend's dad, instead of my mom, I might be giving money to Off-Track Betting.

HOW AND WHEN DO WE MEASURE HAPPINESS?

Now that we have stepped into the confusing realm of figuring out what we mean by happiness, we face another tough task: How and when do we measure happiness? Let's go back to Mother Teresa. Mother Teresa seemed to grow unhappy as she got older, yet seemed to possess a more saintly, deeply joyous spirit during much of her life. Let's take the opposite case: a deathbed confession of happiness. What do we say about that legendary Viennese-Cambridge philosopher Ludwig Wittgenstein, whose handsome profile could appear on a Hollywood poster for a movie called *Tortured Genius*? Wittgenstein almost always seemed miserable (though he did apparently enjoy Carmen

Miranda movies), yet left a happy final note. On his deathbed he uttered these words: "Tell them I've had a wonderful life." Nobody believed him. But was he happy? He certainly brought meaning to generations of graduate students in philosophy (although ironically, his work sometimes appeared to aim at destroying the very idea of meaning). So: Is happiness an average of many moments? Or a random sample of moments? Or the final, deathbed moment? The linguist and broadcaster Barry Farber said that "in Russian tragedies, everyone dies. In Russian comedies, everyone dies too. But they die happy." The Athenian philosopher and legislator Solon argued that the final moments count most. (Calvinists later postponed that reckoning until the hereafter, for which it is exceedingly difficult to take stock, even with MRI scans.) A story is told of Solon listening to his young nephew singing a song of Sappho. Solon asks the boy to teach him the tune, when a smart aleck asks, "Why bother? You won't be around much longer to sing it." Solon replies, "So I may learn it and then die."

For years economists and psychologists have been taking surveys to collect data on happiness issues, but in recent years it's become a frenzy. From 1991 to 1995 only four economics papers were published on analyzing and measuring happiness; from 2001 to 2005, there were over one hundred. But how are these done? In the same way that a weight-loss clinic could strap a pedometer on you to measure how many steps you take in a day, Mihaly Csikszentmihalyi has equipped volunteers with electronic survey machines (perhaps more like Nielsen rating boxes) that beep and prompt people to register their level of happiness at regular intervals. It's called the Experience Sampling Method. But equipping thousands of volunteers with sophisticated beepers and recorders can be expensive. To avoid the cost and complexity of this approach, other researchers, like the Nobel laureate Daniel Kahneman, have used the Day Reconstruction Method, asking subjects to fill out questionnaires and record their feelings about the preceding day. How did you spend your afternoon? Did you play with your children? Wash your car? Attend an office meeting? How did the activities make you feel? Survey evidence from the beeper method (Experience Sampling) and the Day Reconstruction Method shows a fairly high correlation.

The General Social Survey, run by the University of Chicago, deploys a more traditional system, sending pollsters out to ask Americans in person, "Taken all together, how would you say things are these days? Would you say that you are very happy, pretty happy, or not too happy?"

Of course, self-reports on happiness cannot be as accurate as pedometers. The physical distance of a meter cannot be argued with. But a unit of happiness is more flimsy and faulty. People can be toyed with and their perceptions skewed. Neuroeconomists and psychologists have shown that reports can be prejudiced by even the simplest changes to environment. In one example, surveyors concocted a situation in which participants happened to discover a dime on a photocopier before taking a survey. Sure enough, those who found a dime reported a greater sense of satisfaction in life. Ten cents can buy happiness! The beauty care pioneer Estée Lauder discovered early in her career that "even rich people love freebies," because it puts them in a more cheerful frame of mind. Lauder shrewdly gave away sample lipsticks and face creams, igniting the now commonplace "gift with purchase." Economists call this concept "framing." Another experiment: Go to your thesaurus and look up the word "happy." Then read all the synonyms: "delighted, cheery, glad, jovial, blissful, ecstatic. . . ." You probably feel better already just reading that sentence. Experimenters who ask volunteers to read a list of upbeat words find that the volunteers then report feeling happier.

So where does this leave us? We have seen that every definition of happiness has gaps, conflicts, and ambiguities. And we have seen that surveys can be twisted. Should we then take a nihilistic view that happiness is like the taste of snow on the tongue, swiftly gone and indeterminate? I don't think so. It turns out that while every kind of survey on happiness has flaws, when taken together they do hold some water, if not snow. For example, when we ask people whether they are happy, their answers tend to correlate with how their friends and family perceive them. Their answers also correlate with brain scans, word choices, and even the number of smiles they flash. Remember that synonym quiz you took just a moment ago? People who report being happy have an easier time coming up with pleasant synonyms. They also sleep better. So while this happiness survey story is full of holes, like Swiss cheese, it is still cheese and worth pursuing. Happiness matters to us, and in Justice Potter Stewart's words, we know it when we see it.

As for my definition, I cannot separate happiness from a desire to live life. When do we know that we have grown happier? When we feel more joy in seeing a new day, a new decade, and when we hope that children, friends, and loved ones feel the same way.

CHAPTER 3

Rush to Action: The Biology
of Risk and Happiness

What's the Big Idea?
Our brain chemistry likes a new challenge.

Jerome Hanna Dean was an ace pitcher for the St. Louis Cardinals and Chicago Cubs in the 1930s. But he was best known for mangling the English language and for his nickname, "Dizzy." In one World Series game, while trying to break up a double play, Dean got smacked in the head with the ball. He crumpled to the ground unconscious and was rushed to the hospital. Upon his release from the hospital, Dizzy reported, "I'm okay. The doctors x-rayed my head and found nothing."

The story of neuroscience and neuroeconomics is now packed with fMRI, DTI, and MEG scans. Just as expectant parents proudly post sonograms of fetuses on their refrigerators, doctors, psychologists, and economists post brain scans in their books and journal articles. Researchers marvel at their newfound ability to show brain patterns, electrical circuit wiring, and flashes of color as different parts of the brain fire up under different circumstances: Which part of the brain flashes when you win a poker hand? When the IRS audits you? When you see a photo of your mother?

YOU HAVE THREE BRAINS

Our roughly three-pound brain requires a lot of energy, around one-fifth of our caloric intake. From a purely Newtonian point of view, much of the work we do in life is just to keep the brain humming. In fact, it is pretty well known now that we have three brains, named after their evolutionary development.

The first to come along was the reptilian brain (the brain stem), which controls basic functions to keep your heart beating and your lungs breathing. Without this part of the brain, dinosaurs would have forgotten to get hungry or to flee from larger dinosaurs. The reptilian brain also stirs basic emotions, which allow even geckos to act scared. Tiny circuits stimulate nerves, spur blood flow to organs and muscles, and can make us run faster or blush.

Second was the limbic or mammalian brain, which evolved as small mammals gave birth to live young, allowing them to learn which foods are poisonous, which family members are friendly, and which predators may stalk them. The limbic brain includes the hippocampus and amygdala, which support memories and emotions. Without the amygdala mammals would act not just forgetful but, well, nutty. For example, after suffering lesions of the amygdala, a rat or monkey may try to eat nonfoods or even mate with inanimate objects. A woman who lost her amygdala through surgery could no longer detect the difference between angry and joyful voices. The limbic brain gives mammals an urge to nurture and protect. For example, it inspires a cat to nurse its kittens, in contrast to a crocodile, who may chase its own babies down for lunch. To imagine the human race without the limbic brain is to imagine a horror movie, devoid of caring and compassion. I recall a scene in the 1986 movie *The Fly*, starring Jeff Goldblum, where the hero is beginning to grow thick hairs on his back, and he warns his girlfriend to flee:

> You have to leave now . . . and never come back here . . . Have you ever heard of insect politics? Neither have I . . . Insects don't have politics. They're very brutal. No compassion. No compromise. We can't trust the insect . . . I'd like to become the first insect politician . . . I'm saying I'm an insect who dreamt he was a man, and loved it, but now the dream is over and the insect is awake . . . I'm saying . . . I'll hurt you if you stay.

While this quotation might seem to give too much credit to politicians, it makes the point that flies lack a limbic brain and would be even more annoying to us if they grew larger.

But the true jewel of evolution is the third brain, the neocortical (human) brain, which sits like a dome above all the rest. Whales, gorillas, and pigs developed this brain over millions of years, and it allows mammals complex social behaviors, like social grooming among apes, hunting expeditions among wolves, and dolphin shows at SeaWorld. The human neocortical brain has developed even further, permitting us to have more sophisticated languages, plan for the future, and experience empathy. We can learn, but we can also deliberately ponder and make choices. We can learn to deceive a predator or outwit prey. We can try to suppress bad moods and entertain pleasurable thoughts and fantasies. Consider: All animals have sex, but only humans scratched out naked figures thirty thousand years ago in a cave, or on a junior high locker last week.

Moralists may debate whether humans are "higher" beings, but we can leave such judgments aside for now. It is clear that humans developed by borrowing the circuitry of simpler creatures and adding more wattage and more conscious willpower. When biologists and DNA researchers explore the three basic cranial structures and then trace back the genetic codes embedded in us, it appears that human beings, like other living things, crawled out of a single source. And the singularity even goes beyond animals. The writer Bill Bryson has pointed out that about "half the chemical functions that take place in a banana are fundamentally the same as the chemical functions that take place in you." This might explain why Theodore Roosevelt complained that he could carve a stronger backbone out of a banana than out of Justice Oliver Wendell Holmes.

In this chapter we will look into that three-pound mass we call the human brain and try to understand how it evolved, what it operates, and how it can guide us in our search for happiness. Of course, this is not a textbook on neurology. You would have to be crazy to trust an economist to teach you brain surgery. But a look into the human brain can bring us closer to seeing why our drives can drive us toward happiness. Eighty years ago, economists, psychologists, and social philosophers could not use scanning devices to unpack the circuitry of the brain. Heck, up until the very late 1800s, surgeons didn't even know they should wash their hands. Modern technologies make X-rays of the 1930s so antique, that in comparison to today's penetrating scans, those doctors who examined Dizzy Dean probably did find nothing.

THE TOMORROW MACHINE—OUR FRONTAL LOBE

Thinking about tomorrow is a vital evolutionary gift to humans and a critical part of mental health. Without the ability—or the desire—to think about tomorrow, we devolve into misery, into a lower form of life. Take Bart Simpson. In one episode of *The Simpsons*, Bart swallows a bunch of prescription pills and sings "Don't Stop Thinking About Tomorrow" while madly driving a tank through Springfield, rolling over and crushing cars.

We are the animals that can conjure up tomorrow out of thin air. In modern countries, parents, aunts, and teachers routinely ask children, "What do you want to be when you grow up?" This is, of course, a thoroughly modern question. Human brains have been thinking about the future for tens of thousands of years, but two hundred years ago, the son of a blacksmith who made horseshoes would have little choice but to start staring at horse hooves at a young age. That was a cultural constraint for the job market. Let's think about other questions. For millennia, religious people have wondered about a hereafter: Are you going to heaven? Hell? Do you have good karma? Will you come back as a rugby star? Or a squirrel? You can sit back in your chair and imagine a sunny summer day; a cruise to Barcelona; or a scene when you out-drive and out-putt Tiger Woods. We can even take surreal steps in our minds and imagine that our strict sixth-grade teacher turned into a gerbil and is gnawing on woodchips. More important, we can compare and analyze alternative scenarios and then choose which route to take. Robert Frost may have spoken of the road not taken, but that untrod road *was taken* in his mind—and in the mind of any reader of the poem! How do we do this? The frontal lobe of our brain is our future machine. We do not have to deposit a dime, buy a ticket, or push a button to take off into a new world of possibilities. We are born with this ability, though it develops slowly and probably does not mature until about age twenty-five. Until then people have trouble focusing on long-term plans. A four-year-old can't wait to gobble up a handful of M&Ms, and a teenage boy can't wait to get his driver's license and speed to his prom date. Adults who cannot think about tomorrow often end up in debt, impoverished, and in prison. Walter Mischel of Stanford conducted heralded studies on four-year-olds with a simple tool: the marshmallow. He placed a marshmallow in front of them and then left the room. Would the kids be willing to keep their hands in their pockets for a few minutes if they were told they would receive two marshmallows as a reward for waiting? Would you? Children tend to perceive much shorter time frames than adults, and so most children gobbled up the marshmallow within a few minutes. Those who immediately fidgeted and got ready to snatch the treat ended up more likely to score lower on their SATs, and higher on the probability of detention and expulsion. That might explain why many of the teenagers of the 1990s who impatiently shouted "I want my MTV [now]!" are still living in their parents' basements.

Self-control is tightly linked with imagining the future. If you can't imagine the future, there's no reason to exhibit any discipline or self-control. You might as well steal a candy bar from the supermarket or swipe a DVD player from Best Buy, since you cannot picture yourself in handcuffs. Self-control is tough for a four-year-old. (It was probably tough for *Homo erectus*, too, since his brain was more simple.) For children the future is *so* far away. When we were in second grade, the fall term seemed *so* long. But not to our parents. I heard an older actress once announce onstage: "When I was young, the days dragged on. Once you hit sixty: every fifteen minutes, it's lunch."

Adults should have an easier time showing self-control because our neocortical brain encourages pondering about the future. Most adults do, after all, know how to set an alarm clock and show up for work. Those who don't, whether because they are mentally challenged or were taught bad habits by their parents, often end up struggling with debt and chemical dependency. And they have an uncanny habit of showing up to wrestle each other to the ground on *The Jerry Springer Show*.

Waiting is important for the economy, too. We associate waiting with frustrating lines at the DMV, but as the great Victorian economist Alfred Marshall explained, profits and interest are partly a reward for waiting. For an economy, "Now, now, now!" could mean "Never, never never!" Without highly developed frontal lobes, earlier *Homo* species were stuck in what Daniel Gilbert calls a "permanent present." No wonder they were wedged into a Stone Age. They could not imagine picking up those stones and building fortresses or cathedrals. They could learn only through the pain or pleasure of actual experience. Now, learning from experience is crucial, but it still leaves you at the mercy of your surroundings. *Homo sapiens* spend about 12 percent of their lives thinking about the future. Given the gift of the frontal lobe and the structure of the neocortical brain, what kind of economy would offer the best chance of approaching happiness? A system that encourages us to move forward, to ponder, to plan, and to hope.

Before we go further, some readers might indignantly look down at their pet dog and declare: My pooch is so smart, she thinks about the future. She knows what time I come home at night, and she waits with a tennis ball gripped in her teeth, ready for an exhilarating game of catch. As I write this sentence, I am glancing at my brilliant dog, Amaretto. She appears to be nodding. Heck, I've known birdbrained ducks that came to the front door quacking for bread crumbs at the same hour each day. And many animals take action to defend themselves against future threats. Let's look briefly at a beaver living in, say, Colorado. The beaver prepares for a bitter winter by chomping on trees and building a dam. The dam creates a pond, which will later freeze. Before it freezes, though, the beaver drags some aspen leaves in its jaws and buries those leaves under the water in the mud of the dam. Later that winter, the beaver can retrieve and munch on those tasty, nutritious leaves. Now, I must admit I know quite a few humans who would not have the diligence or the foresight to accomplish this feat—even if they had the overbite. But unlike a human being, the beaver does not imagine the frigid winter. He does not consciously consider whether it would be a good idea to build a dam. Lacking a human-scale frontal lobe, he works from instinct or from the lessons he has been taught by his elders, or the lessons he has learned from experiencing last winter. He does not imagine the cold winds and think, "Gosh, can I catch a last-minute Southwest flight to Miami?" The thought does not occur because he is a beaver and his frontal lobe is too modest. But don't feel bad. Evolution continues. Your forefathers once had the brain of a beaver, and so in millions of years that beaver might be able to negotiate a better deal to Miami than you.

FORWARD MOTION + HOPE = ENTERPRISE AND ENTREPRENEURSHIP

Our brains allow us to "see" the future. Not predict the future but envisage a future, whether it be a vision of tonight, next week, or after our death. However, seeing is not enough to bring happiness. Even achieving goals is insufficient. We also need hope. Our greatest moments of happiness come when we are engaged in an effort, trying to achieve, armed with a vision and with hope. A slave feels demoralized because even if he can concoct a vision of freedom, he loses hope. Spirituals sound so powerful because they cry with despair—"Nobody knows the trouble I've seen," but at the same time those spirituals try to find a reason for hope "nobody knows, but Jesus." A serf might also look to heaven for hope, because it is unlikely his economic situation can bring freedom. In contrast, a fluid economic, political, and social system encourages escape. A system that honors entrepreneurs in their garages offers hope to a laid-off worker or a college dropout. True, there are many hard-luck cases, and many neighborhoods of entrenched poverty. But look at the mobility in competitive societies. In the United States, a majority of the poorest children grow up and out of poverty. Even in a brief ten-year period of time, there is fluidity. A study of poor adults beginning in 1979 showed that by 1988 half had climbed out of the lowest quintile of the population. (There's downward mobility, too, as 47 percent of the richest people in 1979 had tumbled from the highest quintile by 1995.) There will always be rich people and poor people, but in a competitive society the poor people will usually not stay desperately poor, and the rich people may yet have to trade their filet mignon for hot dogs.

In competitive economic systems people have a legitimate reason to look forward and a legitimate reason to hold out hope that they can deploy their talents and achieve material rewards as well as a spiritual glow. I am lucky to be a coproducer of the Broadway smash *Jersey Boys*. In the play, after conquering the music world, Frankie Valli reminisces about success: "They ask you, what was the high point? The Hall of Fame? Selling all those records? Pulling 'Sherry' out of the hat? It was all great. But four guys under a streetlamp, when it was all still ahead of us. . . ." That was the sweetest moment. To imagine the future is an evolutionary gift. But this gift needs hope and an economic and political system that permits change and progress.

MAN IS NOT A LOGIC MACHINE

In addition to allowing us to imagine the future, the frontal lobe helps us manage our emotions. The frontal lobe helps us assess our behavior and how others will perceive our behavioral choices. In Freud's world, the frontal lobe is home to the superego. How do we know the role of the frontal lobe? Is this a lot of hocus-pocus, like palm reading? Ancient Egyptians thought the heart was the center of the soul and of thought. For them the brain was spare baggage. Before burying and mummifying, they would scoop out the brain through the nostrils. Aristotle thought the brain was basically a radiator for cooling blood. In the end, we learned about the frontal lobe's function the hard way, because every now and then in the course of human events, a spear, railroad spike, or axe will smash through someone's brain but not kill him. Scientists will then test their remaining faculties to see how the injury damaged the victim. Frontal lobe injuries give scientists gory but marvelously robust results.

Listen to this strange story. A man fell off a stagecoach, smashed his frontal lobe, and then revolutionized motion pictures. Along the way he turned into a madman and murdered his wife's lover in cold blood. Meet Eadweard Muybridge. He wasn't born with that name, but changed his name from Edward James Muggeridge. That was the least of his bizarre behavior. Photography fans know him as one of the fathers of stop-motion techniques. His photographs proved to California governor Leland Stanford that when a horse races down a track, all four hooves leave the ground in midgallop. You can learn about his work at the Smithsonian Institution, see footage of his work on youtube.com, or watch a music video by U2 that celebrates it (the song is "Lemon"). Born near London in 1830, Muybridge immigrated to San Francisco and ran an antiquarian bookshop. Colleagues and customers described him as friendly, orderly, and candid. Then in 1860 he missed a boat to Europe and decided instead to take a stagecoach to the East Coast. Along the way he lost his mind, or at least his prefrontal cortex. The coach to St. Louis carried seven other passengers through craggy mountains. In northeastern Texas, the driver lost control of the horses and the coach raced down the side of the mountain. According to the *San Francisco Daily Evening Bulletin*, "In an effort to stop the horses, the driver drove out off the road, and they came in collision with a tree, literally smashing the coach in pieces. . . ." From this point forward, Muybridge was a changed man. In three days, his long hair turned from black to gray. His personality turned cold, distant, yet sometimes volcanic in temper. He cared little for his appearance or what others thought of him. He missed appointments and lost contacts. He photographed himself naked, and did not care who saw. He still had the rational capability to invent, devise, and design new cameras and photographic methods, but others could barely recognize his new speech patterns and glassy-eyed appearance. By 1872, despite his emotional defects, he had taken a young bride. Flora Shallcross Stone was twenty-one years younger and had worked as an aide in Muybridge's studio. Soon she became pregnant. Muybridge traveled a great deal, and Flora apparently did not like to be alone. A "dashing and handsome" fellow named Harry Larkyns escorted her to the theater but did more than walk her home after the curtain call. In 1874, Muybridge noticed a photograph of his baby on the table of Flora's midwife. Being a curious type, he examined the photo and turned it over to see the following inscription—in his wife's handwriting: "Little Harry." Muybridge stomped on the floor wildly, trembled and gasped for breath. Frightened, the midwife divulged love letters between Flora and Harry.

The next day Muybridge hopped on a ferry, a train, and then drove a horse and buggy to Harry's ranch in Napa Valley. He knocked at the door, and when Harry answered, announced: "I am Muybridge, and this is a message from my wife." He drew a Smith & Wesson six-shooter and fired. Harry was dead. Flora and "Little Harry" survived, and the city of San Francisco would enjoy the greatest celebrity trial of the era.

Muybridge pled insanity and the courtroom was filled with witnesses who testified to his changed personality and character. It made no difference, however. The jury declared Muybridge "not guilty," because they believed he was justified in killing his wife's lover. For neuroscientists, though, the case was breathtaking. Muybridge exhibited all the signs of frontal lobe trauma. In addition to being unable to control his emotions, and lurching back and forth between coldness and hot anger, he disregarded risks. His business associate testified that Muybridge photographed himself on a dangerous rock in Yosemite, "where a biscuit, if slightly tilted, would have fallen down 2,000 feet."

Some might argue that Muybridge's head trauma might have actually energized his photographic artistry. His emotional swings and disregard for risk pushed him to take more chances, pushing his art forward. Artists often claim to have a different risk profile, a different set of antennae from regular folks, which bestows creativity. Perhaps. Recently, David Mamet has suggested that many of Hollywood's top directors and studio heads are mentally ill: "I think it is not impossible that Asperger's syndrome helped make the movies." How else to explain their "indifference to social norms," egos the size of the *Titanic*, and hearts the size of Munchkins'?

Muybridge was not the only accident victim to inadvertently provide neurological research. A dozen years before Muybridge, a railroad foreman named Phineas Gage was blasting train routes in Vermont with powerful explosives. He was known as a kind, even-tempered supervisor. The job entailed planting powder explosives into rocks and then tamping it down with heavy iron rods. On September 13, 1848, Gage was pushing the rod into the rock when sparks flew. The explosive powder ignited, sending the rod, like a harpoon, straight through Gage's cheek, up through the frontal cortex, and out of his skull. It landed eighty feet behind, laced with blood and brain. Gage did the sensible thing at this point and made his way to a coach and to a clinic. He lived another dozen years, a fitful wreck of a personality—irreverent, profane, and annoying. The old Phineas Gage was gone. A new Phineas Gage was born.

YOU CAN'T THINK STRAIGHT WITHOUT EMOTIONS

Cases like Muybridge's and Gage's show up again and again, whether through tumors, industrial accidents, or torn arteries. When that modest web of tissue just behind the eyes, more specifically the orbitofrontal cortex, rips, it is like offering another drink to Dr. Jekyll or letting Lon Chaney watch the rise of a full moon. To be fair, the results are seldom murderous or sociopathic. Instead the warmth of human personality tends to chill. In fact, patients with frontal lobe damage can perform wonderfully on IQ tests, and they might beat you at Trivial Pursuit. But if you give them a test that requires any planning, or if you ask them to plan a picnic in the park, they will either not show up or appear at midnight dressed in scuba gear. They cannot begin "thinking about tomorrow" in any way that makes sense.

What does the frontal lobe have to do with competition and the human race for happiness? Here is the argument: Evolution gives us the frontal lobe—our windshield looking out to the future—which then allows and inspires us to think about tomorrow and the day after. Mentally ill people struggle to do so. The frontal lobe, then, is the part of the brain that tells us we will be happy only if we have some forward momentum in our lives. A life of stasis, a life of murmuring mantras, a life of staring endlessly at the surf armed with a piña colada will confound and frustrate the frontal lobe. *It is literally in the front of our brains, but metaphorically our frontal lobe is aiming human beings to go forward.* When we aim to go forward we cannot help but see where others stand. Just as you cannot enter a moving freeway without adjusting for the cars speeding down the lanes of traffic, you cannot make or enact plans without sensing where your fellow human beings are, and attempting to nudge your way into the flow of things. The entrepreneur tries to get financing for his great (or not so great) idea; the professor seeks to publish one more article to seal his bid for tenure; the cancer researcher stays up till three a.m. finishing her grant proposal; the seven-year-old girl wakes up at seven a.m. to tie back her ponytail and strap on her shin pads for the Saturday soccer game. A competitive economic system acknowledges and applauds such drive and ambition. Attempts to staunch competition simply induce guilt, and worse, gear us up for an emotional and economic car wreck. Part of our brain yearns to feel progress; another part bubbles with hope. The trick to pursuing happiness is to marry the two, and that frequently leads to rushing around rather than sitting at home.

YOUR BRAIN DOES NOT LIKE ALGEBRA: LEFT ≠ RIGHT

You can look at a top view of a brain scan and see a fairly symmetrical image. But the symmetry is a trick. Inside, the left and right sides of the brain are vastly different, yet are so interconnected that we cannot make rational decisions with only the rational part of our brains. Nor can we show emotion if we use only the emotional part. Here are a couple of startling examples.

Justice William O. Douglas, the eminent liberal jurist, achieved numerous records in his career on the Supreme Court: most years served, most opinions, most dissents, and most wives (he married his fourth when she was twenty-three and he was sixty-seven). He loved the outdoors and boasted of hiking the two-thousand-mile Appalachian Trail. In a court opinion he even argued on behalf of trees. Then in 1974, while the seventy-six-year-old was vacationing in Bermuda, a clot suddenly blocked the blood flow from the right side of his brain, creating a brutal stroke. Douglas refused to admit that the stroke had paralyzed the left side of his body. He refused to give up his seat on the Supreme Court, though he could barely focus on testimony. Seven of his colleagues agreed to postpone any decisions until he had left. Not until nearly a year later did Douglas step down. Was it just pride? Anger at President Gerald Ford? More likely, it was the brain damage that prevented him from making a reasonable choice. Reporters figured this out one day in 1975 when they quizzed Douglas about his physical limits. Could he walk? Douglas waved off the question. Paralysis is a myth, he said. Can't walk? Why, Douglas invited the reporters to hike the Appalachian Trail with him! The reporters wondered whether this was a joke. But Douglas went on. My legs are fine, he insisted. Just this morning I was in the exercise room kicking forty-yard field goals. I'm trying out for the Redskins, Douglas confided, without winking or blushing. Doctors term this condition *anosognosia*, from the Greek *nosos* and *gnosis*, meaning disease and knowledge.

At a hospital in San Diego a sharp-witted seventy-six-year-old crisply answers her doctor's questions. What day is it? "Tuesday."

Where are you? "In a hospital." How did you get here? "My daughter brought me." She denies that a few days ago her left side became paralyzed. The doctor asks her to point with her right hand. She does. Now point with your left. She refuses. She really believes she could, but she does not. Finally, she looks at her *own* left hand in her lap and asks the doctor, "Whose hand is this? It's certainly not mine." How can she deny her own hand? Is this a Freudian defense mechanism so she does not have to deal with the searing reality of her devastated body? Is this a neurological lapse that prevents the brain from recognizing anything on the left side? Again, it is not a simple matter of ego; it is an authentic inability to witness the damage. In one case a man with a paralyzed leg actually threw the leg off the hospital bed and was shocked to find himself following it onto the floor.

Mark Twain once joked that no one should use the "royal We" except kings, presidents, editors—and someone with a tapeworm. While we think of ourselves as a single "I," the left and right sides can play tricks on our "I." When the neuroscientists Roger Sperry and Michael Gazzaniga experimented with cutting the corpus callosum, which joins the two cerebral hemispheres, in order to reduce epileptic seizures, the patient could still walk properly and score well on IQ tests. And yet the experiment seemed to produce more or less two individuals—more or less—each with his own free will. Neither side of the brain could share information. A patient could solve a jigsaw puzzle with either the right or the left hand, but could not do so with both. Another patient might go shopping and put items in the cart with his left hand, and then replace them onto the shelf with the right. If the patient's right brain was flashed a signal to walk, he would begin to do so, but the left would have no idea why. The left makes up its own story about why it is walking, and the patient might say, "To get a Coke."

WINK, BLINK, AND THINK

These bizarre and sometimes sad stories about mismatched hemispheres now bring us to three important concepts in any pursuit of happiness. First, happier people tend to have more left-side brain activity. Second, happiness is not the exact opposite of sadness. This is not simple algebra, where one unit of sadness on the right side of the brain can be wiped out by a unit of happiness on the left. Third, while the left side of the brain is often touted as the "analytical side," it needs to consult with the right side in order to make reasonable decisions.

The old slogan is "blondes have more fun," but now it's left-brained people who have more fun—or, more accurately, people whose left cerebral cortex is firing up. How do we know this? It was harder in Dizzy Dean's day. Now we look at an fMRI of a crying baby's brain and see the right hemispheres lighting up, while a cooing baby's lights up on the left. The brains of severe introverts and neurotics gleam right. Think of your worst nightmare, or worst day at the office: You get fired; your colleague spills coffee on your favorite tie; a TSA officer at the airport launches a full-body search. The right side of your brain will flash as radiant as a Christmas tree in Rockefeller Center.

Now imagine a good day: a salary raise, a compliment on your haircut, a wink from a paramour. The left side of your brain feels the glow and sends warm signals throughout your body. Blood pulses faster, your heartbeat quickens, your surface skin temperature pops up, and you may literally and figuratively feel a tingle. The left-side reaction explains why stroke victims damaged on the left side struggle to feel any sense of happiness, while right-side victims sometimes seem oddly elated, despite their predicament. Likewise, when depression sufferers reach a curative stage, whether through drugs or therapy, brain scans show more activity on the left.

It would be nice if the cure for sadness were simply to think "left," much as a football coach can send his offensive guards pushing to the left. Nor can we become happy simply by stomping on our unhappy thoughts. Since happiness tends to reside on the left and sadness on the right, stomping on sadness does not somehow create happiness on the opposite side. P. G. Wodehouse describes a character who "if not actually disgruntled, he was far from being gruntled." This is why effective psychotherapy is not simply a matter of taking patients to Disney World and "cheering them up." Patients need both to cheer up and to tamp sadness down. Like football, our emotional well-being has a left, a right, an offense, and a defense. All we lack is a battalion of coaches with binoculars looking down on the field, calling the plays, and guiding us through our lives.

The third key concept—we cannot make reasonable decisions without both sides of our brains—separates modern thinking from the speculation of ancient philosophers. Plato portrayed emotions as the enemy of rationality. In Plato's world we are like charioteers trying to control a wild, snarling horse within us. One horse, named Reason, is handsome and tends to "behave magnificently." The other, Emotion, is "crooked, lumbering, stiff-necked . . . with bloodshot eyes." We must whip emotions into submission and tame the beast inside us so that we can pursue reason. Plato might have thought differently if he'd spent less time imagining caves and more time in radiology labs, for as the Gage and Muybridge cases demonstrate, when people are robbed of those emotional horses, they do not simply revert to pure reason. They revert to a paralysis that prevents them from making rational plans or rational choices. They do not just become callous zombies; they become callous zombies who cannot harness their intellect for useful purposes.

Kant once said that the insane should be taught by philosophers because the insane reason wrongly. Apparently so did Kant, because the problem at asylums is not so much faulty reasoning as faulty feeling. In order to live a reasoned life we must integrate emotions into our decisions. Let's put it this way: Would you feel safer in a dark alley with someone who can do a tough crossword puzzle but feels no sympathy for a hungry child, or with someone who would feed a hungry child but is stumped by acrostics? As in the famous Goya etching, "The sleep of reason produces monsters."

In *Descartes' Error*, the neurologist Antonio Damasio points to numerous examples where patients with access to pure reason divorced from emotion become socially paralyzed. They would even have trouble ordering a baloney sandwich at a deli because they could not call upon their memories and tastes for salty meat. Our emotions, feelings, and memories penetrate decision making. Army sharpshooters are trained to call on all of their mental functions, not just telemetry and ballistics, as they decide when to squeeze the trigger. A sniper must constantly gauge his surroundings and be sensitive to every breeze and every wave of a tree branch, behind which an enemy may hide. Babe Ruth was known for the ability to read the label on a spinning 78 rpm record. No wonder, sports reporters wrote, he could see the seams on a fastball and swat the ball over the right-field fence. More likely, Ruth saw seams, but also angles, twitches in the pitcher's windup, tiny movements by the catcher, and a draft of air from behind him, all of which figured into his decision to swing. Ruth would have subconsciously gauged the pitcher's demeanor. Were his shoulder's shrugged, anticipating defeat? Was he sweating in fear? Exhaustion? Was he swearing in rage? Did he have the confidence to throw a fastball, or the gutsiness to gamble with a changeup? The pitcher Sandy Koufax compiled an amazing earned run average of less than 1.00 in his many World Series appearances. Was his fastball blazing so much faster than ever to rack up fifteen strikeouts, including Mickey Mantle twice in Game One of the 1963 matchup against the Yankees? More likely, Koufax read the batters better and fit their twinges and twitches into his calculation of which pitch to hurl. After the game, Yogi Berra reflected on Koufax's win-loss record for the season: "I can see how he won twenty-five games. What I don't see is how he lost five."

Malcolm Gladwell's book *Blink* argues that our instantaneous impressions are often right because they actually take into account nearly all of our prior experience—even if not laid out in an analytical spreadsheet. Gladwell begins with a statue of an anatomically correct man bought for $7 million by the Getty Museum in 1985. Many experts deem the statue a legitimate sixth-century BC dolomite specimen. Yet George Despinis, the chief of the Acropolis Museum in Athens, opined, "Anyone who has ever seen a sculpture coming out of the ground could tell that that thing has never been in the ground." Despinis's instant analysis may have the edge. Today the Getty Museum display states: "Greek, about 530 B.C., or modern forgery." Despinis is not relying solely on a spreadsheet in his prefrontal cortex; he is also relying on his impressions, feelings, and emotions. When he first saw the statue he might have noticed a lack of a tingle on his skin, a sudden plunge in excitement.

Now, I think that Gladwell can take a blink too far, and it is difficult to separate instant impressions from stereotypes and prejudices. Nonetheless, recent research shows us that our instant impressions do seem to call upon our lifetime of experiences and whatever helpful tools are encoded in our DNA, allowing us to distinguish friend, foe, predator, and prey. The sharpshooter aiming his rifle at the possible terrorist won't squeeze the trigger unless he "feels" that the target is a terrorist, not a passing civilian.

We can see the link between reason and emotions among investors. Andrew Lo of MIT and Dmitry Repin of Boston University have wired traders to monitor their pulse rates, respiration, and temperature. Those traders who let emotions run amok ruin their portfolios. But those traders who are so calm and cool that they seem to exhibit no emotions perform poorly, too. The highest-scoring traders do not deny their emotions. Instead they used the emotional firepower to psych up their energy level and transmit more impulses to the rational part of their brains.

I have seen the world's top hedge fund gurus in their corner offices slam their fists on tables, shatter glass with rage, and then sort through a corporate balance sheet with the penetrating eye of a laser. Those who slam the table but lose their focus seldom keep their corner offices. They cannot find success unless they can find a way to blend their emotional power with a logical algorithm. In my experience discretionary investment funds often crash when emotions run away from logic. Two scenarios frequently recur: First, a manager "falls in love" with certain stocks and refuses to reevaluate his holdings even as their values plunge. The more a stock falls, the more he thinks that the market is wrong to spurn the unloved stock. He identifies with the stock and ties it up with his own psychological thorns. In the heat of a stock meltdown, I heard a manager actually say, "I don't care if nobody loves Enron anymore; nobody loves me either." Second, a fund manager may do the opposite, sticking too closely to his purely logical algorithm, without admitting that market psychology has shifted. A manager may pull out an Excel spreadsheet "proving" that there is a 95 percent correlation between, say, gold prices and the Canadian dollar. But when the two suddenly diverge because, for example, fear builds that the Bank of Canada may cut interest rates (hurting the Canadian dollar, which is nicknamed "the Loony") or South African miners threaten a strike (helping gold prices), he cannot recalibrate the little boxes on his spreadsheet.

A good investment manager must figure out how to be focused but not closed off. A few years back, a pension fund investor, who prided himself on psychological methods, interviewed me over lunch. I noticed that during the lunch, while I was spelling out my views on the Japanese yen, he was frequently pushing the silverware around, encroaching on my space at the table. What was going on? It turned out he was performing a psychological test on me: Could I stay focused on the Japanese economy while he tried to distract me, toying with my sense of space and ownership? I don't know whether I passed the test, but next time I would make him pick up the check.

Edenists will disdain busy working people. They will portray them as heartless robots of a soulless capitalist system. They don't understand that most of those purported robots are driven both by their rational and emotional brains. They do not represent pure reason or pure greed. Most of those who succeed in moving toward their personal and business goals have integrated their drives for forward motion and hope. There are exceptions, of course, and you can find them in white-collar prisons. But when you consider the enormous charitable gifts establishing and enabling museums, libraries, and theaters across the United States, it's easy to see that successful people have more on their minds than simply making money or pushing other people out of the way.

MIND OVER MATTER OR MATTER OVER MIND?

William James was tone-deaf, depressive, hypochondriacal, cosseted, and closeted. Naturally, he has much to teach us about psychological well-being. While most of this chapter has suggested that our emotions and nervous centers send signals to parts of our body—run, eat, laugh—James turned that model upside down. James argued that the body first creates a signal, and then afterward the brain feels the impulse.

Why is James's view important to us in this study of happiness and competition? Because in the James worldview, we need external stimulus in order to generate internal energy. A life of meditation and inner searching leads to a dead end of boredom and stasis. In contrast, a life of engagement and, yes, competition will kindle our brains and allow us to generate new sources of emotional power. *A busy life actively engaged in the world allows our bodies to take in external stimuli and convert them into internal energy.* We may even get a rush to the left side of our brains. Rushing around puts us in better sync with our selves and the world than putting our feet up.

The father of pragmatism and the brother of the novelist Henry, William James presented his ideas in simple but cogent fashion: In his parable of the bear, James argued that we do not see a bear, fear it, and then decide to run. No, we see the bear, begin to run, and our bodies become aroused as we get ready to run. Our palms sweat, pupils dilate, veins pop, all of which are pathways to transmit fear to our brains. Nanoseconds later we recognize we are scared to death. Emotions are bodily functions, not signals to the body. Our bodies are like a piano with dozens of keys, sharps, and flats. Our bodies transmit rage, fear, love, and desire in various signals of skin tension, temperature, and muscle change. James said that "man has a far greater variety of impulses than any other lower animal." If man plays on a Steinway grand, a ferret is tooting a kazoo.

James's ideas were mocked and discarded during the reign of behavioralists like B. F. Skinner, who thought emotions were bad for our well-being and did not see much difference between laboratory rats and graduate students. More modern science has given James a break. Back in 1966 during the bitterest part of the Cold War, a young anthropologist from Berkeley named Paul Ekman landed in a rickety plane in New Guinea, paid for by the Defense Department. Was he going to study launch pads aimed at China? Methods of Soviet infiltration? No.

Ekman was going to study faces. Ekman had read Darwin and a French neurologist named Duchenne de Boulogne, who had mapped faces and the emotions they signaled. Ekman's task: to prove that there was a universality among facial expressions. If he could do this on Margaret Mead's terrain, he would also kick sand on her contention that the people in New Guinea were emotionally distinct from Westerners. Sure enough, Ekman found that a curled lip in New Guinea indicates that something is revolting, just like a curled lip in California does. And an authentic smile delivers a similar message of pleasure. For discovering universal laughter, Ekman was pilloried in the profession and faced protests led by Mead, who declared him a "disgrace," and the ethnomusicologist Alan Lomax, who stood up at a meeting of the American Anthropological Association, called Ekman's ideas fascist, and said he should not be allowed to speak.

For this chapter, though, Ekman brings a different message. While Ekman was developing a coding system for faces, he noticed an odd sensation: changing his facial expression somehow seemed to change his mood. When he furrowed his brow, "his heart seemed to race and his blood pressure seemed to rise. When he wrinkled his nose, opened his mouth, and stuck out his tongue, his heart seemed to slow, and his stomach felt as if it was turning over." Ekman and his colleagues then took this observation to the subjects in New Guinea and wired them to test blood flow, skin temperature, heart beats, and breathing. According to one of Ekman's students, Dacher Keltner, getting the subjects to make the correct expression required some unusual coaching: "No, don't flare your nostrils, instead wrinkle your nose . . . as you pull your lips sideways, try not to grit your teeth." Sure enough, Ekman's findings seemed to back up Darwin, de Boulogne, and James. The external stimulation can inspire the internal reaction. Moreover, common terms like "cold feet" and "hotheaded" are not just metaphors but actual descriptions of our bodily sensations during emotional changes. When we are angry, blood flows quickly to the hands (so we can wring the necks of adversaries? Keltner ponders); when we are scared, veins constrict. After testing his hypotheses on the New Guineans, Ekman packed up the gear and moved on to West Sumatra, Indonesia, where he recorded similar results. No doubt West Sumatra was safer for him than the coffeehouses of Berkeley.

NEUROTRANSMITTERS AND MUHAMMAD ALI

The ideas of Darwin, James, and Ekman do beg a central question: How do these signals get transmitted from the body to the brain and back to the body? How did early man feel hunger, see a chicken, and then contemplate plucking it and throwing it on the fire to satisfy his hunger? What happens when a cat sees a dog and wonders, should I scratch out his eyes, or run up a tree?

Although we always have three brains, they are not themselves static. Our thinking and feeling systems are infused with neurotransmitters that send signals across our sixty miles of neuro-wiring and perhaps 100 billion nerve cells in the brain. When these cells vibrate, buzz, chirp, and zap, we may feel hunger, joy, longing, or fear. Nerve wiring takes place across threads about one-hundredth the width of one hair on your head. The wiring is critical. Scientists have toyed with neurotransmitter circuits and found, for example, they could re-wire nerves back to front so that little furry animals would see upside down or walk backward. While the most common neurotransmitters are amino acids, like glutamate, neurologists and psychologists studying moods and happiness most often focus on dopamine, serotonin, and opioids. This book is not a chemistry textbook, so let us take a more familiar and vivid story to illustrate the role of neurotransmitters.

About twenty years ago, I met Muhammad Ali in a Washington, D.C., restaurant. At first I was thrilled. As a little boy I was a huge fan. No heavyweight had ever boxed so gracefully nor verbally sparred so briskly outside the ring. He would leave motormouth Howard Cosell dumbfounded. I placed my first real monetary bet ($1) on Ali against Joe Frazier (my grandfather, who boxed as a young man under the name Buck Roberts, bet against me). As a young boxer Ali (then Cassius Clay) was not just unbeatable; he was uncontrollable. He fought for the heavyweight crown in 1964 against a menacing bear of a man named Sonny Liston. Liston had shoulders that could span the Rio Grande and a scowl that frightened Mafia hit men. Ali would fight Liston with psychology. He bought a bus, painted it with his name, and then pulled up on Sonny Liston's lawn at midnight, screaming for the "bear" to come out. At the weigh-in before the fight, Ali's blood pressure rocketed to a dangerous 200/100, and the ring doctor warned that Ali was literally "scared to death." The doctor declared that if Ali's blood pressure did not come down before the fight, he would cancel the fight. Later that day, the reading was a relaxed 120/80. It was all a fake, and it worked. Liston was so rattled by Ali's antics and confused by his style that he collapsed to the canvas in round six.

Now, as I approached Ali in the restaurant, our eyes met. I said, "Hi, Champ." He began to raise his right arm to shake my hand. Time froze. One, two, three, I kept waiting for his forearm to get perpendicular to his body. Finally, it did and his eyes lit up. He tossed out some witty remarks. It was apparent that his Parkinson's syndrome (pugilistic Parkinson's is referred to as a syndrome rather than a disease) had robbed more from his physical reflexes than from his verbal skills. Then remarkably, he drew a pen from his pocket and began to scribble a doodle. A very nicely drawn boxing glove on which he penned his name and mine. That's when the story gets really sad. Stupidly, I neglected to immediately frame the sketch. And today I have no idea where it is.

Beyond my addled response, what can we learn about Ali? He illustrates the story of neurotransmitters. When Ali seemed to go crazy at the Liston weigh-in, he acted as if CCK (cholecystokinin), a neurotransmitter that signals panic attacks, was surging through his system. He could not stop screaming and his heart apparently could not stop beating rapid-fire. Of course, Ali and his team maintain that he was just faking. In fact, when Ali stepped into the ring to take on Liston, dopamine (along with adrenaline) was surging through his system. Dopamine excites and energizes, so that people take more risks. It is sometimes called the "pleasure" transmitter because it is released by eating, having sex—or knocking out an opponent in the ring. Dopamine urges us to take action, to engage, to try new things, and it gives us a feeling of pleasure when we do so. Dopamine may also help people see patterns of behavior so they can assess and refine their predictions about cause and effect. To take a boxing analogy, let us say that Ali notices that every time Liston throws a left hook, Liston first dips his shoulder. Dopamine helps Ali test this hypothesis, and focuses his mind on the prediction that a dipped shoulder signals a left hook. If Liston breaks the pattern, Ali's dopamine neurons would send up a flare.

Sadly, for about twenty-five years now, Ali has been a victim of Parkinson's syndrome, and the dopamine-producing cells in his body are dying off, giving him a masklike expression, a slow gait, and muscle rigidity. A man whose dopamine production allowed him to skip into the boxing ring, anticipate punches, and enjoy the raving crowd has lost that capacity.

For healthy people, though, dopamine is an elixir, a chemical that delivers a rush, a natural high. It makes us feel alert, interested, and, well, alive. It wakes us up to new opportunities, and helps us remember happy memories. Even (as Cole Porter would say) "bees do it" with their own form of dopamine (called octopamine). When a bee lands on a sweet nectar flower field, it activates his neuron for dopamine, marking the spot for a future trip. A lousy-tasting blossom keeps the neuron asleep, teaching the bee to skip this field on the next trip. With its prediction role, dopamine helps us make sense of the world and enjoy making sense in the world. Our bodies are engineered to learn, to relearn, to create powerful feedback circuits if we make a mistake. When dopamine neurons make a false prediction, they spark an electrical signal in the brain (in the anterior cingulate cortex). Intuition is not mystical; it's biological and electrical. We tend to remember mistakes more than successes. And the more urgent the mistake, the more violently the dopamine neurons buzz. They can then call upon the adrenal glands and other biomechanisms to quicken the pulse, dampen the palms, and impel us to move, run, frown, punch, duck, or yell.

Because our bodies are engineered for pleasure and learning feedback, I argue that any economic or social system must do the same, if it is going to allow human beings to flourish and search for happiness. Let's go shopping for a moment. Right at the start, I must admit, I am not an enthusiastic shopper. As soon as I enter a mall, my energy level plummets like Superman near kryptonite. Still, I will go from time to time, if only to see what all the fuss is about. Consider Costco. Though known for planet-size packs of paper towels and other necessities, Costco excites shoppers by turning shopping into an expedition. What's on the shelf today? Can I nab an extra free sample? How long will the inventory last? It's like hunting, without having to wear earmuffs and plaid and orange vests. Costco continuously turns over its product offerings and creates surprises for customers. Our brains like this. Further, Costco limits its profit margins on any item, and therefore engenders trust with its customers. Compare this to a state-run liquor store or post office, where the prices are fixed, the inventory is fixed, and the workers have no incentive to deliver a "rush" to the folks who rush in. Costco also hires better-qualified employees than other retailers and pays them more. All of this leads consumers and employees to rank the store near the top on the list of most-admired firms. "What we do, we do for our customers and employees, and it pays great dividends for our shareholders," Chief Financial Officer Richard Galanti says. Costco sells stuff in bulk, but it prospers because it gives away dopamine, and creates a divine circular flow between customers and employees.

At the same time that dopamine helps us predict and learn, dopamine is the molecule of urge. When we reach for a chocolate éclair, or the hand of a lover, dopamine is at work. Dopamine is an expectation transmitter. We feel the flow *before* we get the result we seek. And this is key. Dopamine is not the reward for winning, for conquering, for finishing the race, the task, or the job. *Dopamine is the reward for trying.* As dopamine flows, the goal seems within our reach, and we thrust our hands outward to grasp it. This is the key to human life, the key to successful social and economic systems, and the great flaw in the thinking of happiness gurus and egalitarian political regimes. Our bodies evolved to crave and to compete. We will discuss this in detail in later chapters, but that craving may be for food, love, sex, and occasionally shiny objects, whether jewelry or fancy telephones or big-screen televisions. Descartes believed "I think, therefore I am." But without an urge or craving, even thinking doesn't make us feel alive. Does this mean we are no higher than beasts? Of course not. It simply means our frontal cortex is linked to our neurotransmitters in sophisticated ways that took millions of years to create.

BEYOND DOPAMINE: OTHER IMPORTANT NEUROTRANSMITTERS OF HAPPINESS

Dopamine does not work alone, of course. Athletes often speak of another set of chemicals, which deliver a bolt of energy to competitors when they've moved into high gear, or when they tear across the finish line. These are called *beta-endorphins*. While dopamine charges us up for a new task, beta-endorphins flow when we feel the thrill of victory, or the agony of defeat. (Endorphins are opioids, similar to opium, and the word comes from the words "inner morphine." When rats or humans get more opioids in their system, tasty foods taste even more luscious. When they are drained of natural opioids, even a warm chocolate-chip cookie brings forth a "blah.")

Serotonin, which is found in fruits, mollusks, and humans, is one of the earth's oldest transmitters. It stabilizes moods and feelings of dominance and submission. There is a scene in Woody Allen's *Annie Hall*, when Alvy and Annie are preparing to boil lobsters in a pot. Suddenly the lobsters escape, claws snapping. Annie grabs her camera. Alvy looks for an escape and says, "Next time we'll get steaks; since they don't have legs, they don't run around." This is not just a scene about lobsters, country WASPs, and city Jews. It is also a scene about serotonin. In the scene, the lobsters are scared to death. They try to assert dominance, as serotonin streams through their bodies. In fact, neurotransmitter studies have been done on lobsters and crayfish. Likewise, Annie and Alvy are juggling their feelings for each other, wondering who is on top, and who will be on top. Will the lobsters win? Will Alvy win? In crustaceans, serotonin tends to enhance the power of dominant beings, yet discourage submissive lobsters from fleeing. In the movie scene, ultimately, the lobster loses while dinner and evolution move forward. In tests of monkeys, high-ranking monkeys enjoy more serotonin, suffer less stress, and thereby have the luxury of spending more time grooming, which no doubt makes them handsomer monkeys and reinforces their lofty status. When dopamine, serotonin, and opioids flow more freely, they engage new neural connections, enhancing the brain's capacity and durability. The stream of transmitters is like a stream in the fountain of youth.

In contrast to dopamine and beta-endorphins, whose molecules shout "action!" our bodies also produce a neurotransmitter that gets us to cuddle. *Oxytocin* triggers caring and maternal feelings through the nervous system. When scientists injected oxytocin into the brains of virgin female rats, the rats quickly "adopt" nearby babies as their own.

Earlier we saw that happiness in our cranial structure does not appear as the simple algebraic negative of unhappiness. Our brain chemistry makes the same point. Happy-making transmitters like dopamine, oxytocin, and endorphins charge us up with desire and sexual energy, and can grant us feelings of contentment. But a different set of chemicals, like the stress hormone cortisol and acetylcholine, make our muscles tense, and prod our hearts to ache with sadness or fear. We can in fact feel both heartache and pleasure at the same time. A tragicomedy story is not an oxymoron, but more likely the effect of some oxytocin sloshing around near some cortisol.

At this point you might be tempted to throw up your hands and say, "Hell, if it's all molecules in my head, 'I' have nothing to do with my own happiness. I might as well mope, or gamble, or take drugs." But this misses the point: Our chemicals are linked to our behavior, external stimuli, and also to the social system in which we live. Perhaps 50 percent of the variance in happiness is genetic and hard to manipulate, but that leaves about 50 percent open for us to tangle with. We have seen in this chapter that our minds and chemistry have evolved so that in order to feel happiness, we had best be (1) moving forward, and (2) anticipating new surprises and experiences. Despite the calming counsel of yogis, vacation packages, and kindergarten—all of which try to dampen the amplitude of our emotions—human beings have a treacherous time trying to achieve a happy state of mind without these two conditions. We may share some DNA with the sloths, but we are the ones who learned to stand upright, propel ourselves forward, and hope for a new day. Not just a rerun of yesterday.

We seem to live in a world where political correctness and egalitarian/communitarian/socialistic voices want to level our urges, and plug our dopamine channels. I am not arguing here that such policies are illegal or immoral or fattening (though they may be the last, if we spend too much time sitting around), but I am arguing that they fight against our natural neuro-structures. Psychologists and neuro-economists who blame competition for unhappiness are simply bad psychologists and neuroeconomists, who want to remake man in their own idealistic image or refuse to accept man as he is. They are free to argue for a "new man," just as Mao Tse-tung did. But they are not free to misrepresent our current biology. Nor should they present "solutions" that would staunch our flow of dopamine and turn faces into Parkinsonian masks. Before the fall of the Berlin Wall, visitors to East Germany would often comment on drab colors, drab clothing, and drab faces. Movie buffs admire the famed Polish director Krzysztof Kieslowski's 1980 film *The Station*, in which the tired, drained, inanimate faces at the Warsaw train station seem to search for something, perhaps a long-lost spark of human energy. Is this where we want to end up?

Please note, my critique of an egalitarian society does not therefore argue for a vicious, dark, Dickensian world, where men simply try to trounce each other at every step. Nor do I believe that Thomas Hobbes is right—that man's essence is a selfish brute. Nothing in this chapter suggests that men do not naturally have good impulses, which create sympathy, empathy, and that naturally lead our eyes to tear up at both sad and happy occasions. The mother who nurses the child, the father who carries his daughter on his shoulders and beams when she swings a softball bat but did not learn this sitting in a modern classroom. A fascinating study of 132 students showed that when they watched a film about Mother Teresa aiding orphans in the slums of Calcutta, their bodies released more of the antibody immunoglobulin, which protects against respiratory illness and disease. Back in Plato's day, the doctor Eryximachus, who takes part in the Symposium (and whose name translates as "combating retching"), argued that good emotions bind us together and put our body chemistry in balance.

If we want to pursue happiness, as individuals and as a society, we would be foolish to ignore our DNA, to ignore our cerebral structure and the neurotransmitters that inspire us to take another bite, whether of an apple or that proverbial slice of life. We have inside of us the stuff of goodness; but we need the puckish, plucky surge of dopamine and other neurotransmitters to feel the spark of life. The milk of human kindness may require a splash of vodka or Baileys Irish Cream.

CHAPTER 4

We Are All Control Freaks—and Need to Be

*What's the Big Idea? You can't and shouldn't
avoid the anxiety that comes with work and
freedom.*

Good luck trying to erase anxiety from your life. There is no
escape route from anxiety even if one withdraws from contact with
other people. Do you think hermits are happy? You won't get cheery by
simply avoiding anxiety and stress. While I sometimes encourage
stressed-out friends to think of their "happy place"—a favorite ski
resort, Disney park, or symphony hall—this is a ten-minute tactic, not
a solution. Escapism cannot make us happy for a meaningful period of
time. We feel greater exhilaration from *mastering* our anxiety than
steering clear of it: the stay-at-home who conquers the fear of flying;
the tongue-tied best man who attends Toastmasters and finally clinks
a glass to salute the groom; the nail-biting groom who hugs his new

bride; the student plagued with "math-phobia" who finally understands how to follow the FOIL rubric in algebra; the laid-off worker who gets the courage to start up his own business. All of them find that it's far better to direct our lives toward mastering rather than fleeing anxiety.

There is an exhilaration in facing up to the twists of life. We see it even in children. Why do kids like to be tossed in the air or whirled overhead like the Scottish hammer throw at the Highland games? When a child is tossed or swung in the air, his heart races, his pulse quickens, and he feels some fear—but the greater thrill is defeating that fear. Watch a one-year-old smile (and drool) while taking those first steps. The smile bespeaks self-gratification—he is proud of himself—but it is enhanced by the risk of falling on his bottom (or crashing into a coffee table).

The toddling child is not just playing a physical game with himself—he is also *re-creating* himself, morphing from a crawling character into a walking character. The smile is the pleasure, the happiness that comes with creation. Before the child has mastered walking, the walking world is a world of chaos, where taking a step is a game of chance, and the odds are incalculable. Yet every child is willing to take the risk, to play the odds no matter how steep. We are, simply put, programmed to take risks, to create something better out of chaos. Those evolutionary ancestors who refused to take risks never emerged much beyond the stage of mollusk.

Unfortunately, as adults we are often discouraged from going beyond baby steps. We even talk ourselves out of taking prudent risks. Why bother studying for that GRE to get into grad school? We might flunk. Why bother asking the attractive woman out on a date? She might turn us down. Why bother asking the boss for a raise? He might laugh. These are all stressful situations. But we are seldom made happier if we shrink from them.

It's spectacularly easy to find doubters who will reinforce our fears. On the eve of launching her cosmetics company, Mary Kay Ash was sitting with her husband at the breakfast table, going through their business plans. They had saved up $5,000 and were ready to commit their entire bank account to secure a small office with a few desks and to start manufacturing sample skin creams. Suddenly, her husband grabbed his chest and slumped over. A fatal heart attack killed him. All of Mary Kay's professional advisers told her to tear up her plans. She went forward anyway, noting that accountants and lawyers make very good accountants and lawyers. But she had a dream to pursue and was willing to plow her life savings into that dream.

TWO KINDS OF ANXIETY

Life is filled with anxiety but there are two dramatically different kinds of anxiety that lead us to bite our fingernails. The first comes from recognizing all the confounding choices we have to make in life. Should I quit my job? Where should I send my kids to school? Should I file my tax return using the 1040 long form or short form? Should I return the phone call from my mother (yes!)? Kierkegaard called anxiety "the dizziness of freedom." He coined the phrase many years before the IRS came up with the 1040 form, but his point stands. When we have choices to make, we get a little jittery, worried we might tick off the wrong box, or tick off our spouse or our boss.

There is, of course, a different type of anxiety, and it is more dangerous and hurtful than the dizziness of freedom. It comes not from facing too *many* choices, but from seeing *too few* choices, a lack of freedom. This anxiety can emerge on a macro scale—for example, the Chinese government that won't let you have a second child or move to another province. It can emerge on the micro front, too—for example, the tyrannical father who dictates that you must take over the family bakery and wake up at four a.m. to fry doughnuts. In either case the gates of freedom clang shut around you, creating anxiety and despair. Given the choice, the anxiety of freedom is far more inviting because it gives people the potential to re-create themselves. Just as men evolved from lesser forms, we must evolve over the course of our lives in order to sustain our mental health.

In this chapter we will put ourselves on the couch of the psychoanalyst, in the laboratory of the psychologist, and in the marketplace of the economist. We'll examine our inner need for freedom, a need that shows itself even among children. What kind of freedom? The freedom to choose where to live, what kind of job to take, and what to do with the money we earn. A free society with a free-wheeling economy offers the best hope for fulfilling these primal desires.

THE TYRANNY OF THE TODDLER

Little children teach us a valuable lesson about the pursuit of happiness. This pursuit requires us to test limits and to exert some control over our lives. Babies start, of course, with virtually no control. To toddlers, the rule of parents is both mysterious and awesome. I recall when my first daughter began to issue her own orders—"yes," "no," "do this," "not that." Often they seemed like a totally senseless game of Simon Says, like "put your feet in the refrigerator." Then it occurred to me that our instructions to her, "eat your chicken" and "brush your teeth," seemed like the arbitrary barking of a potentate. A two-year-old understands the command, but not the rationale. She understands "cause and effect" only when she is the prime mover, or when she witnesses the catalyst. She sees that some things she likes to do elicit applause, while other acts generate a scold. This dichotomy, write Ralph Ross and Ernest van den Haag, "literally puts the fear of God into us—the conviction that our actions must follow a path laid out by a Being whose word is law, whose will is inscrutable, and on whose benevolence we depend—who is as omnipotent, incomprehensible, and unaccountable as parents are to infants."

Even though human babies need physical contact for nurturing and for sustenance, toddlers yearn to break free. We are all control freaks compared to animals with lesser brains. In fact, research shows we get a high from exerting control over our environment; in contrast, we plumb depths of despair when we are shackled. Toddlers *enjoy* deliberately dumping their applesauce onto the floor and watching us clean up. Even strapped into their high chairs, they seek some control and need to ask, "Who's the boss?" A toddler who never dumps his plate will grow up emotionally stunted. Little kids need to make things happen. It's not enough for Mommy to push the stroller. The kid needs a steering wheel on his stroller and wants to believe that he can steer it. The kid needs to vocalize. Often the kid will sing louder to drown out Daddy. Happiness is partly a function of control and social interaction that call forth our competitive spirit. As the child grows older the spirit glows brighter. A ten-year-old on a bicycle looks at his mother and says, "Look, Mom, no hands!" What is he doing? He's showing that he can control the bicycle without help from his parents. Not only that, he can even control and ride the aluminum beast without even touching the handlebars!

These days some child-rearing experts worry that parents allow children too much control. The parent no longer provides a figure of authority but instead one of comic relief. The comedian Dana Carvey performs a routine in which he claims that toddlers today require two parents to accomplish any one task. For example, taking a bath. The mother will suggest, "Johnny, would you like to take a bath?" And the father, playing the role of an enthusiastic yes-man moron, croons, "Ooooh, a bath! That's a good idea!" In the black-and-white days of Beaver Cleaver, a bucking kid would be submerged, as if in the brutal training exercise of a Navy SEAL. No doubt, parents should not give children unfettered control, but it seems undeniable that we naturally yearn for some freedom, and that desire begins at a very early age.

THE SCIENCE OF CONTROL

You have allowed me to discuss beavers, Mary Kay Ash, and Kierkegaard, but where do we find any proof for my claims? This is not supposed to be a freshman dormitory bull session. The evidence comes when we look at people and animals that are denied freedom. Living things feel terrible when they lose their freedom. Freedom may be dizzying, but the lack of freedom is downright debilitating. And the impact is even more dramatic when freedom is taken away without reason. Kafka's Gregor Samsa turns without warning into a bug. In *The Trial*, Josef K., accused of an unnamed crime by an unnamed authority, suffers humiliation, and devolves into a jittery wreck, so helpless he cannot even kill himself. His last words: "Like a dog!"

Kafka's final line gives us a scientific starting point, for Martin Seligman conducted some pathbreaking work with twenty-four mutts in 1967. This came long before Seligman turned into the dean of positive psychology dogma. The canines taught Seligman a great deal about people and led him to develop the concept of "learned helplessness." Think back to Viktor Frankl's brutal experiences in the Theresienstadt concentration camp. He created moments of sanity among insane evil by creating programs, therapies, and outlets for despair. He tried to save his "patients" not from bullets but from a dark helplessness that paralyzed their minds. In the 1960s, Seligman wondered whether such a state of crippling helplessness could be induced. Is it a state of mind? If so, could therapists point to an escape route from this state of mind? We will see that people learn helplessness when they are denied freedom and blocked from seeing cause and effect. They become infantilized, and their world reverts to a capricious, sad chaos.

For Seligman's experiment, the immediate question was this: Could he demoralize mutts? Seligman harnessed a variety of dogs and divided them into three groups. One group would receive electric shocks but have the ability to turn off the shock by pressing on a panel. The second group would feel the shocks but have no tool to stop them. For this key group, the world became a place of unknown and unpredictable danger. Shocks were inescapable. Finally, a control group received no shocks.

Seligman then devised a clever apparatus to test the impact of this conditioning. He put each dog in a "shuttle box," essentially a box with two rooms divided by a low barrier. In the first room, the dog would again receive a shock. But the dog could avoid further shocks simply by jumping over the divider. Here was the question: Would the dogs take advantage of the easy escape route? Seligman witnessed that overwhelmingly the control group jumped away from the pain. Most of the first group, which had learned how to shut off a shock, leaped to safety. Yet about two-thirds of the second group, which had been demoralized by inescapable, mysterious shocks in a prior setting, could not muster the energy, drive, intellect, or morale to climb over the barrier. They lay down, whined, and resigned themselves to pain in a chaotic world. Eventually, Seligman and his coresearchers "rehabilitated" the distressed dogs by tugging on their leashes and showing them that escape was possible and not pointless. Some of the dogs needed fifty tugs on the leash to liberate themselves from helplessness.

Learned helplessness turns us into emotional wrecks by robbing us of motivation and our ability to learn. In Solzhenitsyn's *Gulag Archipelago*, prisoners are not emotionally destroyed simply because they are shivering in frigid "reeducation" camps. The brutal weather does not do them in. They are dehumanized because they feel they cannot escape the irrational, petty despots who run their lives. This is why any economic system, any lifestyle you choose, or job you seek, must allow for freedom. Mutts are not human beings, of course, even if Stalin treated people like dogs. Experiments on rats, monkeys, and mongrels give us powerful clues for human therapy, but you wouldn't want to eat a bowl of Alpo just because your pooch gobbles it up. Here are some key differences to keep in mind when trying to apply animal research to human beings, especially when the research concerns babies: First, human infants are generally more fragile for a longer period of time. A mother giraffe gives birth to her baby while standing up, and the gangly animal manages to lumber around almost immediately. Human infants cannot walk or feed themselves for years. (Lazy teenagers may temporarily reverse the forward momentum.) With such a long period of child rearing, it's likely that nurture among human beings counts for more in this early period. Instincts program behavior more in squirrels than humans. Second, humans learn more about how to take care of themselves and manage their surroundings, whether from parents, television, books, movies, or peers. Even the victim of a sorry childhood can learn to deal with the damage. And, of course, a human who enjoys a charmed childhood can be messed up by hanging around with the "wrong crowd." In 1998 a grandmother from New Jersey, who could not get tenure at a university, riled child psychologists everywhere with her argument that parents hardly matter, but that peers and childhood chums do. The basic message was that Ward and June Cleaver's pontificating was pointless—but watch out for Eddie Haskell! Judith Rich Harris's late-life bloom was celebrated by *Newsweek* and even the American Psychological Association. The association awarded her research (found in *The Nurture Assumption*) the George A. Miller Award, named after the Harvard professor who dismissed Harris from its Ph.D. program in 1960 because he said her research was not original enough for Harvard's standards!

Because animals are not humans, Seligman needed some research that extended beyond mutts. While it would be difficult to find even graduate students who would strap on leashes, welcome electrical shocks, and jump into shuttle boxes, Seligman's colleague Donald Hiroto devised a clever alternative. As Seligman did with mutts, Hiroto divided students into three groups. The first group would wear headphones through which they would hear loud, irritating noises. A button on the headphone would allow them to stop the sound. Thus, the noise was *escapable*. The second group wore headphones and was told they could turn off the sound. However, the experimenter lied, and the button on the headphones did nothing. Their irritation was *inescapable*. The third group received no noise stimulus.

Following this conditioning, Hiroto tried to discover whether the headphone test had robbed the second group of their coping skills. He sent all the students not into shuttle boxes for dogs but into rooms where they would hear a noxious, loud noise. But this time all groups had the ability to spot a lever and then push on it to turn off the sound. They even received a five-second warning light before the noise would commence. Would the students push on the lever, or endure the pain? Almost all of the control group and the first group quickly grasped the task, found the lever, and escaped the noise 88 percent of the time. The second group, hobbled by their prior experience, fumbled with the lever, deployed it inconsistently, and thus suffered through the noise in about 50 percent of the instances. In similar experiments, the hobbled group later stumbled when trying to solve simple word problems.

We are born helpless, quickly become control freaks as babies, and then spend our lives deciding when to relinquish power and when to take it. We call people "well-adjusted" when they make prudent decisions about taking and relinquishing control. Perhaps this overriding issue in our lives explains why the Alcoholics Anonymous "Serenity Prayer," made most famous (and likely composed) by the theologian Reinhold Niebuhr, shows up glazed onto coffee mugs, printed on posters, and knitted into wool caps sold at church flea markets: "God, grant me the serenity to accept the things I cannot change; Courage to change the things I can; and Wisdom to know the difference."

WATER PLANTS, SAVE LIVES

More control over our lives tends to build up confidence. Now, I am perfectly aware that overconfident people can do a lot of damage. Just look at all those financial fund managers drunk on illusions of their own talent. Why do casinos let players throw craps dice? Why does your state lottery let you pick numbers rather than just accept a pre-numbered card? Why are those "coin-scratch" promotions so popular? Because when we think we control a game, our confidence rises—and we bet more money!

The mistake of so many happiness gurus is this: They do not value the pleasure of power. Wait, I don't mean a domineering Übermensch-like, Nietzschean power that stomps on lesser mortals like a young, brutal Siegfried wielding a deadly blade. I mean power as effectiveness. The effectiveness that a child experiences when he figures out how to hold a cup of milk without spilling, or how to tie his own shoes. This boosts pride, and it is a pride based on actual accomplishment, not based on feckless self-esteem training. *The best way to achieve self-esteem is to do something worthy of esteem.* After years of self-esteem training and self-help mantras, Washington, D.C., students scored first in an international survey of self-esteem. They also believed they developed superior math skills compared to their peers in other districts and countries. Unfortunately, when they were asked to put down the cheerleading pom-poms and instead take standardized math tests, they finished just one spot above dead last. Of course, they finished first in self-delusion. And so, power cannot be defined simply as self-confidence. But it should not be defined and disdained as sheer dominance over others. Power can lead to happiness when people learn to use tools effectively in order to create order out of chaos.

More control can help avoid misery; it can also help avoid death. In 1976, Ellen Langer and Judith Rodin, two intrepid psychologists, visited a 360-bed nursing home in New England called Arden House. On one of the floors, they placed houseplants in each of the rooms. Caretakers watered the plants. This was the "baseline" floor. On the fourth floor, they put the old people to work, forcing them to choose the plants, the location for the pots, and then left it to the elderly to fetch and pour water into the pots from time to time. Eighteen months later the psychologists returned, expecting to see a lot of dead rhododendrons. They tested the residents and found that though all the participants were quite frail at the start, the fourth-floor residents proved more alert and cheerful. Then Langer and Rodin were shocked to learn that only half as many of the engaged, "empowered" people on the fourth floor had died. The easier life was an easier path to the grave. Langer later explained that she was inspired to conduct this experiment while visiting her grandmother in a nursing home, where she witnessed her frustrating and debilitating lack of control.

The houseplant example demonstrates that the desire for freedom and control need not be one of dominance over other people. It can also be a desire for creativity. Composers and painters may speak of a higher calling, but in the end they are taking ink, paper, pixels, and paints to turn chaos into their version of order, whether they are realists like John Singer Sargent or surrealists. John Cage provides experimental "chance" music, and Dali bends dreamy watches like limp body parts, but they still end up with more order than the buckets of ink they start with. Even artists who feel dominated by others can try to express freedom. Michelangelo sought the financial freedom to pursue his own sculptures, but had to nod to patrons at the House of Medici in order to pay for it. After being bullied by Pope Julius II, he got his revenge in the Sistine Chapel by painting the pope's face on the prophet Zechariah with a cherub forever aiming an obscene gesture at him.

So many of the critics who portray our lives as an empty rat race, in which we display the moral character of acquisitive rodents, misperceive this race. We are engaged in an effort to create value in the world, to take the stuff we see about us and reimagine it. We could leave it on the ground and do nothing—preserve the environment as it is—but that would be a life of witnessing the earth's erosion and entropy. Not a very piquant recipe for human happiness.

WHY DO PEOPLE WHO DON'T NEED TO WORK, WORK MORE?

Here is a simple question: If the world is a wicked rat race, why do people with so much money work so many hours? Shouldn't they take more vacation? Let's start with some wrong answers to this question: First, "they just want more stuff so they can show off." But if bragging were the motivation, what is more boast-worthy than a vacation in Tuscany, or lounging around your built-in swimming pool when your neighbor peers over the fence? Second, "they may be paid a lot of money as lawyers or bankers, but they are like slaves to their bosses." But if hardworking people put in extra hours because they must kow-tow to some pooh-bah, why do entrepreneurs and the self-employed work even more hours than anyone else?

Thorstein Veblen, the colorful Midwestern economist born the son of Norwegian immigrants, suggested in *The Theory of the Leisure Class* (1899) that rich people love to lounge around and hope others catch them with umbrellas in their drinks. Veblen thought the walking stick was a great advertisement, for a man with a stick in his hand, rather than a wrench, must have time on his hands.

Now, I have seen enough clips of Paris Hilton and other "celebri-ties" to know that rich, ninny layabouts do exist. And I will sprain my finger to flip a television channel as fast as I can to avoid seeing them. (But, my gosh, don't Paris Hilton and her cohorts work awfully hard to get themselves looked at?) When we examine the data for high-earning people, we see far less conspicuous hours at the spa and far more hours at the office or in traffic trying to get to the office.

Though I am loath to give Paris Hilton one more pixel of attention, let me contrast her to the patriarch of the family fortune, Conrad Hilton. Like Veblen, Conrad's folk came from Norway, but while Veblen's folks settled in Wisconsin, Conrad's headed south to the New Mexico Territory, where Conrad was born in 1887. A tall, lean man who always watched his weight, Conrad built a worldwide hotel brand from a small boardinghouse in a two-horse town. And he did it with hard work. That first hotel, bought in 1919 in Cisco, Texas, was in his eyes a "cross between a flophouse and goldmine." In the 1920s he added a dozen more. Then the Great Depression hit, the hotels suddenly emptied, and the remaining guests ducked out without paying their bills. Conrad lost his fortune. But he climbed out of debt working six days a week and scanning the country and the globe for new opportunities. In 1963, *Time* magazine paid tribute to his work ethic: "In his 76th year, a full decade after most businessmen retire, Hilton is busy spotting the world with hotels wherever the U.S. tourist and businessman alight, girding the globe with new links in the longest hotel chain ever made." His hotels boasted of the most comfortable beds, but somehow Conrad never seemed to sleep. He was rich, he was famous, and he was busy. He also seemed rather happy, except for a few brief years when he was wed to Zsa Zsa Gabor. How focused was Conrad on work? One evening Conrad appeared as a guest on *The Tonight Show Starring Johnny Carson*. Carson asked whether Conrad had a message for the American people. Conrad paused, pondered, and answered in a sagely voice: "Please," he pleaded, "put the shower curtain *inside* the tub."

When I was doing research for a book on legendary CEOs, I was stunned to learn how bold, fearless, and energetic entrepreneurs like Akio Morita from Sony and Estée Lauder were. After World War II, Morita crawled on his hands and knees, a badger brush in hand, trying to figure out how to paint magnetized goo on tape (so he could compete with U.S. audiotape companies like 3M). Estée Lauder, who imagined herself a descendent of Austrian aristocrats, sweated over an old

restaurant stove at two a.m., trying to mix up the freshest facial mois-
turizers. Lauder's only family connection to royalty was being born
in the New York borough called Queens, yet she soon found herself
hobnobbing with Princess Grace of Monaco. She had Churchill's de-
termination and Princess Grace's waistline. Any one of these people—
Morita, Lauder, Hilton—could have retired very early and enjoyed
Veblenesque splendor. They could have bought Edens for themselves
and luxuriated under the swaying palms.

This phenomenon is not limited to the phenomenally rich. Wide-
ranging surveys show that highly paid people do put in more hours than
just about anyone else. Are they tricked into putting in more hours?
Unlikely, since the hardest-working people seem to be the ones with the
most education. Those with postgraduate degrees work more hours
than those with bachelor degrees, who work more than high school
graduates. In the last few decades, the number of college-educated men
working more than fifty hours a week has jumped over 37 percent. The
highest-paid workers are twice as likely to work long hours as the bottom 20 percent. This certainly turns a Dickensian view on its head,
which would have portrayed low-wage workers stuck in sweatshops all
night, while the white-collar swells waltz at the Waldorf.

When I was teaching economics to Harvard undergraduates, I
would occasionally bring up the "backward bending supply curve."
This was a fancy graph that basically conjectured that if you paid
people too much, they would cut back their hours. Obviously, having
reached their financial goals, they would substitute leisure for work. In
reality, few people cut back on their hours when they get a raise. Over
the years opponents of income tax rate cuts have argued that tax cuts
might lead to less work, but those claims have often proved flimsy.
While an employee may envy a coworker's dimples, or the praise of a
supervisor, vacation time is among the least envied features in the
workplace.

So, why do rich people keep working? Why do smart, highly paid
people work more hours? Why do the self-employed work more than
anyone else? Get ready for this answer: Work makes us happier, more
eager to wake up the next morning. Those frontal cortexes of ours like

us to move forward. Our hominid ancestors who survived thousands of years of struggle against predators, competitors, and the brutal environment had to be thinkers and tinkerers. Adam Smith said man was driven by a deep human need to better his life. By nature, we are not potted plants (though government policies can turn us into a vegetative state, as we'll see in chapter 9). Staying home feels like we are staying put. Most people prefer the surge of dopamine that comes with new challenges, and the brain bath of oxytocin that comes when we banter with coworkers around the photocopier.

Why do the wealthy and the self-employed work the most? Because they can! Because they have the control and power to put in more hours. Moreover, they clearly see a connection between working harder and achieving the psychological glow that comes with success. They want to be proud of themselves more than they want to be surrounded by fawning waiters at the beach club. Self-employed people are 29 percent more likely to work over forty-four hours a week than the average, and 63 percent more likely than those who work at nonprofit foundations. All of this makes a soggy, bitter soufflé of the foolish French legislation in 2000, which prevented employees from working more than thirty-five hours each week. French politicians thought the cap would magically conjure up more jobs. They got the economics wrong. Banning people from working longer hours hurt people and hurt the economy. Policymakers should have flipped back the pages of their manuals to the nineteenth century: Back then the French economist Frederic Bastiat blasted such thinking in a parody, proposing the government should slice off everyone's right arm. That way it would take twice as many workers to get anything done! In 2005, faced with a 10 percent jobless rate, France threw in the towel on the thirty-five-hour cap, which had neither created more jobs nor more joy.

PEOPLE LIKE THEIR JOBS, EVEN IF THEY DO GRIPE

Now, I am perfectly aware that jobs do not seem as secure as they used to be, that defined benefit pension plans have faded, and that hardly anyone gets a gold watch after twenty years. And, of course, some people have lousy jobs and hate their bosses, as well as the annoying guy in the next cubicle. When you hate your job during the day, or when your detestable boss hates you, it is very hard to be nice to your spouse and children in the evening. This is beyond doubt. But might the grumbling sometimes be exaggerated? While Adam Smith posed a desire "to better," William Safire proposed a deep human desire "to complain." The *Dilbert* concept of a cubicle surely sounds demeaning—nothing says "your job is safe" more clearly than an "office" made out of dusty Nerf material that a two-year-old could knock over. Why do people share *Dilbert* comics and watch a send-up on TV like *The Office*? I suspect these are popular not because they remind millions of people of their own daily misery, but because they show readers/viewers an alternate, exaggerated work universe filled with misery and absurdity.

In fact, most people really like their jobs. A random sample of over twenty-seven thousand Americans between 1972 and 2006 showed that 86 percent were satisfied with their jobs, with nearly half describing themselves as very satisfied. For the past twenty years around Labor Day, the Gallup pollsters have released an annual poll on job satisfaction. The percentage of employees either "completely" or "somewhat" satisfied has ranged between 85 and 94 percent. Looking at similar data, Syracuse University's Arthur Brooks concluded that even those who call themselves "working class, those 'nickel and dimed' folks," scored just a few points below average in satisfaction. Most people felt satisfied, regardless of how much money they made. Naturally, those who truly believed they were in "dead-end" jobs planned to quit and find something else.

If the social critics are right and we are in a vicious rat race, shackled to a quick-spinning hedonic treadmill, wouldn't you think that knowing someone's income would help you predict his happiness level? After all, those who slip in income would slide off the treadmill as their "superiors" go shopping at Saks. But here's the truth: Personal control predicts happiness much better than income. Someone who earns peanuts at the zoo, but decides when to feed the elephants and when to take his own break, may be happier than (a) the emeritus executive who still gets a fat paycheck though no one listens to him anymore, or (b) the harried dentist who has to ask his office manager when he can slip out to the bathroom. As little kids, we want to demonstrate that we can change the world, or at least dump our oatmeal. As adults we want to show that we can play a role in our workplace and have some impact.

I made a strategic error in my hedge fund consulting company back in the 1990s. Most of my employees were in their late twenties and early thirties, with graduate degrees. We were publishing a daily analysis linking economics, financial markets, and politics. Our clients, a who's who of hedge fund moguls, including George Soros and top portfolio managers at Goldman Sachs and Morgan Stanley, eagerly awaited our missives forecasting the yen, the dollar, and the next move by the Federal Reserve Board. Bill Clinton's top advisers, George Stephanopoulos, Bob Rubin, and Larry Summers, read our briefings. We were powerful, but we were exhausted from the daily grind. I wanted to alleviate the stress, and therefore directed each employee to take off every other Friday. I thought they would like the idea—some R&R, after fighting in the trenches of financial markets and politics. They nodded their heads and followed the plan for a few weeks. Then I noticed something interesting. The scheduled vacationers started to rebel against me and acted like scabs on the picket line, refusing *not* to show up for work. Why? Because they were trying to build their careers, trying to unleash their creativity. I had wounded their pride in a scheme that seemed to make everybody dispensable except for me.

GO WITH THE FLOW—TO WORK

Mihaly Csikszentmihalyi developed the concept of "flow," a state of mind that arises when we are completely entranced, enthralled, and absorbed by an activity. Time flies when you are a potter and love the whirl of the wheel, or when you are Dizzy Gillespie lost in a bebop riff. Flow seems to require a high level of concentration, a love of the activity. It's not just washing dishes and "zoning out." Fans of flow tell people to pursue their bliss and lose themselves in the whoosh of time. Since a real job is a drag, tell the boss to kiss off, grab an easel and tubes of oil paint, and go off to Provence. That's the romantic story. And it has certainly worked for some authors and moviemakers in Provence. But for most of us, it doesn't. Researchers were startled to discover that we have more flow experiences at *work* than at our homes. Hanging out in our game room and playing with the toys of our hobbies, whether stamps, toy trains, or video games, would not induce as much flow as plain old work. Our minds like work, even if we tape *Dilbert* cartoons all around our desks. For achieving flow, the workplace beats listening to our favorite music or hanging out in our free time.

Do you ever wonder why Norman Mailer always looked like he was scowling? Writers, musicians, and artists, who would seem to score high on a flow scale, tend to be more prone to depression. Extroverts are happier. Showing up for work and bumping into coworkers in the restroom and around the coffeepot points us toward happiness. Entrepreneurs are happiest when they begin bringing other people into their venture, and sharing their enthusiasm. In contrast, flow in front of a lonely typewriter is not a recipe for happiness, it turns out. Eugene O'Neill and Tennessee Williams achieved flow but often in a stupor. Their literary flow barely kept pace with the flow from the bottle.

We mistakenly suspect that people work harder than necessary because they want to trump each other at the country club, or leave skid marks in the parking lot as they zoom away in their new Ferraris. This is true of some and is certainly the reputation of someone like Donald Trump, but friends of mine who have worked with him assure me that the glitz is more a pose to support the Trump brand. In reality, they describe him as a "schlump" (with crop-circle hair). He may be daring with other people's money, but he's a lot more shrewd than the bling suggests. He may get this genetically. My grandfather was a developer and a friend of Trump's father, Fred, when they were building houses along the East Coast in the 1940s and 1950s, along with Bill Levitt of Levittown. My grandfather told me that while he and Levitt played pinochle and poker every night, Fred Trump refused to join in. "He was too cautious to gamble," my grandfather said.

WORK HELPS US RE-CREATE OURSELVES AND CREATE TOMORROW

Greed and envy do not explain the extra hours of work, despite the Edenist screeds. A different psychological/neurological drive is playing out: Work rides the waves of chemicals we discussed in the previous chapter. Work charges up our brains with dopamine when we start anticipating a new success. It does not matter whether the anticipation comes from a stock that has been upgraded, a poker hand that suddenly starts looking like a winner, or a new breakthrough project at the office.

Those neighbors of yours rushing to work are inspired by new activities. They would drive much more slowly and sluggishly to a dreary assembly-line operation dictated by a Stalinist potentate. We want the hope of a new tomorrow. Not because we want to brag about our bangles, beads, and BMWs, but because we want to feel better. I don't care whether you believe in God, Darwin, Richard Dawkins, or Richard Pryor, you cannot believe that our species would have survived fifty thousand years if we did not have some inner mechanism that made us want to see tomorrow and play a role in it.

Daniel Gilbert has cleverly noted that we get no kick from watching a recording of *Monday Night Football* on Tuesday, even if we did not know who won: "Because the fact that the game has already been played precludes the possibility that our cheering will somehow penetrate the television, travel through the cable system, find its way to the stadium, and influence the trajectory of the ball as it hurtles toward the goalposts!"

We want the freedom to control or at least influence our world. We want to feel the freedom to succeed. People in free countries are happier than those in countries that feel like prisons. Remember, the Berlin Wall was not intended to keep out Westerners. It was intended to keep in East Germans. But sheer freedom is not enough, of course, to create happiness. *We want to feel good about our success.* We want to deserve our pleasure. Guilty pleasures are reserved for Godiva chocolate. People who do not feel responsible for their own success feel sadder 25 percent of the time. That's why lottery winners usually lose their giddy smiles pretty quickly.

It's easy to misunderstand the motivation of entrepreneurs. Sure, money is important, but Bill Gates did not have a vision of dollar bills stacked up to the moon and back. He had this vision: I can see a computer on every desk. Steve Jobs imagined an iPhone in every hand. Mary Kay Ash imagined soft skin on the cheeks of every housewife. Today at laboratories in San Diego, Geneva, and San Juan, Puerto Rico, scientists imagine a vaccine to prevent breast cancer. There are easier ways to pay your mortgage, but working hard and fighting for success makes us happier.

Flip the dictionary to the word "drive." You will quickly see a verb and a noun. These homonyms are not a mere verbal coincidence. The verb "to drive" means to steer a vehicle. The noun "drive" means a strong internal motivation to succeed. We drive our cars forward, not because the car pushes its own transmission to the "D" slot, but because we shift the car and step on the accelerator. We do this deliberately. We try to control the vehicle. Our hearts pump, our muscles twitch. We are driven to go. We are driven to succeed. We cannot lift ourselves to a happy state without both kinds of drive. We need tools, but we also need the guts to pick them up. When Churchill pleaded with the United States to send ammo, he assured, "Give us the tools, and we will do the job." Previously, he called upon the British to supply the "blood, toil, sweat and tears." Churchill was fighting for freedom. To fight is a verb. But to be happy is also a verb—a word of action that calls on all the organs, juices, and muscles that evolved so that we could survive as a species. The freer we are to choose our jobs and to exercise some control over our tasks, the more likely we are to taste our share of happiness.

CHAPTER 5

Darwin and a Tale of Three Apes:
Why Competition Does Not Make Us Evil

*What's the Big Idea? We weren't hardwired to be
happy or good, but engaging in competition can
help make us both.*

I have bad news to share: Our minds and bodies were neither designed nor did they evolve to maximize happiness, contentment, glee, or kindness to animals. We are animated to maximize survival—to live, to fight on behalf of our children and the possibility that our genes will be passed on to new generations. Sometimes in the course of human events that comes from holding hands or forming teams to stack sandbags to stop a flood. Sometimes—very, very rarely—it means eating human flesh. Of course, nature does not literally scream "live!" in our ears or give us a paperback survival guide. *Nature merely dangles the hope of positive feelings if we do useful things that promote survival.*

For example, our bodies need sugars. Mother Nature gives us a tongue that likes sweetness. Having children gives our genes a future life. So, the idea of sex kindles our loins, our dreams, and our dopamine and nitric oxide circuits. Nature dangles bad feelings, too. Venomous snakes can kill us. Mother Nature gives most of us the willies when we see one slither by.

WE'RE ASKING THE WRONG QUESTION

Once we understand this million-year backdrop, we should realize that *"Why aren't you happy?" is the wrong question.* Happiness is not a default position for our species. It isn't a given. Considering all that we face, from nosy neighbors to jealous boyfriends to skinflint bosses, it's amazing that we can become happy at all! Quite often social scientists ask the wrong question. How many times have you heard someone ask, "What causes poverty?" That's a simple question. I can create poverty in a few days. I'll just stop working. That's no great mystery. Poverty is the default for the human race. We've got, oh, thirty thousand years' experience creating it. The challenge—the miracle of the past two hundred years—is creating wealth and *escaping* poverty. Like escaping poverty, escaping a state of misery is the challenge for all human beings. The default case is not Eden. We cannot go back to paradise, and should not assume that taking out an eraser (or a pill) to wipe away our stress and competitive urges will somehow deliver us back to a natural, happy state. We must fight for our happiness, and while we may come out bloodied and bruised, we usually come out as better people. It took a long time for Charles Darwin to figure some of this out. He did not get off to a strong start. Darwin's father himself told young Charles: "You care for nothing but shooting, dogs and rat-catching, and you will be a disgrace to yourself and all your family."

THE MAN WITH THE PLUMP GIRLFRIEND

At age twenty-eight after five years at sea, Charles Darwin called his girlfriend "plump"—and he survived! In 1838 "plump" was a compliment. He was deciding whether to propose marriage. So he did the logical thing for an awkward, nerdy young man: He penned a cost-benefit analysis in his sloppy handwriting. While he dreaded giving up "the conversation of clever men at clubs," he took comfort knowing he would have a wife "to be beloved & played with—better than a dog, anyhow." He worried about the expense of furnishing a house, and that he would be a "poor slave," no longer able to travel, even to "go up in a balloon." On the positive side, he could picture himself with "a nice soft wife on a sofa with good fire, & books & music." Darwin's situation suggests four important things about human nature: First, humans prefer *companionship*, whether canine or connubial. Second, humans must make *choices* in their lives—they are not as instinctually predetermined as simpler beasts. As Mary Poppins says to her openmouthed young ward, Michael: "We are not a codfish." Third, when Darwin praises plumpness, he reminds us that *eating* is primary. Early human beings spent most of their daylight hours foraging for nuts and berries, or tracking animals, hoping to put meat on their own bones. Even today in poorer countries, people will spend 50 percent of their income on food. And in wealthy countries, well, consider how much time you might spend with friends plotting where to have dinner. Fourth, *cultural tastes* change, for few eighteen-year-old lads in England today would list "plump" among the pros in a list of pros and cons. Back in Darwin's day plumpness indicated someone was wealthy enough to buy a lot of food. If the British model Twiggy had shown up in London in the 1860s rather than the 1960s, she would have been rushed to a hospital or returned to some debtor's prison. These four items are key to understanding where we come from, our search for happiness, and our hardwired drive to compete.

By uncovering the brutal logic of survival, Darwin peeled back embarrassing secrets of our species. We care what others think; we care what they possess; and we strive to keep up with them. There's an old joke about a rich lady who discovers that her husband has taken a young mistress. She's outraged and demands to see a photo of the hussy. The husband shows her a photo and defends himself. "Everyone's got one. Even Sam Green." "Sam Green?" she replies astonished. "Sure," says the husband, "he's sleeping with that waitress at the club." "Her?" snips the wife. "Well, *our* mistress is much better-looking."

There may be nothing pretty about the evolution of our species, but we are what we are. And the truth is our evolution has imprinted the urge to compete in our genes, to ensure our survival and allow us glimpses of elusive happiness. Darwin was no Dr. Frankenstein, and *Homo sapiens* are not monsters.

SURVIVAL OF THE MOST COMPETITIVE

The career guide *What Color Is Your Parachute?* has sold millions of copies and its rainbow cover peeks out from the shelf in school guidance counselors' offices around the world. The book's logic makes sense: First figure out what kind of person you are; then find a career that matches your skills and interests. We might ask the same question before choosing our economic system. What kind of ape are we? Deep down, at the genetic level, are we ruthless, kind, rapacious, sympathetic? What kind of acts and emotions fire up our chemical transmitters? Darwin did not know anything about neurotransmitters. In fact, he did not know much about the human body when he sailed on the HMS *Beagle* in 1831. While critics of free markets often link Darwin to a dog-eat-dog, zero-sum world, where one man's lunch is another's empty lunch pail, Darwin did not board the *Beagle* looking for blood. He had much humbler aims. He was looking for bugs and leaves. As for man, Darwin had a fairly charitable view of the species. He was clubbable, good company, but naïve about business. The only thing he seemed to compete for was the best collection of bugs. At Cambridge University, a friend drew wonderful cartoons of Charles riding on the back of a bug with the caption: "Go to it, Charles!" Though

Charles came to believe he was descended from apes, his most immediate lineage was more illustrious: His domineering father, Robert, was a physician and a wealthy financier. His maternal grandfather was Josiah Wedgwood, patriarch of the Wedgwood china family.

Robert thought Charles was a bit of a ninny and tried to shame him into skipping the voyage of the *Beagle*. It was just another useless escapade for his luftmensch son. Charles was too timid to take on his father alone, so he pleaded with a Wedgwood uncle to persuade Robert that Charles was not wasting his life. Wedgwood won the day, and Charles got the trip of a lifetime, which seemed like a lifetime on a ninety-foot, three-masted boat that sailed around Africa, Asia, South America, and across the Atlantic. Charles was dirty, often sick and hungry, but always fascinated. He particularly liked the finches in the Galapagos. He could not figure out how two islands near each other could be home to similar but not identical finches. And why did each kind of finch seem best-suited for the trees and insects of its island? He surmised that the finches had adapted to the environmental conditions of their island. But how? Darwin had read *An Essay on Population* by the English economist Thomas Malthus, which argued that population will outstrip food, and therefore there will be a continuing struggle to see who gets to eat. Remember, the search for nourishment never ends, and eating is primary.

Darwin then conjectured that if there is a constant struggle for survival, those who adapt best to environmental conditions will prevail. When he gazed at finches, he was looking at the winners in life's sweet and bitter skirmish. "Natural selection" was born in Darwin's mind. (Darwin did not actually use the expression "survival of the fittest," a catchphrase that debuted in Herbert Spencer's 1864 *Principles of Biology*.) Sure, the process of natural selection had been going on for millions, if not billions, of years, but the thought did not occur until the 1830s. Now, if you had an earth-shattering, or species-shattering, idea, you would most likely share it at least with some friends or colleagues at the lunch table. Darwin, however, kept quiet for about fifteen years. Perhaps he worried that his idea was also "church-shattering" (he later stated that he felt like confessing to the murder of God). Perhaps he was too busy fathering ten children and writing a treatise on barnacles. After five years at sea on the *Beagle*, he never left England again, and he seldom left his study in Down House, his home southeast of London. He didn't turn into a bug à la Kafka, but he almost turned into a hermit. He aimed a mirror outside his window so he could detect any visitors and hide before they knocked on his door. We also know he was often distracted by depression, listlessness, indigestion, and awful itches perhaps contracted from tropical insect bites. He resorted to experimental treatments, including vinegar baths and electric shocks, presumably not at the same time. Ironically, the man who would become identified with "survival of the fittest" was fitted with fits and proved most unfit.

Finally, in the 1850s, Darwin started to hear of other scientists working on vaguely similar ideas. Snippets of Darwinian thought even showed up in fiction. In 1847, the future prime minister Benjamin Disraeli wrote a political novel, *Tancred*, which was worthy of Oscar Wilde and made fun of socialites who put too much faith in pseudoscience. In the novel a daffy Lady Constance lauds a new book called *The Revelation of Chaos*, which "explains everything. . . . First there was nothing, then there was something; then I forget the next, I think there were shells, then fishes; then we came. Let me see, did we come next? Never mind that; we came at last. And the next stage will be something very superior to us; something with wings. Ah! That's it: we were fishes, and I believe we shall be crows. But you must read it."

With so much nonsense and sense floating around, Darwin grew worried that he was at risk of losing his ideas to others. At a badly attended London meeting of the Linnean Society in 1858, Darwin's ideas were presented alongside a paper by the naturalist Alfred Russel Wallace, whose thesis was so close to Darwin's that Darwin said, "I never saw a more striking coincidence . . . even his terms now stand as heads of my chapters." Wallace may have spoken of monkeys in the Amazon, but those monkeys sounded a lot like Darwin's finches. Wallace had sent his papers to Darwin, and now Darwin had two worries. First, he wanted to maintain his first-in-line claim, knowing he had written down his ideas in the 1840s. Second, having a big heart, Darwin fretted that Wallace would think him petty for pressing that claim: "I would far rather burn my whole book, than that he or any other man should think that I had behaved in a paltry spirit."

Motivated by the spirit of competition and comforted that his work preceded Wallace's by over a decade, Darwin finally sent his full manuscript to a publisher named John Murray. Murray sent the treatise to a lawyer named George Pollock, who called it "beyond the comprehension of any living scientist." Then Murray sent it to Whitwell Elwin, who edited the *Quarterly Review*. Elwin thought it "wild and foolish," and suggested that Darwin instead write about pigeons. "Everybody is interested in pigeons," he counseled. Nonetheless, Murray went forward in November 1859, selling out the first run of 1,250 copies in a single day. The world has not been the same since. The eminent biologist Thomas Henry Huxley declared, "How stupid of me not to have thought of it!" and became known as Darwin's bulldog, spreading the word against all sorts of attackers.

Take a moment and think about Darwin as a metaphor for natural selection. Equipped with the idea of natural selection in his head, Darwin was himself a kind of mutant. At the time he first had the idea, he was radically different from other scientists and biologists (except Wallace and Huxley). He had learned a new way to look at the world. The new method proved potent and spread (today we might say it "went viral"). Those scientists who shared and adapted to Darwin's view ultimately won the race for university chairs.

Of course, Darwin did not agree with all of the Darwinists who embraced his ideas and then ran with them. Huxley and Herbert Spencer took Darwin's biology into the social realm and soon "survival of the fittest" took on a moral tone. The winners in life's competition must be morally superior, not just physically superior. This violated the logic of the great Scottish philosopher David Hume, who a hundred years earlier argued that you cannot deduce an "ought" from an "is." In other words, just because something does exist does not mean it ought to exist from a moral point of view. Just because a Galapagos lizard suns itself on the rocks better than another does not mean that the more successful lizard has a nobler conscience. He isn't a good lizard or a bad lizard; he's just a lizard. But because he is alive, he was probably born from a competitive family.

Darwin did not see only fierce competition in species; he also thought kindness and sympathy might be built into our bodies and brains. While Huxley tended to see sympathy as a cultural artifice taught in the churches, in the schools, and at the dining room table, Darwin suspected that it was innate. He loved to study animals and documented the facial expressions and moods of monkeys, dogs, and people. He spent a lot of time sketching and interpreting the gaze of his "sharp-witted" white fox terrier, Polly. Polly apparently had a very expressive face, filled with emotion, no more so than when Darwin taught her to catch biscuits off her nose. In work that predated Paul Ekman's research by a hundred years, Darwin asked missionaries to report their observations on facial expressions, and often reviewed his own notes on meeting "primitive" islanders while on the *Beagle* voyage. The point is that Darwin did not believe that man was simply violent, rapacious, and brutish. He also saw a softer side in our apish past. Now let's look at the three apes in each of us: the bad ape, the good ape, and the competitive ape.

THE BAD APE

Woody Allen said modern business life is not dog-eat-dog. That would be direct and predictable. It's worse than that; it's "dog doesn't return other dog's phone call." Try as we might, we cannot ignore our violent and selfish impulses. You can stomp on them, you can try to rise above them, but whatever you do, they'll still lurk, waiting to pounce on you, for they were shaped a million years ago. Our ability to grow violent quickly protected us against rampaging invaders with clubs and stalking wolves with fangs.

In France a paleontologist brushed off the dust of a skeleton. The stocky hominid, probably thickly muscled, lacked a strong chin. It was *Homo neanderthalensis*, our crude, stupid, and hairy relative from back east. But this Neanderthal from forty thousand years ago looked different. The left side of his skull was dented, and jammed into the rib cage was the head of a spear. Was this an accident? Forensic scientists concluded that another Neanderthal had thrust a spear into the rib cage, and delivered a fatal blow to the skull as well. The victim was a male, as most victims and most perpetrators of violence have been. The same rule holds mostly true today for *Homo sapiens*. Just as Little Red Riding Hood observes that Grandmother has big teeth, and the wolf replies, "All the better to eat you with!" we observe that males have bigger shoulders and arms, "All the better to beat you with." True, a single murder among Neanderthals does not prove that they were especially violent cousins. Yet life among the Neanderthals probably did involve a lot of snarling and the turning of outstretched hands into shaking fists. These are reflexes and impulses, not the conscious choice of actors portraying violence. As Steven Pinker has pointed out, "boys in all cultures spontaneously engage in rough and tumble play, which is obviously practice for fighting."

Last year I took my daughters to York in northern England. York (Jorvik) was an old Viking port, dominated by the Danes around AD 900. The Jorvik Viking Centre has wonderful displays of decaying Vikings, showcasing the skeletal dents of spears and battle-axes. And, of course, the gift shop was packed with schoolkids menacingly waving foam rubber swords. I have to admit that most of the sword swingers were boys. Does this mean that girls and women are less competitive? No; it simply means they may direct their competitive spirits in different directions.

Studies on patriarchal and matrilineal societies show that when society gives women the upper hand, they are quite happy to take it and swing it hard. Compare the Maasai of Tanzania and the Khasi of India. Among the Maasai, women are chattel. Among the Khasi, they control the money and the power. Researchers challenged men and women in each tribe to throw a ball into baskets, earning money for each basket scored. If they beat their competitors, they would earn triple the amount. The dominating women of the Khasi played hardest, beating the Khasi men. The dominating Maasai men outplayed the submissive Maasai women. Most interesting, perhaps, the dominating Khasi women narrowly outhustled the dominating Maasai men. All this suggests that the spirit of competition is inborn among both sexes, but can be enhanced or tamped down by the structure of rewards in society.

The comedian Jack Benny boasted that in forty years of marriage he and his wife never considered divorce. Not once. Murder? Yes! But divorce, never. Sure enough, psychologists report that 90 percent of men and 80 percent of women fantasize about killing someone, though not necessarily a spouse. Violence may not be "random and senseless" from an evolutionary point of view. A male may resort to violence to wipe out a sexual rival, access food, or scare off other men by proving he is willing to kill in order to defend his family. A woman might kill to defend her body or her children.

If *Homo sapiens* can be moved to kill, then there is little point arguing that we can also act in ways that are petty, envious, acquisitive, and every other fault that puts you at the back of Deepak Chopra's class. I am not aware of any religion anywhere that denies man's fallibility. The question is whether man's fallibility comes from within, or whether he is just a victim of circumstances. In *West Side Story*, Stephen Sondheim's brilliant lyrics to "Gee, Officer Krupke" list just about every excuse to exonerate members of the Jets gang:

> We ain't no delinquents, we're misunderstood.
> Deep down inside of us there is good . . .
> My parents treat me rough. With all their marijuana,
> They won't give me a puff.
> They didn't want to have me,
> But somehow I was had,
> Leapin' lizards! That's why I'm so bad . . .
> Gee, Officer Krupke, we're down on our knees,
> 'Cause no one wants a fellow with a social disease . . .*

---

* "Gee, Officer Krupke" by Leonard Bernstein, lyrics by Stephen Sondheim. Copyright © 1956, 1957, 1958, 1959 by Amberson Holdings and Stephen Sondheim. Copyright renewed. Leonard Bernstein Music Publishing Company LLC, publisher Boosey & Hawkes, Inc., sole agent. International copyright secured. Reprinted by permission.

Clearly, there are times when bad parenting, lousy schools, and dangerous circumstances propel people to grievous acts. Sometimes we may fight a just war, but just as clearly we have evil impulses that explode from within. Even kids brought up in pristine suburbs with white picket fences will occasionally pick up a fence post and smack a neighbor. People are people, sheep are sheep, and foxes are foxes. You might be able to train a sheep to act nastily and bite like a fox. But just try to persuade a fox to stand in the meadow innocently bleating a "baaah" as a meal saunters by. The real question is whether the spirit of competition is the culprit in the evil we see around us. The charge is misplaced. The competitive drive is a tool that motivates us. It does not tell us what exactly we should be interested in achieving. That's where parents, preachers, and teachers come in. We have seen competitive drives used to conquer famine, plague, and invading marauders. You can see the spirit of competition spurring a farmer to plant more crops, or a biologist to stay late at the laboratory testing a new vaccine. To blame competitiveness for evil is like blaming thirst for a drunk stumbling down an alley.

THE GOOD APE

In just the past few years, it has become more fashionable among psychologists to find the good ape in all of us. Sure, we have impulses to steal, cheat, and kill. But we have impulses to hug and cuddle. And these impulses are long-standing. Millions of years ago our ancestors may have been chimpanzees. Then some of their progeny began to stand up and roam the open savannas of Africa. We still share over 98 percent of our DNA with modern chimps, less difference than you would find between a horse and a zebra. But we are no longer chimps. Though chimps have played starring roles in movies, primatologists now admit that they can be more violent than even a drugged-up Hollywood egotist. A chimp could not have written *Hamlet*, but might readily murder his uncle for the status. Romantics find this difficult to accept.

When Jane Goodall first went to Tanzania she was twenty-six. She was pretty, unmarried, adventurous, and nervy. She had bucked the traditional British college system and managed to get into Cambridge University's graduate school program with a prior degree from a secretarial school. By the 1970s she had spent about thirty years in the jungle, reporting on chimps, mostly saying nice things. Documentaries and articles about her work tended to marvel at the chimp and wonder why men could not act as civilly as our cousins. Clearly, it seemed that human society, with all its envy, competition, and stress, had fouled up our branch of the family.

Then Goodall witnessed the "Four Year War" of the 1970s. It was a chimp war. Males broke into two groups and attacked each other. While Goodall had seen much tenderness and hand-holding among the chimps, suddenly she was seeing fangs come out, even among chimps who had lived together in peace. When she woke in the night, "horrific pictures sprang unbidden to my mind"—a female chewing on an infant's flesh, "her mouth smeared with blood like some grotesque vampire from the legends of childhood." Even more wrenching for Goodall, she had named the predators and knew the nicknames of the bleeding victims. She described the wounds and atrocities the way a family member would after visiting the scene of a crime. How could the chimps act so viciously, so human? Chimps have long memories and can remember individuals years after separation. But they do not have loyalties. All that matters is whether another chimp belongs to the territorial breeding group.

Some critics suggest that the Four Year War may have been inadvertently instigated by Goodall. By feeding the chimps, she disturbed their natural balance. Among these critics is an affable best-selling author and Dutch primatologist at Emory University named Frans de Waal. De Waal is less well known for criticizing Goodall and better known for popularizing the "kinder, gentler" cousin of the chimp, the bonobo ape.

Bonobos look like smaller chimps, but their less arched eyebrows make them look less cartoonish and more professorial. They are also more matriarchal, more promiscuous, and more into kissing on the lips than the chimp. They have more sex than residents of a co-ed dorm in Amsterdam. And they are the toast of the town among primatologists and socialites as well. At least that is the reputation for this chimp cousin that lives in Congo, and now at many zoos. In a superb *New Yorker* article called "Swingers," Ian Parker describes a fund-raiser for bonobos held in a downtown Manhattan yoga club. The audience of "young, shoeless people sat cross-legged . . . listening to Indian-accented music and eating snacks prepared by Bonobos," a restaurant that serves raw vegetarian food. The restaurant's menu declares: "Wild bonobos are happy, pleasure-loving creatures whose lifestyle is dictated by instinct and Mother Nature." The founder of a bonobo support group stood up at the yoga club and said that bonobos were "into peace and love and harmony . . . They might even have been the first ape to discover marijuana." The last time Manhattanites were treated to such an odd fete, Leonard Bernstein served Roquefort cheese hors d'oeuvres to the Black Panthers in his Park Avenue duplex. The bonobos are, however, far more sympathetic than Eldridge Cleaver ever was.

The *New York Times* and *Washington Post* have quoted primatologists who report that when bonobos are not copulating, they are comforting the sick and supporting each other during labor. They're like Gandhi letting his robe down at the Playboy mansion.

But could these bonobo traits be exaggerated? Is it possible that, like Margaret Mead, some primatologists are going a bit far in nearly nominating these apes for Nobel peace prizes? De Waal calls the animals "elegant" and says they enjoy "love and peace." He points out that "no bonobo has ever been observed eliminating its own kind, neither in the wild nor in captivity." True. However, the crucial words are "in the wild." It turns out that hardly anyone observes bonobos in the wild. The Congo forest is remote and dangerous, both because of marauding elephants and marauding humans. I watched the bonobos literally hang out at the San Diego Zoo. I was surprised to find out that this is where a large proportion of professional primatologists do their bonobo research. The weather's great, and there's a Starbucks down the road. But captivity is an odd environment. Bonobos face a different kind of hunting challenge when they are fed by polite, tanned Southern

Californians, instead of chasing down antelope and ripping out their intestines. Remember, human prison behavior is not the same as street behavior, either. Human prisoners at a penitentiary are known to have different sex lives in their cells than they do in their bedrooms back home.

ARE WE BUILT TO BE NICE?

A few years ago Jorge Moll, an Argentine researcher at the U.S. National Institutes of Health, sent an urgent e-mail to a colleague, Jordan Grafman: "You gotta see this!"

Grafman, a gap-toothed neuroscientist who had led the Vietnam War Head Injury project at the Walter Reed Army Medical Center, began to read the results of a brain-imaging test, thinking, "Whoa—wait a minute!" Just then Moll burst through the door and the two scientists stared at each other, stunned.

What had they found? The neuroscientists had hooked up volunteers to an MRI machine and gave them the choice of keeping money or donating money to charity. When the volunteers chose to give the money away, the MRIs showed a glow coming from the primitive limbic brain that usually signals a desire for food and sex. Moll and Grafman surmised that altruism may be a primitive, inherited genetic code, not just a moral code handed down from Mount Sinai. Several studies show that when we give to charity or share our winnings at the gaming table, our prefrontal cortexes light up. The "joy of giving" turns out to be a physical pleasure, not just a Sunday sermon. Sunday sermons, therefore, are not invented by moralists but are the result of our biology.

Psychologists sometimes refer to "helper's high," when volunteering seems to lift endorphin levels, and scientists have wondered whether they could induce it. We know that we can alter our chemical balances. Just as the caffeine in a huge mug of coffee can make some people twitch and tap their fingers nervously, other drugs can enhance emotional activity. So in a Los Angeles laboratory researchers gave volunteers a shot of oxytocin (the "cuddle hormone") and then tested whether they would be willing to share money with strangers. Sure enough, the thirty-four volunteers were 80 percent more generous than those who received a placebo. All this proves that drugs can be effective. But it would seem a dubious strategy for society to inject or dope people into kindness.

In Aldous Huxley's (the grandson of Thomas Huxley) *Brave New World*, people escape the pain and stress of life by ingesting "soma," a magical drug that packs up troubles and leaves people smiling. The novel gets its title from Shakespeare's *The Tempest*, in which Miranda, for the first time, sees what a young man looks like: "How many goodly creatures are there here! How beauteous mankind is! O brave new world! That has such people in't!" She'll learn that not all the men are goodly, and even the goodliest is not all good.

Just as Miranda infers too quickly and extrapolates too far, I am concerned that in the interest of showing the good side of humanity, some researchers may sometimes shade the darker side and infer weighty conclusions from little study. It is one thing to observe limbic brains light up in a few dozen graduate students; it is another to want to tear up social and economic systems affecting hundreds of millions of people, as Richard Layard, Juliet Schor, and other economists urge. It is one thing to observe bonobos and people helping relatives and neighbors; it is another to propose a new system that expects people to treat strangers like blood brothers.

U.C. Berkeley's Dacher Keltner published a book in 2009 called *Born to Be Good* that traced physiological impulses toward kindness. Keltner does a fine job when he describes the workings of the vagus nerve, also known as the "wandering" or "rambling" nerve, since it shares its etymologic route with vagabond. The vagus nerve gives us feelings for which we often use metaphors, whether butterflies in the stomach, a lump in your throat, or a warm feeling in your heart. The nerve runs from the brain past the jugular and the carotid through the chest down to the belly. The vagus nerve releases neurotransmitters that can slow down your heartbeat and make you faint, or make you sweat when you are fearful. The vagus may be the "nerve of compassion," for it can gin up your oxytocin levels, leading you to care more, feel more, and trust more. You may find yourself feeling warm and fuzzy at the sight of a puppy rolling next to its mother. Keltner asserts that the vagus nerve developed in mammals to support a new, "caretaking" behavior. People with more active vagus nerves often seem to act in a more nurturing way, although the research is somewhat mixed. We do know that people in all lands have some sense of fairness and capacity for sympathy. I recall when, for the first time, my baby daughter in her high chair picked up her spoon and offered her oatmeal to me. Children and pet dogs will offer comfort and share their toys.

Keltner, who likes to speak in terms of Asian philosophy, also promotes "jen," a Confucian term his mother taught him, meaning love of fellow man. He concludes that survival of the kindest may be a more accurate description of our evolution than survival of the fittest. (Leo Durocher, who argued that "Nice guys finish last," would disagree. Then again, 1940s Brooklyn was more ruthless than today's Berkeley.) Keltner himself may be too kind. Despite his fine work, he seems to try very hard to exonerate mankind and Charles Darwin from transgressions. Where were those vagus nerves in the 1930s and 1940s when so many Germans, Poles, and Latvians *volunteered* to round up Jews, Gypsies, and homosexuals? Humans have a bad habit of dehumanizing other humans, which somehow blocks the vagus nerve from doing its protective duty. The vagus nerve receives a much fainter signal when we consider distant strangers rather than close family. George Orwell wrote of his service in the Spanish Civil War, lying in a ditch, grasping a rifle, with "hardly enough cover for a rabbit." Airplanes screamed in the sky above. Suddenly, he saw a young Fascist solider jump up from a trench, tearing across the field. Orwell's job was to kill him. He aimed his gun, but then saw the man's trousers slipping and the soldier trying to run while hoisting them up. Orwell couldn't fire: "I had come here to shoot at 'Fascists,' but a man who is holding up his trousers isn't a 'fascist,' he is visibly a fellow creature, similar to yourself, and you don't feel like shooting at him." There but for the grace of loose trousers went a dead man. The answer is not to humanize people by giving them loose trousers. We cannot design a society that is based on these chance feelings of humanity, even if there is some evolutionary basis.

Keltner writes that when Darwin stopped at Tierra del Fuego and "met the Fuegians, who greeted passengers of the disembarking *Beagle* naked, with arms flailing and long hair streaming, Darwin was the first to make friends with them by reciprocating their friendly chest slaps." That makes Darwin sound magnanimous and nonjudgmental—if not the Bono of biologists, at least the bonobo of researchers. Yet, Keltner fails to quote Darwin's disgusted opinion of the Fuegians. Darwin thought their shacks were "like what children make in summer." He reported that he "could not have believed how wide was the difference between savage and civilised man: it is greater than between a wild and domesticated animal. . . . These poor wretches were stunted in their growth, their hideous faces bedaubed with white paint, their skins filthy and greasy, their hair entangled, their voices discordant and their gestures violent. Viewing such men, one can hardly make oneself believe that they are fellow-creatures. . . ." Scientists should not argue that man is intrinsically good by citing isolated instances of man on his best behavior. The "good" ape is not the whole ape.

THE COMPETITIVE APE

People have noble drives and ignoble drives, strong impulses and weak impulses. For societies to hang together, they must rest not on the highest motives, but on the strongest motives. The challenge, then, is to harness the strongest motives and ride them to a more peaceful, prosperous future.

The problem with socialism is that it takes up too many evenings. The problem with relying on the human impulse for kindness is that it is hard to get anything done. Baking pies and making pottery for each other is nice in a small community but does not allow an economy to grow. An advanced economy relies on transactions among strangers, not neighbors. The old African proverb states it "takes a village to raise a child," but it takes at least two villages to come up with a vaccine for malaria. The word "economy" comes from the Greek *oikos*, meaning household, but there is a logical fallacy in thinking a household economy is the same as an economy of strangers. In ancient Greece the mothers and fathers owned small farms that served as family and business units. Everybody in the *oikos* knew everybody else. They broke bread each night and slept in each other's rooms. But Aristotle knew that a model based on kindness and familiarity could not be extended very far. That's why he stated that a town should only grow so large— the townspeople all need to be able to hear the voice of the herald.

A free-enterprise system based on trade among strangers works more dynamically. A price system allows you to assess whether a job is worth doing. If a system is based on kindness, we would be stumped pretty fast. In Keltner's book he tries to create a jen pricing mechanism— for example, watching kids at his daughter's playground delivers a 1.5 jen ratio but standing in line at the post office yields a paltry and exasperating .125. Now, let's say somebody starts a business and will stand in line for you, would you give him .12 jens? What would he do with it? What is a jen? Can it be traded? Invested? Is 1 jen to me equal to 1 jen to you? I do not mean to make fun of jen. But jen is obviously a personal matter. An economy is not. The point of a market-based system is that it allows transactions on like terms. We don't need Confucius or palm readers looking into our souls in order to take $10.00 out of our pocket to buy a book of postage stamps.

Rather than rely solely on the kindness of strangers, we must appreciate and use all our drives. The Talmudists had a memorable way of putting this forward. They debated and recorded biblical teaching after the fall of Jerusalem, and did not deny man's less noble impulses. In the beginning, according to Genesis, God *formed* man from dust and breathed life into him, giving him a living soul. He also *formed* the beasts in the field and the fowl in the air. But Genesis spells the word for "form" differently in the case of man and animals. The root of the word for form is the ancient Hebrew *yetzer*. The Talmudic rabbis note that the spelling used to "form" mankind has a double meaning. It also means drives. In other words, man has more drives than animals. A cheetah might rip the throat of an antelope—that is his drive. Can you blame him? Even the cartoon animals in Disney's *Lion King* sing of the "Circle of Life." Catholic priests do not expect a coyote to trot up to the confessional booth. But a man has a conscience, a drive to help, a drive to grieve, and a drive to be greedy, too. The rabbis spoke of *yetzer hatov* (good drive) and *yetzer hara* (evil drive). The evil drive propels us to cut off a slow driver in traffic, to get our kid into a better school than our neighbor's kid, to shove the change into our pockets instead of putting it into the tip container. It also makes us randy, stirs our loins, and leads us to admire the shapely bottom of the young thing who walks in front of us. Freud's id hosts the *yetzer hara*. Unlike the good drive that is to be cultivated in pews, prayers, and around kitchen tables, the evil drive we try to bolt behind the door or keep zipped up.

Here is the important contribution of the rabbis—they realized that even the evil drive can be constructive. A famous legend in the Talmud tells of a town where the rabbis figure out how to capture and lock up the evil drive. All evil thoughts are banished. Oh, happy day! Then a strange thing happens. Nothing. Nobody gets out of bed, nobody goes to work. Soon there is not one fertilized egg in the chicken coops, not one baby in the village. No female becomes pregnant. It turns out that horniness springs from natural, not always honorable, urges. The Shakers in New England banished sexy thoughts and reproduced nothing but uncomfortable furniture. All that is left is the memory of stern people on hard benches crossing their legs tightly.

We cannot provide a future for ourselves or for our children—or even have children—without accepting our natural drive to strive, to control, to express our humanity. Sometimes the results are embarrassing, of course. For example, "to covet" sounds bad and looks bad. But what if we covet others' wisdom? Or their patience? Or their ingenuity? More important, what if our coveting leads us to study more, work harder, or work more carefully?

WHERE HAVE ALL THE PEOPLE GONE?

Be very careful about scholars who claim to find an overwhelming, in-born human chemistry that pushes us toward happiness or toward moral goodness. Sure, lots of people are nice; maybe most. But evidence for anything universally good is skimpy. A big problem here is that many, many prehistoric and ancient *Homo* societies have died out. We only know about those that: (1) created something lasting, like language, architecture, or art; (2) lived on through their children, like the Israelites and Han Chinese; or (3) left bones that archaeologists have been lucky enough to dig up. Our knowledge of prehistoric and ancient peoples is puny compared to the number and variety of people that have actually walked the earth, or perhaps swung from branch to branch. We can take malaria and yellow fever shots and travel to the Amazon to visit foragers today, but we cannot do time travel. Archaeologists have discovered maybe five thousand prehistoric bodies, not enough to fill up the bleacher seats at Wrigley Field, even if each body was in one piece. But most of them come as bone shards, not whole skeletons.

My point is we know more about the survivors. It is a matter of logic and of statistics. Ancient peoples who had poor economic and political systems died out sooner and were less likely to survive the earth's onslaught of natural disasters. Moreover, they were less able to defend themselves from invaders and bandits. Somewhere buried under the earth across the world are the ground-up bodies of ancient Shakers—people who failed in their struggle against the earth, against beasts, and against fellow humans. Many of them failed because they chose or inherited political and economic systems that failed to take full advantage of their natural drives and capabilities. Many may have failed because they chose or inherited systems of morality or religious practice that ended up fostering diseases or leading to a biological dead end. Consider: though the Hindu civilization has survived, millions of Indians who took ritual baths in the Ganges River subjected themselves to waters heavily contaminated with fecal matter harboring *Vibrio cholera*. One can easily imagine extinct societies that required similar bathing rituals, and failed to emerge from contaminated waters.

Despite what Moll and Grafman discovered about the limbic brain, I am dubious about claims that mankind is chemically born with a universal, chemically triggered revulsion to murder, incest (Darwin married his first cousin), theft, and so on. Yes, almost every civilization we know of condemns these acts. But those are the civilizations we know about today! We cannot, from a scientific point of view, prove the case. There may have been numerous places where theft, incest, and murder were accepted, or even lauded. A universal good remains theory, while the digging continues. Now, it is true that those surviving civilizations seem to share a similar moral code and promote similar emotions ("honor thy father and mother"). But that does not prove that all the groups of *Homo sapiens* who ever existed did likewise. Maybe those without our emotional palette died out because they could not cope, cooperate, or compete.

Utopian researchers tend to speak loudly about good behavior and clam up when bad behavior emerges from the evidence of bones and burial plots. Some anthropologists in Colorado were embarrassed recently when a twelfth-century AD burial ground revealed the remains of twelve humans who had been either grilled or stewed like animals by the Anasazi tribe. To avoid blushing, disappointed experts use a pseudonym for cannibalism: the "C word."

Mankind is capable of all sorts of behavior that seem unnatural and odd, to say the least, to our "modern" minds. In New Guinea today, a tribe segregates young men from young women and then secretly requires the males to regularly ingest the semen of older adolescents, believing that semen will make them braver warriors. I am sure there are plenty of euphemisms to apply to this behavior. The point is that evolution has given us instincts, impulses, and gifts. But without a clear set of directions, people can follow their hearts, brains, and genitals in all kinds of ways.

Why is economic, political, and social anthropology so difficult and such a young field of inquiry? Quite simply, when people are worried about their next meal and surviving the winter, they do not have the luxury of academic pursuits. Until recently, few countries had the wealth to look on their old bones as valuable history. Villagers tended to dump them where convenient. Before World War II, at Dragon Bone Hill in China, a Canadian archaeologist discovered the jaws of "Peking Man," *Homo erectus*. Other digs followed. After the occupation by the Japanese, the fossils were gone. Where did they go? Chinese locals ground them up into medicines. They probably made good calcium pills. In Alan Bennett's brilliant play *The History Boys*, the old schoolteacher recalls that historically all soldiers were unknown soldiers, and "so far from being revered there was a firm in the nineteenth century, in Yorkshire of course, which swept up their bones from the battlefields of Europe in order to ground them into fertilizer." It turns out there may be less world history in textbooks than at your pharmacy and local gardening center.

Still, historians have no choice but to work with what is left. They may also consult people living today in aboriginal cultures, for those who forage in the forests of South America, Africa, and Asia give clues to ancient and prehistoric peoples. What do we know? First, that modern scholars have a tendency to romanticize. So desperate are researchers to uncover and honor peaceful, loving hunter-gatherers in our midst that every decade seems to bring if not a hoax, a display of fantasy and suspension of disbelief. In the 1970s *National Geographic* magazine placed the Tasaday tribe on its cover, a Stone Age clan of cave dwellers on the Philippine island of Mindanao. The cover showed a young boy peacefully climbing a vine looking much like *The Jungle Book*'s Mowgli, in an era when American battleships were steaming toward Vietnam. The Tasaday ate yams and tadpoles, and this meager diet kept them healthy and mentally well. They did not suffer from modern afflictions like divorce or adultery. And, of course, they didn't shop at any place like Kmart. It turned out a Filipino playboy had masterminded the scheme, luring poor villagers to take off their clothes and climb trees in exchange for cigarettes. A best-selling book in the 1960s was called *The Harmless People*, about !Kung Bushmen in the Kalahari. Apparently, Bushmen healers could chase away lions with just their spirits and could cure terrible illnesses using only their hands, which they first washed in fire. It did not take too long to discover that the murder rate among the Bushmen surpassed Baltimore's many times over. Today the author of *The Harmless People* is best known as the author of the beloved, million-copy hit *The Hidden Life of Dogs*.

I do not cite such hoaxes to create cynicism about researchers. Obviously, all but a small number are dedicated and careful. I cite these cases to suggest that the search for Eden, the yearning for Eden, is powerful and prolonged in human history. That means the burden of proof—a very heavy burden of proof—must be placed on the shoulders of those who believe that we can create paradise here, that man's ignoble drives can be staunched, and that we can build an economic system based on Zen, jen, or !Kung principles. In the next few chapters, we will look at the history of economic relationships and the history of competition. We will see how competition actually breeds cooperation. And that this cooperation, instigated by competition, has doubled our life expectancy in the past 150 years. Is that not something to be happy about?

PART 2

HAPPINESS IS HARD WORK

PART 2

CHAPTER 6

Whistle While You Work

What's the Big Idea? You will be happier if you work, even if work sometimes doesn't make you very happy.

When I was a kid I had a favorite relative named "Aunt K," for Kathryn. She was a cross between Madam Curie and Annie Oakley. She had greenish eyes, wore her hair in a bun, and had, my mother said, "a face like the map of Ireland." When Aunt K took us fishing, she fearlessly hooked the bloodworms. She water-skied until age seventy, knew how a carburetor worked, and built her own house of Tennessee stone. She also sang opera, did calculus, and sewed my favorite Halloween costume, a Snoopy dog that won me prizes in parades all through grade school. She hopped the early train into Newark and worked as an actuary for the Mutual Benefit Life Company. She was a pretty good judge of how long people would live. Why did some people live longer? They worked and did not sit down on their behinds. Aunt K had no time for laziness. She *hated* the expression she'd hear at the office, "Take it easy." She grew up in the Depression, and so whenever we happened to pass some construction worker leaning on his shovel, she'd shrug dismissively and say, "Looks just like the WPA."

We think we hate work, but we are wrong. Work extends life; it even makes us happy. Lazy societies die off, and lazy people die off sooner. Competition drives us to improve our lives, which gives us a better chance of achieving good cheer. According to the Bible, human beings once had the chance for a life of contemplation, meditation, and harmony, but the temptations of that darn snake ruined it for all of us. Thus, we are forced to work. Michelangelo's Sistine Chapel frieze of Adam and Eve's expulsion shows Eve looking longingly back to the Garden—possibly worried that she left something behind. Both feel anguish that they will now labor for their bread. They realize they are naked, the sun is setting, and the temperature will drop. They better figure out how to yank down some fig leaves and cover up. They feel a stirring in their stomachs. Where will we get dinner? This is the unavoidable story of life as a hominid on planet Earth.

Happiness gurus associate work with the callous behavior that creates an evil planet. The Cornell economist Robert Frank thinks most of us want to work much less, but we are afraid others won't go along and so we'll fall behind. He thinks we would like living in smaller homes, watching smaller televisions, and cashing smaller paychecks. Frank laments traffic, but by his own logic he should like it, since it creates an obstacle and raises the cost of showing up for work. To the happiness gurus, we are padlocked inside the Prisoner's Dilemma. But they have it wrong. Idle hands are the devil's tools. Busy hands fight evil. Thomas Aquinas argued (and who would argue with Thomas Aquinas?) that indolence makes us sad. The Book of Ecclesiastes states that when our hands are idle, the roof sinks in and the house leaks. The Bible is not literally forecasting a wet floor; it's forecasting a soggy spirit. Confucius warned that an emperor who did not work hard would be wiped away by earthquakes and floods, reflecting a discontented populace. The route to happiness, uncertain though it may be, must include some sweat.

Think again about "idle hands" and "the devil's tools." Human beings have hands with opposable thumbs. As early hominids evolved, we were able to grip more firmly, more finely, and more securely than chimps, bonobos, or orangutans. Our ancestors could count their fingers, and they could count their blessings for this evolutionary gift. This evolving grip put the world in our hands, allowed us to make tools, whether sharp arrowheads for hunting or dainty baskets for carrying fruits. This made work easier and gave us the hope of developing innovations and inventions. Many management experts these days give speeches with titles like "The Innovation Economy," but it has been going on ever since the first hominids realized that not only could they shake a tree to get coconuts to fall off, but they could shape a tool that would cut down the tree.

Recently, neuroscientists have jumped into the act, investigating the role of work on brain activity. When we show ambition and take on a new project at work, serotonin and dopamine start flowing more vigorously. Neurons begin to grow and make new connections. Gray cells, which process information for the central nervous system, become invigorated, allowing the brain to renew itself. When you allow yourself to feel ambition it is like sipping from the fountain of youth. In contrast, when we become less active and less ambitious, advanced scanners and microscopes show serotonin levels slipping and gray cells dying. If you don't show up for work, or simply lean against the shovel or the photocopier, hoping someone else will do the job, you are skipping a sip at the fountain of youth. For those who are big fans of *The 4-Hour Workweek*, I would ask, What will you do the rest of the day? Do you want to take the *risk* of working only four hours? The act of work is like a form of applause, a validation that you are spending your time well. The paycheck comes later. It is like the glow of an encore.

Do you want to get dumb, fast? Retire today. Retirement appears to spark a drop in cognitive abilities, even when controlling for age and health issues. When people decide to retire and when they actually do retire, they cannot recall as many words or think as clearly as those of the same age and health who keep at it. We can see this in international comparisons. Countries that urge people to retire early by heavily taxing work and awarding handsome public pension benefits end up with stupider old people. Forgive me for reporting the research in such crude terms, but the evidence is striking. In the United States and Denmark, for example, a man in his early sixties is one-third less likely to be working than a man in his early fifties. In France and Austria, the older men are 80 to 90 percent less likely to be working. The early retirees pay a price. Cognitive ability of men in their sixties dropped twice as much in Austria and France as in the United States and Denmark. The retired Viennese and Parisians may enjoy tastier pastries while lounging in their cafes, but they can no longer follow the recipe to bake pastries themselves.

Two forces conspire to whittle away at the brain's functions. First, work continually keeps testing and reorienting our mental circuits. Disengaging from work tends to disengage those circuits. Second, anticipating early retirement likely discourages older workers from learning new tricks. Why bother mastering the latest software if you are planning to become obsolete yourself? It's the geriatric version of high school "senioritis"; the graduating class coasts to a close, and learns pretty much nothing in those final months. For most of the twentieth century, Americans followed a trend toward retiring earlier than their parents. But in the past ten years, this trend has reversed a bit. As the authors of an international study on cognitive ability point out, "This is good news for the standard of living of elderly Americans, as well as the fiscal balance of Social Security and Medicare systems . . . it may also be good news for the cognitive capacities of our aging nation."

What is work? I don't want to quibble over definitions. The Department of Labor Statistics categorizes hundreds of jobs, from the mundane insurance adjuster to the nightclub musician. For my purposes here, work is what you do to put food on the table. In an advanced society, that means a job that pays you money. In a primitive society it means a task like hunting or fishing that literally puts a trout or an elk chop on the dinner plate. What about rich people who would have enough money without working? Well, many of them work anyway, perhaps to save wealth for their children or maintain their self-esteem. Both of those are honorable motivations.

YOU ARE WHAT YOU DO AND HOW YOU DO IT

It would be stupid to argue that all jobs make us younger. Thousands of coal miners in the past 150 years emerged from mines with deadly diseases and rotting lungs. Clearly, this book is focused on people who have jobs or can get jobs that do not require them to descend on rickety elevators to perilous depths. It's also true that many feel stuck in boring, deadening jobs, washing dishes or staring at a security monitor. (The key word is "stuck." Are they really stuck? Have they explored all alternative opportunities, including moving across town, or across the world?) The longshoreman philosopher Eric Hoffer observed that "every great cause begins as a movement, becomes a business and eventually degenerates into a racket." Few of us can think of our everyday employment as a "great cause," but as long as it is not a racket or a wretched activity, the effort can make us better off, and not just financially. How one describes a job is pretty subjective. Take the janitor of a hospital. It sounds dreary: sick people, dying people, patients who cannot control their bodily functions. But what do the janitors themselves say? Amy Wrzesniewski of NYU and her colleagues interviewed hospital janitors and discovered that some hated the work and others loved it. Who actually liked cleaning up after others? Those who touched the hands of patients, added water to the flowers, exchanged smiles with visitors, and saw their work as a career or a calling. Those who saw the job simply as mopping up waste thought they were wasting their lives.

Now let's look at an example of another modestly paying job that seems to generate lasting psychic rewards. The hairdresser or barber who counsels his clients, allows his client to sound off about a spouse, or suggests new styles gets more psychic satisfaction than the one who merely picks up scissors and snips. No wonder a UK study showed that hairdressers were the happiest workers, happier than better-paid lawyers and accountants. After a day off, 60 percent of hairdressers in the UK look forward to returning to the salon. Child-care workers and plumbers also scored highly. In Britain, barbers have always had a special role. I recall my first haircut as a graduate student in the UK. After the man had done his work, he looked me in the eye and asked, "Would you be needing anything else, sir?" "Um, no, I don't think so." He then gestured to a drawer with a selection of condoms. I guess the idea was after looking so good, I would have a busy evening. In any event, it showed the role of barber as both haircutter and confidant.

Poets, better known for staring at clouds in the sky or the bottom of wineglasses, have praised work when that labor arouses devotion. A W. H. Auden poem states that one does not even have to know what a man is doing in order to tell if he is devoted to it. Whether a surgeon preparing an incision, a clerk preparing a bill, or a cook mixing his sauce, all you need to do is watch for a "rapt expression" in his eyes. They are all "forgetting themselves in a function."

My Aunt K, who hated "take it easy," thought that we discouraged work with the language we use, even prejudicing children against work because it sounds like punishment. "Labor" sounds like labor camps. When I was a kid we heard about "reform schools," and they sounded like a place where kids were forced to break rocks in the hot sun. However, Donald Hebb, a legendary neuropsychologist, was known for turning work and play on their heads. He took hundreds of children in classrooms and told them that if they misbehaved they would have to go outside and play. If they behaved well, they could stay inside and work. Sure enough, within a few days the children absorbed the cues and preferred work. They also improved their math scores. Hebb knew a great deal about education, if only because he failed the eleventh grade and had to repeat it.

Hebb could have learned a lesson on work/play preferences from Tom Sawyer, Mark Twain's feisty, original American boy. In a celebrated scene, Tom is painting a fence when his friend Ben stops by, hoping to entice Tom to go swimming. At first Ben can't understand how Tom could prefer painting. But Tom replies, "Does a boy get a chance to whitewash a fence every day?" Soon Ben gets caught up in Tom's enthusiasm and asks whether he could have a turn with the brush.

Then Tom states a philosophy worthy of Aquinas or John Locke:

> to make a man or a boy covet a thing, it is only necessary to make the thing difficult to attain. . . . Work consists of whatever a body is OBLIGED to do, and that Play consists of whatever a body is not obliged to do. . . . There are wealthy gentlemen in England who drive four-horse twenty or thirty miles on a daily line, in the summer, because the privilege costs them considerable money; but if they were offered wages for the service, that would turn it into work and then they would resign.

THERE'S A REASON IT'S CALLED A DEPRESSION

What happens when there is no work? In the early 1930s, several years before being thrown in prison by fascists, a young Viennese woman named Marie Jahoda and her new husband, Paul Lazarsfeld, began regular visits to a depressed community in Austria called Marienthal. The town had reason to be downcast. The hundred-year-old textile factory, which started as a flax mill, bolted its doors, and the company town went bankrupt. Marienthal had been a thriving place, with social clubs, libraries, and active political debate. But with three-quarters of the people getting by on government support, life seeped out of the town. Moreover, if government bureaucrats caught sight of anyone actually doing any paid work, they would snatch the relief check from the offender's hand. This included chopping firewood and delivering milk in return for keeping some milk. One man lost his support when he was caught accepting change for blowing into a harmonica. "During the summer we used to go . . . [to] all those dances! Now I don't feel like going out anymore," one woman lamented. This truly was the day that music died. No one was surprised when Jahoda and her husband reported that the people were downhearted. They had lost control, and seemed little more lively than the dogs in Seligman's tests of learned helplessness. Perhaps that was to be expected. But the striking news in this staggering study was how the lack of work seemed to rip the souls out of Marienthalers. People certainly had leisure time, but even free leisure activities exhausted them. The libraries had books, people had time, but few bothered to sit down to read. Just about the only club that seemed to function was the cremation society. Near the end of the data-gathering expedition, one researcher noticed that men were walking more slowly and stopping more often than women when they crossed the street. Wives (who could still stay busy with housework and nonfactory work) put food on the table, but their husbands showed up late. The researchers passed out time surveys, but most of the men could not even remember how they had spent the day. People felt more tired, even though they went to bed earlier. Bedtime shifted back to nine p.m., when it had been eleven p.m. What was the point of staying up? Of course, if MRI and electron microscope devices had been available back then, neuroscientists would have witnessed gray matter retreating, serotonin levels plummeting, and neural connections fading away.

After the Marienthal factory failed, citizens became too dependent on an unstable government. Living on government relief, while necessary in the short term, became fertile ground for depression, mental disease, and a social disease called Nazism. Support for the Nazi Party closely tracked the rising unemployment rate. Despair and idle Austrian hands—not goose-stepping soldiers—are what brought Hitler back to Austria.

Marienthal serves as a loud warning about what happens when government welfare checks attempt to replace lost work. They can partly replace the paycheck, but not the psychic compensation, and they can lead to disaster. Government welfare programs seldom lift spirits, and usually reinforce miserable moods. Arthur Brooks cites data showing that if you take two people with the same age, education, and employment characteristics, but if one is collecting welfare, there is a 16 percent higher chance that person will have felt "inconsolably sad" at some point in the prior month. As many of us have found, unemployment has similarly demoralizing effects on those who still have jobs. Obviously, when people get laid off, they spend less, retailers get hurt, and government tax revenues fall. But layoffs also deplete the confidence and happiness of those still working. This runs against the Edenist belief that prosperity is simply a relative matter, that most of all we like to beat other rats in the rat race. *If Edenists are right and the modern economy is just a scrum of unchecked envy, greed, and one-upsmanship, we would feel happier when other people are laid off.* But that is not the case. If it were, presidents who presided over recessions would win elections, since even in a bad recession 90 percent of workers keep their jobs. But you never heard anyone shout, "Hurray for Herbert Hoover!"

THE LAZY INHERIT THE DIRT

Early in this book I described the frontal cortex as a windshield looking to the future. Our biology pleads with us to move forward. Our brains do not like us to sit around like a poached egg on toast. Is this a curse of evolution? I don't think so. I can't deny that one motivation for work is to acquire things, whether rib eye steaks, a Rolex watch, or the suntan gained at a Club Med vacation village. Critics of a free-enterprise economy condemn modern people for scurrying around too much and for being greedy. Take the common sayings about the grass looking greener and keeping up with the Joneses. These expressions do reflect common sentiments. But why do we feel this way? Envy has played a vital role, keeping us alive. We evolved because we were aware of what others were up to. Picture yourself as a Neanderthal, among a large group of Neanderthals living in caves. Now a saber-toothed tiger (more precisely a saber-toothed cat) starts prowling near the caves. The tiger steps toward your neighbor's cave. What would your troglodyte brain tell you to do? Would you ignore the tiger since it seems bent on killing your neighbor, but not you? Of course not. You would keep your eye on the neighbor's cave just long enough to get the hell out of there with your family. Maybe you would pick up a club and light it on fire and wave it to scare off the beast. Here's my point: We have brains that do find the neighbor's yard or cave an irresistible sight. And we do notice what other people are up to. But these behaviors did not evolve because of jealousy. We developed these patterns because they helped increase the odds of our own survival. In today's world, they help prod us out of bed and get us to work because we'd like a nice car like our neighbor's. In the workplace, even if you don't care about your neighbor's car, it's a good idea to keep an eye on your boss and figure out who he really does and does not like.

We survived because we were not content to sit in our caves and watch the world, and the tigers, go by. Our survival instinct is a competitive instinct; caveman Fred wanted to pass on his genes more than he wanted caveman Barney to pass on his. If evolution allowed us to be completely content, our ancestors would have sat in a stupor when the mastodon came stomping by, forgotten to take out their bows and arrows during deer season, and missed the last salmon to leap over the dam during the run.

And so today you may find yourself peering over your neighbor's fence. But you are probably not doing it because you are hoping his house burns down. We do it for entertainment, for curiosity, and because our intelligence impels us to use our skills to raise our standard of living, or at least to ensure that we can continue to survive in a challenging world. The more we learn, the better our odds. Donald Hebb is also known for Hebb's Law, the concept that the firing of neuron cells creates connections to others, and those connections in turn promote cell growth (the slogan is "neurons that fire together wire together"). This cerebral activity reflects our role as human social actors. The more we learn from others, the more we interact with others, the more we grow our brains. That's why work does not threaten our well-being nearly as much as relaxing and retiring.

THE EARTH IS NOT FLAT

I have to admit the Edenists do offer some appealing fantasies and fallacies. Let me tell you the story of young Estée Lauder, who was working in a New York beauty salon when she complimented a wealthy customer on her blouse and asked politely where the patron had purchased it.

The woman smiled and looked straight into her eyes: "What difference could it possibly make? You could never afford it!"

Lauder walked away red-faced and burning inside. "Never, never . . . never will anyone say that to me again, I promised myself. Someday I will have whatever I want: jewels, exquisite art, gracious homes. . . ." Later in life, Lauder assured herself that "wherever she is, I'm sure her skin looks dreadful."

Here's the problem with work. We quickly realize there is a pecking order. At some time, we all feel like Estée Lauder did. Yes, work gives us self-esteem, but it may also steal away our self-esteem. And if we start feeling bad about ourselves, we inevitably start to think that if we could just ditch our competitive urges, we could wipe away the false and frustrating hierarchies that imprison us and depress us. Hey, this sounds good to me! Are you tired of your boss? Or the bossy PTA mom? We have dreams of their getting run over by their own Range Rovers, or maybe watching them slip on a banana peel. No matter who you are, you feel that someone is looking down on you. There's a reason this theme is recurrent in pop culture. In an episode of the television show *The New Adventures of Old Christine*, a Stepford-like PTA mom sneers at Christine and suggests that maybe she could help out at the school fair, after she "punches out from her shift." That's the kind of dig that sent Gatsby packing his bags from North Dakota to Long Island Sound.

Despite the slings and arrows of outrageous snobs, it is a fantasy to think that we can live in a "flat" world, one with no hierarchy. It is not who wins in direct competition that hurls the slings and arrows, but who wins the genetic sweepstakes. Some are born pretty, some not.

Some super-smart, some rather dense. Some have doting parents, some are abandoned. Even if we try to equalize the economic community, inequalities and hierarchies will arise. Before the market system evolved, people were put in their place by other forces, whether political, social, religious, or chemical. They usually accepted their roles and their status. Ancient Hebrews knew that only those of Aaron's blood could serve as priests. Aristotle said that some were born to be slaves.

The Great Chain of Being kept the Elizabethans in line, for it created a hierarchy of beings, beasts, and professions. God ruled from heaven, and as the chain descended downward there came angels, kings, nobles, men, lions, dogs, eagles, fish, insects, snakes, and so on. Under the spell of this chain, the status quo held firm. For a simple man to challenge a prince was like a prince taking on God himself. No surprise "my lord" became the standard greeting to a nobleman. To challenge the Great Chain was to risk a fate like Lucifer and to fall as far as John Milton could imagine in *Paradise Lost*. While the Great Chain recognized that man had the ability to reason, it also recognized that his reason was knotted to base animalistic urges. The Great Chain trapped men to their station in life. (The Catholic Church did not care much for Gutenberg, because when common people got their hands on their own Bibles and could speak directly to God, it tangled up the hierarchical chain.) The Protestant Reformation took a different tack to give solace to the discontented. It taught common people to comfort themselves in the belief that God would eventually rejigger the hierarchy in the hereafter, and they would finally see justice. All they had to do was wait, and God would take a sledgehammer to prideful sinners. St. Augustine assured believers that God was "secretly just and justly secret." In Hinduism, karma might finally transform that snooty boss into a hamster. Ancient Greeks comforted themselves believing that "the mills of the gods grind slowly but exceedingly small." These days people have less confidence in the justice of heaven and hell, and that creates a big problem: We feel more injured by the hierarchies we see now. Today we see a dope in the corner office and say, "Who made him king? Who does he think he is?" A hierarchical work environment often strikes us as morally wrong, since we can't justify it using reli-

gious or ancient philosophical precepts. Still, we can't
archy on Earth without resorting to authoritarian o.
methods, which just make things worse.

Sometimes people will attribute destructive hierarchies to
dominance or testosterone. I have heard many commentators suggest
(partly tongue-in-cheek) that we would not have so many wars if
women dominated the UN and the offices of presidents and prime
ministers. But this, too, is too flippant. Former secretary of state Madeleine Albright pointed out that it sounds good until you think back to
a female-dominated environment, where women ran all the important
institutions—high school! High school did not seem so flat and egalitarian, did it? Women are just as likely as men to establish hierarchies.
A pecking order arises among hens and roosters, among high school
guys and high school girls. Frans de Waal has written of hierarchies
among female chimps. Churchill threw up his hands at the thought of
a flat society among humans. He had studied animals and hierarchies
and announced that he liked pigs best, for dogs look up to you, cats
look down at you—but a pig will look you in the eye as an equal.

Evolution does not give us a flat society, and never did, even when
people believed in a literally flat Earth. Now let me give you a hint
about your great-great-great-great-etc.-grandfather of the BC era. He
was more likely an egotistical blowhard clawing his way to the top than
a pushover. People with higher status tended to have more babies. The
egotists reproduced most. Bertrand Russell (who maintained that
Marx was too obsessed with wealth, and Freud too obsessed with sex)
said that the real human driver is the *power* to make things happen.
And power automatically creates a hierarchy.

Capitalism did not invent hierarchies, and eliminating it does not
wipe them out, either. I won't claim that the results of a competitive
economic system are wondrously fair. I was driving down the freeway
last week. I noticed in my rearview mirror a black Porsche tailgating
me. Suddenly, the Porsche speeds up and sideswipes me. The guy driving it had a vanity license plate that read "I-Doc," so I suppose he was
a rich, egotistical eye surgeon. I don't like him. He's probably the sort
of doctor who plasters his face on billboards advertising laser eye sur-

ry. But then I began to think: These laser eye surgeons have been engaged in heated competition, which has driven down the price of LASIK surgery by about 50 percent in the past ten years (without the government getting involved). Who benefits? Millions of patients, who can now afford the procedure and can give away their old glasses. Sure, the I-Doc in the Porsche feels as if he's the king of the hill. And yes, I hope his air bag suddenly goes off and slaps him in the face (as long as no one is hurt). Nonetheless, we must see that unlike a noncompetitive system, a market yields a hierarchy largely based on actually doing something others find valuable, whether it's performing eye surgery, building a better mousetrap, or engineering a computer mouse. And the market creates only temporary hierarchies that can be tipped over by new upstarts, whereas the robes of noblemen could not even be ruffled unless you could get past the moat and the crocodiles. When Bill Gates and Steve Jobs dropped out of college, no one thought they could ever take on IBM or Xerox.

Take a snapshot of any workplace and you'll see a hierarchy. Even in an office environment where the boss works in an identical cubicle side by side with others, everyone knows which is the boss's cubicle. Even in avowedly Maoist institutions, hierarchies sprung up and became even more stark. A Maoist's climb up the party ladder might include a weekly hot shower when others merely hoped for one cold one. Even in prisons, where everyone is stuck in the same kind of clanking cell, hierarchies emerge, whether for telephone privileges, cigarettes, or sex. American capitalism did not invent hierarchies, but it did create avenues for individuals to break out of them and thumb their noses at the boss in the corner office or cubicle next door. The upshot is this: We need to work and we need to look over our shoulders. No society can eliminate hierarchies, but a free-enterprise system may help you find a better job and a more tolerable hierarchy to live with.

CHAPTER 7

How Time and Interest Rates Bring Us Closer

What's the Big Idea? To thrive, societies need long-term thinking, competitive interest rates, and the ability to deal with the stranger.

Every summer my kids want to go on the fast rides at the county fair that passes through town. And every summer I look at the carnies screwing together the rickety roller coasters, wondering whether those structures can be stable when they are pried apart and tossed onto trucks in the middle of the night for their trip to the next county. Do you trust a fly-by-night salesman? Of course not. He takes your money and hops the next Greyhound out of town. If everyone acted like a fly-by-nighter, the economy would collapse. Back in my graduate school days, I was fascinated by the sudden collapse of countries and societies. Unlike Jared Diamond, I did not chalk it up to bacteria. I was not looking at medical cases; I was researching places like Vietnam in the

1970s. When an invader conquers a country, the economy rapidly self-destructs, tracking a catastrophic mathematical function. What drives the collapse? Not guns. Not nooses. People stop trusting and trading with each other. Their reputations in the old regime become irrelevant, and so people are more likely to act dishonestly. Why? Because time horizons shrink, as if our clocks and calendars are being sucked into black holes. The Latin root for "credit" means trust. In a collapse, nearly every business suddenly turns into a fly-by-nighter. People no longer care about next year, or next month. Instead, they are looking for the last chopper out of Saigon.

Yeats's modernist masterpiece "The Second Coming" warns that the "centre cannot hold." That center turns out to be the structure of time. When we do not prize tomorrow, we devolve. We devolve into cheating and stealing, so that we steal tomorrow from ourselves and from others. Premodern societies care less about tomorrow, and therefore work and save less today. Recall the discussion of the child and the marshmallow in chapter 3. Children who show patience turn out to be more successful and smarter than those who grab what's put in front of them. Older children and girls score higher than boys. We're not talking about politeness; we're talking about forbearance, about having the foresight to imagine that tomorrow could bring a better day, or more marshmallows. Economists sometimes call this *time preference*. Societies with savvier time preferences usually figure out how to trade up from mud huts and outhouses to indoor plumbing. Now, I am not telling you that it is always good or rational to have a long time preference. (During hyperinflation, it makes sense to spend your money before lunch, if prices will quintuple by dinner.)

Foraging societies, those seemingly idyllic places where people work less and relax more, don't think as much about tomorrow. Why should they? They have little reason to imagine anything but a rerun of yesterday, except perhaps punctuated by some exogenous shock: a leopard invading, an attack from a rival tribe, or a school of striped bass swimming into their fishing nets. How can we judge the time preference of hunters, gatherers, and planters? In Tanzania the Hadza tribe live as nomads. They can make huts from branches in a few hours and do not bother developing better tools. They will follow the scent of honey, or the thunder of a migrating herd. What they won't do is spend much time trying to improve their tools. Why? Because a better axe or a second axe will be surrendered to the chief, deleting any incentive to improve. Moreover, when they pick berries, they will often chop down the whole branch, not caring whether that will mean fewer berries in the future. Compare this zero-time focus with Amanda Wingfield from *The Glass Menagerie*, who warns that "the future becomes the present, the present becomes the past, and the past turns into everlasting regret if you don't plan for it!"

Certainly, there are some tribes that care more about future vegetative growth than others. The Mikea forager-farmers in Madagascar have been pressured by conservationists to stop slashing and burning maize fields, and they seem to be doing so (the conservationists have taught them to plant alternatives like manioc). In their culture, the Mikea cite proverbs that argue both for and against saving for the future: "The distant tree is no cure" tells them to snatch immediate rewards; while "What the goat nibbles is quickly gone" tells them to conserve.

Why bother studying foragers? They give us clues to our past and to our evolution. In the years since the earliest *Homo* (*Homo habilis*), 90 percent of those who have walked the earth upright have been hunter-gatherers, and we have been hunter-gatherers for 99 percent of our collective time on Earth. And it has been dreary.

AS INTEREST RATES FALL, CIVILIZATIONS RISE

As an economist, the best measure of time I can find is the prevailing interest rate. When interest rates are high, it tells us that tomorrow counts for less. It is not worth investing today. From a business point of view, very few financed projects will pay off if interest rates are high (the "hurdle rate"). However, when interest rates are low, it tells us that we should invest today because any return will be prized more in the future. During the German hyperinflation of the early 1920s, prices and interest rates jumped higher each hour. The price of a cup of coffee could go up as the waitress was pouring. Teachers got paid at ten a.m. and brought their banknotes to the playground so their relatives could pick them up and then buy things immediately. Likewise, the hyperinflation of Zimbabwe in recent years acted like a neutron bomb on the economy. Coincidentally, in 1919, when Yeats wrote "things fall apart; the centre cannot hold," interest rates were jumping sharply, the British pound slid in value, and Europe was preparing for a terrible bout of post–World War I inflation. Elsewhere, I set out "the Buchholz Hypothesis," arguing that the crime rate is importantly a function of interest rates. This solves the puzzle of the Great Depression. Most commentators on crime say that a lousy economy leads to crime. But during the Great Depression, crime rates fell, as they did in 2008 and 2009. Why? Because interest rates fell, too. People did not give up on tomorrow, even as they suffered economic distress.

If you charted interest rates over the past two thousand years, you'd mostly see a decline. Certainly the advent of banks and enforceable legal contracts have played a huge role. Mostly, though, interest rates have declined because life has become more secure (thanks, in part, to contracts). If your shop looks like it will catch fire tomorrow because bandits will come pillaging through town, lenders will not trust that you will pay them back.

Simply comparing interest rates from Bronze Age Sumer to ancient Greece shows a sharp drop, from 20 percent to 10 percent. From ancient Greek civilization through the ancient Roman civilization rates declined a bit further. Historians have uncovered the accounts of the Temple at Delos from the second century BC. The temple took in money through offerings from pilgrims and from visiting monarchs from Macedon, Egypt, and Pergamum. The temple did not have a modern vault; it kept the funds in jars, and then lent them out to property buyers. For a five-year mortgage, the temple would charge 10 percent. In case of default, the temple could seize the property of the borrower, according to a well-defined contract. Medieval Europe enjoyed falling rates from about AD 1250 to roughly the time of Darwin. Shakespeare would have gotten better terms than Chaucer, and Dickens better terms than Shakespeare. Ironically, Shakespeare set the bitter money-lending of *The Merchant of Venice* in Italy, where interest rates dipped to nearly half of English levels. Bassanio would have gotten worse terms in London.

Competitive societies do a better job of setting interest rates than noncompetitive societies. Interest rates depend on a whole set of purely economic factors, such as inflation and the quantity of money in circulation. But they also rest on the competitive quest for credit. Businesses and entrepreneurs show up at the bank or at the bond market with their plans and spreadsheets, trying to persuade lenders that they have a better plan and prospect for profitability than everybody else. When a couple buying a new home applies for a mortgage they are (unknowingly) arguing that they are a better credit risk than alternative borrowers. A credit-rating system is a competitive system. Not everyone or every business presents the same credit risk. That's why IBM can borrow at 3 percent, but the MGM Mirage gaming and hotel company might issue a junk bond at 11 percent. In 2010, as Mediterranean governments shuddered with bankruptcy fears, Greece had to pay 20 percent for money it promised to repay in two years, while Germany could sell ten-year bonds at just 2.5 percent. That's why you might loan $5,000 to your neighbor and not even $100 to your nephew carrying the skateboard under his arm. If we cut out the competition for credit—if we made sure everyone could borrow on the same terms—we'd punish the economy, discourage lending, and set back our hopes for progress in this world.

Regardless of specific differences in interest rates, this point stands: Societies that make tomorrow more appealing show more progress. And not just material, GDP-measured progress. They also show less bloodshed and longer lives. We all know the cliché used when we send an urgent package: "time is of the essence." *Well, it turns out that time is of the essence of human progress.* Either we imagine progress and move forward, or we sink into entropy and the center does not hold.

WHEN THE STRANGER COMES ALONG

Comics laughed in 2006 when President George W. Bush returned from vacation saying he had read Camus's *The Stranger*. Yet Bush probably did see himself as an outsider, accused of a crime (for invading Iraq). The lure and the danger of the stranger show up in high and low culture, from Camus to the great western *Shane* to Billy Joel's first bestselling album. Here is the crux of economic progress: Trust in tomorrow, and be willing to trust strangers. I don't mean blind trust; I mean a willingness to do business with strangers that must be reinforced by good results (for example, those that earn "Top Rated Seller" status on eBay). Following Robert Axelrod's seminal *The Evolution of Cooperation*, Robert Wright correctly argues that human progress comes from "nonzero-sum" transactions—that is, doing business with others in a way that each gains. This is a lot more motivating for both parties than the zero-sum transaction. In a zero-sum situation, one person can gain only if the other loses; for example, I just stole your chariot. Even before the golden age of Greece, Thucydides, the great historian of the Peloponnesian War, spelled out his case for trade and made clear what the choice between commerce and a mud hut in the wild entailed: "Without commerce, without freedom of communication either by land or sea, cultivating no more of the territory than the exigencies of life required, destitute of capital, never planting their land (for they could never tell when an invader might not come . . .), [nomadic ancient Greeks] cared little for shifting their habitation," and could not rise above nomadic life or achieve any "form of greatness."

But what makes nonzero deals possible, or more likely? I will give you four ingredients: First, a legal construct like enforceable contracts, whether enforced by a court, a king or tribal chief, or social stigma; second, a willingness to wait for results—that is, patience; third, an interest rate structure as discussed above; and fourth, and perhaps most important: *repeat transactions*, expecting to deal with the same person again, and therefore treating the other person as someone closer than an utter stranger. This is what I call the *Rule of Repeats*. When someone expects to do business with you again, they are far less likely to cheat you. It is the Rule of Repeats that turns strangers into partners and counterparties. And this conversion makes all the difference in the world. The Rule of Repeats makes reputations matter.

Let's look at some simple examples: Are you a good tipper? Be honest. All the time? Really? Think of your favorite restaurant or bar. If you're lucky, you've got a place like Cheers, where "everybody knows your name." You enjoy a few glasses of wine, a tasty dinner and dessert. The waiter pats you on the shoulder. I bet you leave a good tip. Now let's say you've flown into some remote town on business. You don't expect to be back, and you don't want to come back. You find a decent restaurant and have a good meal. Do you tip as well? Most of us don't. If we're never coming back, it matters less what they think of us as we walk out the door. Don't feel bad. The restaurant feels the same way about you. That's why I, like most economists, try to avoid eating in touristy, rotating restaurants with city views. Those restaurants don't get repeat customers, simply because just about nobody is a regular in a tourist district.

The Rule of Repeats applies in more serious ways, too. Transient neighborhoods have higher crime rates. "Love your neighbor as yourself" doesn't work too well if people don't perceive others as neighbors, but just some guys passing through. Would you trust a fly-by-night jeweler to clean your diamond ring? Of course not. *Here is an overlooked virtue of a competitive economic system: Reputations count much more.* In a competitive system, businesses feel pressure to act as if their customers will be around tomorrow, and possibly come back for another transaction. These pressures—good pressures, I might add—are stronger than ever because of our Internet-savvy world, where a terrible review on yelp.com, tripadvisor.com, or amazon.com can doom a vendor.

Our animal cousins care about reputation, too. Chimpanzees share more with those who have proved themselves in the past—for example, by helping with grooming. Male rats remember where they enjoyed hot sex and return to those areas of their cages, hoping to experience another romp. Reputations would be pointless and incalculable without memory functions.

In fact, one unnoticed result of national revolution is that it wipes away the solid underpinnings of reputation. One cannot trust that another man will behave as he did under the prior regime. He may not believe that you will stick around for the next Reich.

KITH AND KIN AND OTHERS

Our bodies are equipped with tools to identify our kin. Though everybody knows that dogs and many other animals have keener senses of smell than humans, humans can identify a sibling by scent, but cannot identify a half sibling the same way. We are preprogrammed to trust our mothers and fathers and next of kin. That is easy to do. *But trusting someone we have just met—or even more astounding, trusting someone we will never see face-to-face—that is the trick to moving from mud huts to prosperity. That requires us to be comfortable with an abstraction and it requires more flexible brain patterns.* We are a face-to-face species (like bonobos and gorillas, human beings even tend to copulate face-to-face, although there is enormous creativity and variety in these matters), but have the ability to go beyond that. A competitive system nudges us to do so because it offers the prospect that someone outside our family, outside our clan, may be bringing more to the table than just the threat of theft and plunder.

Let's try a thought experiment. You are standing on the beach, watching your relatives and strangers play in the surf. Suddenly, a huge wave hits and they are drowning. Who do you save first? For whom will you sacrifice your life? Most people will rescue their children before their nephews, their first cousins before their second cousins. The stranger comes last. This is not a moral recommendation. Certainly, we would be furious if a professional lifeguard checked last names and bloodlines before jumping into the surf. Nonetheless, this is the way of most flesh.

In the 1940s, a young British boy of twelve was playing in his yard with a . . . hand grenade. His father had brought the explosives home to Kent after serving in World War II. The grenade exploded and the boy, named William Hamilton, was bloodied. His mother, trained in first aid, rushed him to the hospital. Although the boy lost parts of fingers and was badly scarred, he survived. He spent the next fifty years of his life studying how people behave toward relatives. As a biologist, Hamilton surmised that "survival of the fittest" was too narrow, and seemed too selfish a dictum. After all, why would parents sacrifice to provide for their children if they were so solipsistic? Why would people try to create some kind of wealth just to leave it to their children? Hamilton developed a theory called "inclusive fitness," in which he showed how people sacrifice greatly—but in proportion to how closely they are related to others. A parent shares 50 percent of his genes with a child, a grandparent 25 percent, a first cousin 12.5 percent, and a second cousin 3.125 percent. A stranger? 0. That's why only embittered parents leave money to strangers rather than to their own children. (Sometimes the embittered may be justified. King Lear would have been wiser to cut off two of his daughters.) Naturally, there are other exceptions. Warren Buffett has already told his children they will not be receiving billions or even hundreds of millions (that would rob them of their incentives to work). Buffett presumably believes that his children will grow to be better people by engaging in the competitive world, rather than buying themselves out of it.

Hamilton's idea can be stated in a simple equation: $c < rb$. This means that a person will sacrifice (c for cost) if the cost is less than the benefit (b) multiplied by how closely related (r) the beneficiary is. So, for a closer relative, people will make bigger sacrifices, if the benefit is significant. Let's take an easy example. Let's say your brother asks you for a dollar, because he could trade that dollar in for $2.50. The cost to you (c) is $1. You share 50 percent of your genes with your brother (r), and your brother will benefit by $2.50 (b). Since $2.50 times 50 percent equals $1.25, which is more than $1, you would likely give him the money. Now say a second cousin comes along. In his case, $2.50 times .03125 equals less than 8 cents; you would likely keep your dollar. I know what you are thinking: "Hey, I just bought Girl Scout Cookies and I hate Girl Scout Cookies—I just want to help the children." To which Hamilton might reply, "Would you have bought more if you knew the girls selling them? Or if you were related to them?" Or maybe you are thinking: "I hate my relatives and I dread Thanksgiving family meals!" Or, "I would jump in front of a train for my brother, but push my sister onto the tracks, so how can they have equal weights?" Clearly, the equation does not hold for everyone, and it's too precise to be justified empirically. My task here is not to prove Hamilton correct, but to suggest the obvious: We have a bias toward our children, parents, and other close relatives.

As you consider your Thanksgiving family tensions, and your urge to poison your annoying aunt with spiked cider, consider this: 103 pioneers settled in the original Mayflower colony at Plymouth. Over 50 percent of them perished after the first winter in 1620. Those most likely to die had the fewest genetic relatives. A more recent study asked 300 women in Los Angeles, "Who helps you when you have troubles?" Close kin help most. Even squirrels display a similar behavior. They will warn relatives of a dangerous coyote nearby, but slink off quietly rather than warn a stranger squirrel. We seem to be wired to our kin, even if, as Cain and Abel first showed, we sometimes snip that wire, with great passion and with great guilt. In fact, brother-versus-brother violence makes great literature precisely because it hits us in the gut, or in our genes. The Koran also tells the story of Cain and Abel (among many other biblical stories). No story seems more heart-wrenching than that of a Civil War mother, with two sons going off to battle, clutching bayonets aimed at each other.

When we remove kin from the picture, we are left with neighbors and with strangers. Here again, we have a stronger urge to protect members of our community. This is a historical and biological story. According to Plutarch, Aristotle taught Alexander the Great to look at Greeks as "friends and kindred, but to conduct himself toward other peoples as though they were plants or animals." The Old Testament sounds more kindly, continually reminding the Israelites that as slaves in Egypt they were once "strangers in a strange land," and must protect the stranger and give him equal justice. Clearly, trusting strangers is an uphill fight. Nations have traditionally stuck together because they have exalted shared characteristics—blood, history, culture, language. Politicians and the songwriters of national anthems have always spoken of shared blood, fatherlands, and motherlands. The Soviet Union anthem hailed "our free Motherland!" It helps to have someone to hate, too. Nations have usually repelled foreigners, bonding that much more closely over shared dislikes of people who were different, often attributing vile traits to them. Foreigners smell bad. Crazed mullahs in Iran will announce that Christians and Jews are really pigs and monkeys. In *Planet of the Apes*, the apes sneer at the smell of Charlton Heston, and finally he recoils, "Get your stinking paws off me, you damned dirty ape."

Military leaders have known since Thucydides that they must turn platoons into brotherhoods. In a classic example, Henry V's rallying cry at Agincourt, "We few, we happy few, we . . . band of brothers . . ." allowed a relatively puny assembly of English forces to slaughter the heavily armored, imposing knights of France. And then there are the more laughable calls to phony kinship, like the University of Florida student who disrupted an assembly and badgered Senator John Kerry. As security guards threatened him, the young man pleaded, "Don't Tase me, bro'!" They zapped him anyway, which he may have deserved if only for that elocution.

COMPETITION PRODS US TO TREAT STRANGERS BETTER

Creating brotherhood in a military expedition is tough enough, even when soldiers are willing to put their lives in the hands of others. But creating brotherhood in civilian matters is far more challenging. This brings us to the crux of the argument: *A competitive system prods us to treat strangers like neighbors and kin.* In a simple "small is beautiful" world, we sit by an olive tree alone, or perhaps with close friends and family. The progress of the past two hundred years has destroyed distance and destroyed the walls that used to keep strangers out, and keep ourselves inside. When these walls tumble, we engage with others to cure polio, fight despots, and increase our life expectancy. Think how you are treated by stores competing for your business, compared with institutions that require you to use their services. In a competitive industry, a merchant sees you walk into his store and hopes you will buy something. A salesman with a stack of upholstery samples hopes he has a fabric you like. Federal Express and UPS will eagerly speed to my house to pick up a package. In contrast, the U.S. Post Office, safe with its monopoly, is not in such a rush. Nordstrom wants me to apply for its credit card, and will quickly process the application. The Department of Motor Vehicles likes me to stand in line for a long time. DMV employees are in no rush, and there is certainly no pleasure involved for either party. Two hundred years ago, store owners typically wanted to deal only with customers they already knew. If you never had the chance to buy a chicken leg at a Soviet store, you are lucky, for you would have gotten a flavor for noncompetitive markets. First of all, you would have stood in two lines. One to pay; one to pick up the leg. Oh, yes, then the third line to complain that it wasn't a leg but a meatless wing. Then came the bad news: the brooding, surly sorry souls behind the counters who had absolutely no incentive to do anything but smirk and shrug. Not only were you a stranger, you were an utter imposition. Today, in the United States and the UK, if I cannot find chicken legs at the supermarket, the nearest stock boy will walk me over to the counter. In a market where we are competing, someone can always provide better service. Some Starbucks customers actually have a favorite barista. Now, I will admit some employees can be terrible, even in competitive cultures. But they are less likely to hang on to their jobs if they are spurning customers. David Hume, decades before Adam Smith, noticed that a market system gives even "bad men" a reason to act nicely. Let's say the bad man behind the deli counter is only faking a smile and pretending to be nice. That's certainly better for the customer than if he lets out his true feelings. And, if you follow Aristotle, acting virtuously will eventually improve the soul and spur authentic virtue.

Competitive economies often guide us to cooperative behavior even with our chief competitors. When the Mars chocolate company was starting out with its Milky Ways and Snickers, it actually purchased chocolate coating from Milton Hershey's chocolate company, because it wanted to offer its customers the most enticing coating. In a more recent example, Apple deigned to load Microsoft programs onto its computers because users needed Microsoft software in addition to Apple's. The supply-chain managers at Sony fly to Korea to buy flat-screen technology from rival Samsung.

THE OPPOSITE OF COMPETITION IS NOT TRUST

Here's another fantastic myth, though I do feel its emotional tug. If we just ditched all this competition nonsense, we would all learn to trust each other. But here's the rub: the default case is not trust. Trust is earned. And it turns out that competition raises the level of trust among strangers. As I argued earlier, trust among close family is fairly easy to show. But trusting a stranger, that is the miracle, for it requires abstract reasoning. Increasing trust by 15 percent raises national incomes by 1 percent in every following year, estimates Paul Zak and Stephen Knack. For a U.S. family, that would raise the present value of family wealth by roughly $20,000. Countries that provide more freedom and defend private property rights enjoy higher standards of living. Is this just a random act of oxytocin, for oxytocin is the "trust" transmitter? No, competition and the Rule of Repeats raise trust, give us contact with more people, and perhaps squirt a bit more oxytocin into our bloodstreams.

Trust is hard to come by in the wild. In foraging communities, tribes raid others, not just when food is short but when they seek to abduct women or mete out revenge. In modern times we see that even if most people are sympathetic and kind, all it takes are a few liars and thieves to shake up the balance. In a New Orleans neighborhood, 95 percent of the residents can be saintly, but if a gang takes over 5 percent, suddenly SWAT teams must rush in to protect the cowering saints. In 2003 Iraq, the vast proportion of Iraqis were very peaceful, but a small number of terrorists skulking and plotting made towns impassably lethal. To have survived the millennia of premodern life, our ancestors had to display grit, growls, and the sharp blades they could whittle from timber and splinter from flint. They had to prove toughness. Revenge was not served sweet; it was served bitter and cold-blooded. But it had to be served, lest opportunists trample the village.

BREAKING THE CHAINS

Back to Rousseau, who announced that everywhere man is in chains. More than a jailer's chains enmeshed men (for example, the Great Chain of Being). Of course, there is a comfort in knowing your place in life. If you know your job is to wake up each morning and chop wood, it cuts out a lot of uncertainty. Remember Kierkegaard's explanation of anxiety, the "dizziness of freedom." Who likes to be dizzy? But without that dizziness, the chopper of wood ceases to ask some good questions, like: "What if I'd rather learn how to build a chair? Or teach Latin? Or write a killer app for the iPad? Or break loose from this tintype town?"

A competitive system allows people to break free from those chains, so a stock boy like Sam Walton could end up owning a chain of stores (Walmart), and the son of a welder could end up owning a manor. We should not be ashamed of our urges to improve our lives, even if that means looking over the fence now and then to see what our neighbors are up to.

At Harvard Law School there was a long tradition for the dean to address new students with the story of the two students camping in the woods. A ferocious bear tramples over their campsite. One student starts lacing up his sneakers. "What are you doing? You can't outrace a grizzly!" the other shouts. The student with the sneakers replies, "Oh, I don't have to outrace the grizzly. I just have to outrace you." That is the logic of a zero-sum society, where you are either fast or you're lunch. But that is not the story of a truly competitive system. In a truly competitive system, someone comes along and invents a system to detect grizzlies, or warns campers of bears. Most of human competition makes us more adept at handling the hazards of the world, of learning from our neighbors, of dealing with strangers, and of possibly turning strangers into friends. And few things make us happier than a new friend.

CHAPTER 8

The Era of the Stranger

*What's the Big Idea? Competition not only leads
to innovation, it decreases violent behavior and
increases cooperation.*

Prehistoric people were pretty violent. Foraging tribes today turn
out to be violent, at least compared to citizens of developed countries.
Now, this violent behavior of course rubs against romantic notions of
Rousseau's followers, but it has been documented by archaeologists,
anthropologists, and just about anyone else willing to dig up a grave or
put on a pith helmet. An exhaustive study of indigenous peoples asked
what percentage of the male population died in battle. The typical answer among various tribes: 20 to 40 percent. In contrast to the rivers of
blood that flow from the killing off of almost half the males in the
Jivaro (Peru and Ecuador) and Yanomamo (Amazon) peoples, World

War II looks like a set of isolated skirmishes. In an ancient Nubian cemetery in northeast Africa, one-half of the skeletons had bones that showed the bludgeoning and smashing of violent encounters. More recent graves from nineteenth-century Australia showed that about one-quarter of the occupants had died in a war among the tribes. Skulls are dented with the shapes of axes. Of course, not everyone—maybe not anyone—in these cultures believed that violence was senseless. Warriors achieved status, and successful warriors achieved immortality through their children. Compare two Yanomamo tribesmen of the same age. Let us say one had killed and the other had not. The one who had killed sired more children.

Why are premodern people so violent? If we go back two thousand years to European cities, we certainly see what looks like a bloodthirsty populace to us. Ancient Romans paid for front-row seats to see lions rip out the bellies of slaves. The Romans enjoyed drama, and if they needed to portray a death scene, why hire an actor? Better to drag a slave onstage and let him perform in living color—namely, red. Forget Audrey Hepburn; a visit to such a show was the original "Roman Holiday."

It would be easy to argue that people have been cruel to each other and cruel to animals forever. Samuel Pepys, whose diaries of seventeenth-century England gleam with wit yet give us glimpses into the mundane, attended the punishment of Thomas Harrison for deposing Charles I. Pepys famously wrote that Harrison was "hanged, drawn, and quartered . . . looking as cheerful as any man could do in that condition. He was presently cut down, and his head and heart shown to the people, at which there was great shouts of joy." Apparently, Harrison got off lucky, because others who were "drawn and quartered" were disemboweled and castrated before their own eyes. After watching the show, Pepys enjoyed oysters at a tavern, returned home, and yelled at his wife for making a mess. He was so angry, he kicked and broke a "fine, little basket," which "troubled me after I had done it." Other than the mess in the house and the broken basket, it had been a lovely day.

Every nighttime local television news show seems to begin with a crime report, and the top-rated television program in the United States, France, and Australia is the same: *NCIS* (Naval Criminal Investigative Service). Crime sells. From a historical point of view, there is good news, though: Levels of violence in modern communities seem to be dropping over the centuries. Homicide rates in Europe today are perhaps one-tenth the rate of the year AD 1300. And even the rate in AD 1300 Europe is small compared to the rates we find among foraging communities.

So why were premodern tribes apparently so violent and impulsive? They failed to do three things: (1) think sufficiently about tomorrow; (2) figure out how to trade with strangers; (3) develop persuasive moral codes that humanized the stranger.

Before I get into these points, you may be asking, "What does this have to do with work and our search for happiness?" *Our best chance for happiness comes when we work hard now, anticipating a better tomorrow.* Working for tomorrow looks like a rush, a frenzy of effort that takes us away from the ashram. But evolution, and our neurotransmitters, are all telling us to keep moving, to look to tomorrow.

Neanderthals may have died out because of frigid weather, but then again *Homo sapiens* appeared around the same time and managed to make it through an Ice Age. I would argue the Neanderthalic brain did not look forward to the same extent and, therefore, did not innovate. Why bother innovating and inventing new tools if you cannot picture them leading to bigger crops or healthier children? At the same time, Neanderthalic "culture" could not figure out how to trade with strangers and how to create moral codes that preserved life.

Work makes people less violent and less impulsive. Those foraging tribes today who labor the fewest hours of the day appear to be the most homicidal. Anthropologists who track foraging tribes report that they tend to work about one-third fewer hours than Europeans. Sometimes they work little because they can achieve subsistence nutrition without working harder. And that is enough for them. This brings to mind E. F. Schumacher's concept of "enoughness." Work less, consume less. Other foraging people work little but struggle for subsistence. The Hiwi of Venezuela work just two hours a day—and yet complain of hunger, achieving just 1,705 calories per day. Despite the promises of the Edenist authors, I doubt that "enoughness" would give their readers more peace of mind or a more peaceful neighborhood.

HOW COMPETITION TURNED INTO COOPERATION

There is no doubt that humans must cooperate within the family structure. Hyenas are born with sharp canine teeth that can rip flesh. If a mother gives birth to two males, the stronger will destroy the other. In contrast, human babies are born without teeth, and it takes months for them just to scoot a few feet. Humans need a family more than many other animals. Parents twist open jars of Gerber's baby food at a point in life where a hyena could tear open up the belly of a zebra. For our hominid ancestors, walking on two legs was quite a physical feat, but it made babies more vulnerable. The birth canal of a biped is narrow, and therefore human babies must be born with relatively small heads and small brains. Human brains triple in size, whereas ape brains merely double. Compared to nearly every other mammal, *every* human child is born premature. Other than making cute sounds and loud cries, they can do little. It's a good thing babies have large eyes and make those cute sounds, or they might be abandoned. Even after ten years, a child has little chance of hunting and gathering his own meal. When you consider our physical limits, our flimsy design suggests that God could be a committee running an old version of a spreadsheet with a lot of bugs in it. Or perhaps we are designed for cooperation, for no man could raise himself by himself. During a million-year period the *Homo erectus* brain size grew about 25 percent. As our species developed bigger brains, we developed the ability to look forward and the ability to process oxytocin in a way that feeds feelings of sympathy. Helpless offspring brought men and women together as mates.

But remember, these relationships are all in the family. We are a caretaking species—when we care about the other person. However, as we saw earlier, we care less and less as they become less related to us. But who do we choose to cooperate with outside the family? And how do we cooperate? If our kin come first and easiest, who comes next? Here comes a brief economic history of cooperation.

THE HUNTING TEAM

Thirty thousand years ago, *Homo sapiens* devised joint expeditions. To do what? Pick flowers? No! To hunt mammoths. The need to compete against nature spurred cooperation. Our first competitors were the herds that tried to escape our arrows. Then the neighboring clans who were hunting down the same beasts. Once we left Eden, cooperation became a result of competition, not a rival to it. So who did early man cooperate with? Those who could help us take down a big animal and provide dinner. I saw a bumper sticker recently that read, "If we aren't supposed to eat animals, why are they made out of meat?" That sounds pretty snide, but it might very well reflect our ancestors' cruder view of the wild. Fossils of hominid teeth from 2.5 million years ago show that our ancestors tasted ribs and legs and everything in between. Perhaps it was because bigger brains required more energy and more protein. Perhaps it was from desperation, perhaps curiosity after a million years of grasses. But they liked animal meat, and the long race to the Outback Steakhouse was on. From that point forward hominids would use sharp molars to shear meat. Our physical development and tastes spurred more competition and more cooperation. Though we did not have the jaws to bite the jugular of a wildebeest, we didn't have to. We had the intellect to kill at a distance, with arrows, blades, and even tricks. About a thousand years ago Native Americans tricked herds of buffalo into jumping off cliffs and then feasted on their flesh. In 1805, Meriwether Lewis described how one of the "most active and fleet young men is selected and disguised in a robe of buffalo skin . . . he places himself at a distance between a herd of buffalo and a precipice."

Then with hunters outflanking the herd, the decoy races toward the cliff. At the last moment, the young man ducks into a cranny as the stampede runs into the breach, the empty air. Lewis notes, "the part of the decoy I am informed is extremely dangerous." You can visit such a site at Head-Smashed-In Buffalo Jump in the Canadian Rockies near Alberta.

I am sure the Blackfoot and other tribes took good care of the young decoy after a successful outing. It takes a fairly big brain to remember who has helped you in the past. Luckily, humans have one. It allows us to form bigger social groups. In fact, you can trace a correlation between the size of a primate's frontal cortex and the size of the social group. (Don't worry if you are a loner, you might still be smart.) With our bigger brains and our taste for more protein, we could suss out which neighbors actually helped take down the beast. That let us discern the successful hunters from the free riders. Skilled hunters would share with each other ("reciprocal altruism"). Free riders and clumsy hunters would be shunned.

TRADE MAKES YOU MORE FAIR

Here is an unexpected finding: The civilizations that trade more with outsiders grow more fair, honest, and generous. Confounding noble savage fantasies, an economic system that relies on trade has been shown to promote fairness. Last year *Science* magazine reported a fascinating study by researchers at the University of British Columbia. They tested the fairness of tribesmen in fifteen premodern cultures, from the nomadic, foraging Hadza of Tanzania to the Sanquianga fishermen in Colombia, who will trade the catch of the day. Among the tests was the "dictator game," a well-known device in which one person receives a gift of money and can dictate what portion to share with another. The researchers discovered a striking correlation between fairness and those tribes that engaged in trade. The more insular the tribe, the more capricious and stingy the people. *In other words, the*

more isolated from the rush of modern life, the less noble and generous.
By opening up the world economy, we are opening up the possibility of
more nobility, not locking people into an iron cage of greed.

STRANGERS, PATTERNS, AND THE BIOLOGICAL BASIS
FOR THE RULE OF REPEATS

The happiness gurus who say we have an innate altruism are likely
right—but they have not shown how you deploy it to build a robust
economic system for strangers. That answer comes from competition and the Rule of Repeats. Our brains are wired to detect patterns,
which help us recognize who helps, who slacks off, and which stranger
does honest work. The brain detects repeat transactions and signals
something when we come into contact with faithful counterparties—
including strangers. That signal flashes "fair." When our eyes see a
hungry coyote, our brains flash "run!" A competitive economy evolved
because the Rule of Repeats matched up with the human brain's capacity to discern fairness even from strangers. This sophisticated pattern-
recognition system gave people the capacity to cooperate on economic
matters.

Our brains like to detect patterns. They will even "fill in the
blanks" to complete one. For example, the magic of Hollywood comes
from your brain, which can connect the rapid flashing of still images
into the continuous flow of a film. When we lie on the grass gazing at
the clouds in the sky we can't seem to stop trying to reconfigure cloud
formations into familiar shapes. We're so good at making something
significant out of random stimuli that we've given it a name, pareidolia.
In 1994, pilgrims shed tears when they spied the Virgin Mary in a
grilled cheese sandwich in Florida. The sandwich later fetched $28,000
on eBay.

We are not, however, flawless at pattern detection. Sometimes our
brains do seem to impose a pattern even when they see random marks,
which can lead stock investors to think they've found the Midas touch.
In my career, I have sat through numerous presentations where some

too-smart portfolio manager shows off an investment model, which, using statistical backdating, "proves" that it "would have worked" in the past, and therefore I must fork over my money to him now for future gains. Following Amos Tversky and Thomas Gilovich's debunking, Jonah Lehrer has explained clearly why the "hot hand" in basketball is really in the eye of the beholder, not in the true statistics. A few months after his great-grandmother passed away, my three-year-old nephew looked up at the sky and said, "I see Oma in the clouds. Not all of her, just her butt." She would have been happy to be remembered, but it was probably my nephew's brain playing a pattern-detection trick.

Our hardwired pattern-detection program helps explain why we like familiar things. They give us comfort as they fall into pattern-detection grooves in our minds. Turn on the radio. Let's say you like Frank Sinatra, and you hear Michael Bublé. You are probably pleased. You might like Coldplay, and feel good when you hear the hit song parody "Everything Sounds Like Coldplay." Even if you hate someone's music, if you listen enough, your brain will begin to accommodate it. As Mark Twain said about Wagner, "it's not as bad as it sounds." Impressionism looked like blurry smudges until people saw enough to start bidding up the price. I always wondered about spicy foods, which seem to burn my tongue and lips. Do spice lovers not feel the burn? Are they born with thicker skin? It turns out that children in India are not born with a love of spicy curry. Their mothers feed them curry at a very early age, until it becomes second nature. Soon they begin to like the pattern of flavors. What is a movie sequel but another taste of a similar stew? Likewise, the Rule of Repeats leads us to trade with people we've dealt with before. The Rule of Repeats is a social activity. But when you look at the human brain, you see a neurological structure that supports it.

In 1939, a young man named Robert Zajonc and his parents fled Lodz, Poland, for a safehouse in Warsaw. Suddenly, a Nazi bomb exploded the apartment, killing his parents and leaving sixteen-year-old Robert with a broken body but an unbent spirit. He escaped a Nazi labor camp, joined the French Resistance movement, and ultimately became a distinguished psychology professor at Stanford. Zajonc focused on pattern recognition. In one key experiment he drafted a bunch of American graduate students and flashed before their eyes Chinese characters. The Americans had no idea what the characters meant; they could have come from a fortune cookie wrapper or been made up by a calligrapher. Zajonc discovered, though, that the students developed a liking for those inscrutable characters that they saw most often. Incidentally, Zajonc also did research on birth order and came up with the controversial finding that IQ points correlate with birth order, and decline with each subsequent child. He was an only child himself.

The neurons in our brains embrace patterns. The more often they see a connection, the more securely they create a connection among other neurons. Imagine you own an overgrown plot of land, and you would like to create walking paths through a tangle of woods and vines. The more often you trample on a certain route, the clearer the path becomes. Your footsteps eventually dig a groove in the dirt. Your brain creates grooves, and every time it sees a pattern recur, it becomes easier for the brain to recognize the pattern the next time. In the days before iPods, when CDs ruled (and before that tapes and records), I remember knowing exactly what song would follow another. Not because I consciously memorized the order; it seemed that the final notes—somehow even the silence in between songs—signaled to my brain what tune would follow. Neurons contact each other through dendrite spines. When we see a pattern repeat, bumps literally grow on the dendrites, reinforcing the recognition. If you watched dendrites through an electron microscope while a patient listened to a repetitive, catchy tune—let's say the Village People's "YMCA"—you might literally witness the dendrites transform. Then you might pull your hair out.

THE NEURAL PATH TO YOUR DRY CLEANER

The Rule of Repeats applies similarly to human transactions in a market economy. In other words, every time you drop off your shirts at the dry cleaner and then pick them up clean and neatly folded, you make it easier for yourself to return to the dry cleaner the next time you have soiled shirts. Likewise, in your brain dendrites grow and the neural pathways become etched more deeply so they are more easily accessible. Your brain connects shirts to the dry cleaners, and when you get in your car you find it easier to drive there, having to think less about the directions. Now, let's take the metaphor further. Those dendrites become enhanced with each experience. Imagine you are looking down at a time-lapse Google Earth display of the town you live in. As you (and others) bring more shirts to the cleaners, the dry cleaner's business grows and the owner expands the shop. The dry cleaner is like a dendrite, and the added profits and expansion are the bumps resulting from more transactions.

Neural pathways make good metaphors, but they literally reflect social pathways. Take London taxi driving, a noble tradition since the first horseless carriage roared past a horse in 1897. Now, I've driven all around the UK, and I figure nothing gives my brain a better workout than landing jet-lagged at Heathrow, renting a car with a stick shift, and whipping around the roundabouts on the "wrong" side of the road. It takes several years for would-be London cabbies to learn the location of sixty thousand roads and innumerable pub locations, and then to figure out how to get there. Professional drivers call it "the Knowledge." Three-quarters of the trainees drop out. Only after grueling exams can an applicant earn a coveted license. (Compare that to New York City, where some of the drivers come from places where they have not yet invented the traffic light.) Of course, the London cabbie has a paper map, and often an electronic GPS system. But the driver has another map, too. Driving the streets and learning the routes has literally created a mobile map in his head. A University College, London, study showed that London drivers have larger posterior hippocampi than other people, and that as the driver gains more experience navigating the roundabouts and mazes, neural connections grow deeper. When the head of Cab Drivers Club learned about the research, he said, "I never noticed part of my brain growing—it makes you wonder what happened to the rest of it."

Our emotions also follow the Rule of Repeats and reshape neural pathways. Let's take the negative case: road rage. The shortest measurable time frame is probably the millisecond between when a New York City traffic light turns green and the car behind you honks. Every time you scream and honk your horn, you make it easier to scream and honk the next time. You'll scream and honk more quickly. The hot hand may not exist in basketball, but the hot head certainly does exist elsewhere. Your brain knows exactly how to process the frustration of driving. That's why if you want to become happier, you have to fight against etching negative pathways more deeply into your brain. If road rage becomes your habit, the "path of least resistance" becomes anger, and you are hurtling yourself toward misery.

100 PERCENT ALTRUISM FAILS

Philosophers, preachers, and psychologists fail us when they extol only cooperation and see competition as an enemy. Can't we just depend on altruism, and won't our brains just get used to people trusting each other? As an economist I can assure you that full cooperation and 100 percent charity would be chaotic, pointless, and waste natural resources. Without markets, how would society know what to produce? An example: Suppose that Michael wants a football helmet, and Max makes helmets. Cooperative/charitable Max says, "Here, Michael, take my helmet." Michael asks the price. Max says, "Free." Great, they are both happy. But how many helmets does Max have? How can he afford to buy the plastic materials to make more? Even if everyone is 100 percent charitable and Max can obtain materials for free, how would society decide whether it's worth drilling for the oil to make the plastic to make the helmet? At some point, we need somehow to fess up and answer the following question: "What's it worth to you? How much would you give up for a helmet?"

Go to your dresser drawer and take out the old T-shirt you don't wear anymore. Or maybe the rugby shirt that makes you look like you once hosted *Blue's Clues* on the Nickelodeon channel. Surely, you don't need the shirt, and someone else does. Why not send it to a shirtless guy, sweating in the sun in Namibia? Why don't we all just give away "free" shirts and solve the problem of clotheslessness? In a book called *The Travels of a T-Shirt in the Global Economy*, the Georgetown economist Pietra Rivoli spells out one objection: When we dump our old T-shirts on poor countries, their homegrown T-shirt companies get slaughtered, leading them to fire workers, hurting the overall economy. In this case, "free" is very costly. Looking at the problem, the *New York Times Magazine* "Ethicist" Randy Cohen even wondered whether it would be unethical to give away a shirt to an African. He quoted Bama Athreya, the executive director of the International Labor Rights Fund, who told him that the used-clothing trade "has contributed to the decimation of local garment industries, and therefore contributed to unemployment in Africa." (In the end, Cohen was stumped by his own query.) Rivoli points out, however, that the African textile industry is so riddled with poor quality and management that "free" is just one of many pervasive problems. Rivoli does not tell this story to discourage charity—I strongly encourage it—but we'd better be aware that trying to set up a system to replace or undermine trade usually ends up undermining people, not just undermining an abstraction called "the market."

THE ERA OF THE STRANGER: MORE PEOPLE, MORE COMPETITION, MORE CONNECTIONS

Here's the first thing you need to know about economic history: For most of man's life on earth, he has lived no better on two legs than he had on four. I could show you stylish charts proving that until a few hundred years ago just about everyone lived in poverty, hoping for enough calories to get through the day and expecting many of their children to die before reaching adulthood. The paucity of food, clothing, and medicines three hundred years ago in Europe was downright Paleolithic. Even in the 1990s, I heard reliable reports from rural China of "one-pants families," where the father would wear the pants to work during the day, and his wife would wear them to work at night. The result of Asian poverty was especially heart-wrenching. Female infanticide is practiced even today as a reaction to Beijing's one-child policy, but historically it had been practiced whenever food was short.

Throughout the world in medieval times and up until the 1700s, people competed much as they had as foragers. In Kenya the man with more wealth in the form of cows had more wives and children. In South America, hunters who brought home the most meat spread their seed the most. Whether in forager communities or European villages, the most successful men fathered the most children, and a greater proportion of those children survived. In England in Shakespeare's day, the richer half of the population fathered 40 percent more children than the poorer half. The economist Gregory Clark calls it "Survival of the Richest." Here's the point: *Before* the rush of our current rat race, in a world of village cobblers and potters, there was much misery and it was not distributed on the basis of who "deserved" a happy life.

There was competition prior to the 1700s, but it was not really among strangers. Four hundred years ago people knew the Earth was not flat, but they acted as if it was and seldom traveled more than a few miles to the next village. Then in Europe something remarkable happened in the 1700s, widely called the Industrial Revolution. But that unfortunate term makes the event sound like just the clatter of heavy machines. The time heralded a new work ethic, too. Some have called it the *Industrious* Revolution. The age of colonialism, when kings and queens merely claimed land and precious minerals, turned the world into a crisscross of merchant routes. While Europeans in prior centuries had focused on the afterlife, the hereafter became subsumed in the here and now. I would call it the *Era of the Stranger*. It was a period when trade flourished, when contracts were signed hundreds of miles apart, and when new transportation systems allowed strangers to interact with each other across the globe. This outburst of competition was messy, it was sometimes demeaning, and it was beneath the dignity of the clergy and the noblemen (who felt threatened). Rather suddenly, common people had access to a wider variety of food, better nutrition, and more modern medical techniques. This Era of the Stranger was also about the only thing in human history that began to drive up life expectancy and drive down the number of children who died in infancy. For the first time, despite the warnings of Thomas Malthus, population grew quickly, and so did the overall standard of living.

The world got wealthier when more strangers started trading with and competing with more strangers. This is the story of human progress. Imagine we scroll back the clock five thousand years. The world population is perhaps 4 million. There are no hearing aids for the deaf, antibiotics for the stricken, or air-conditioning for the elderly in the summer. Do you think a small population of 4 million people, made up of self-contained clans, would have come up with these discoveries? Of course not. The "miracles of modern science" did not come until a feverishly competitive system began to create wealth, which allowed populations to grow. More babies were born; more survived. More strangers began to trade goods and ideas. More people on Earth meant more brain waves flowing with scientific and engineering inspiration. More people means more geniuses, whose inspiration and perspiration can improve lives. Up until the 1980s, most developmental economists frowned on population growth, and in the 1960s and 1970s, experts warned of a "population time bomb," and young people swore off childbearing because the world would have another mouth to feed. But in the past twenty-five years, economists have begun to see the upside of having more people around.

An outburst of competition in the 1800s led to another revolution: literacy. The most successful people not only had the most children, they tended to then invest more time and attention in those children. Their children were more literate and numerate than other children. Soon strangers who could read and count began to interact with other strangers who could read and count. By the mid-1800s, the book publishers Charles Scribner's Sons, Macmillan, and Collins were shipping books across the seas, leading to more literacy in a more competitive world. Workers in mills learned how to weigh, measure, and calibrate tools. Similar trends began to emerge in China and Japan. It was competition that created literacy, not mandated school attendance legislated by a king.

All this rushing around was dizzying. Old ways were ripped to shreds. No doubt, there was a lot of nostalgia for the more stable life of the Middle Ages. But that stable life was, well, pretty much like living in a stable. People ate what horses ate, relieved themselves as horses did, and had as much indoor square footage per person as a horse. The old ways were replaced by expanding literacy and a rising standard of living. As I mentioned earlier, incidents of violence began to fall. As people traded more, they smacked each other around less. With less violence, murder, and vandalism, life seemed more secure. Interest rates fell, which made investment more attractive, reinforcing a rising standard of living. People became more thrifty, more hardworking, and less likely to kill each other. Who prospered? Those who learned to save, invest, read, write, add, subtract, and avoid solving disputes with daggers. Competition bred cooperation with strangers and replaced an insular, "communal" society that had all the characteristics of inbreeding: disease, retardation, and deadly family infighting. In communal societies, most people could not count, and did not even know how old they were.

Most of us are descended from those who learned to compete and cooperate in the economy. Those men who did not learn spread less of their seed. Women who did not learn these behaviors gave birth to fewer babies. Did mankind evolve during this process? Is it possible that Darwinian adaptation favored those whose brains and genes tilted them toward competing hard, working hard, and avoiding violence? The "Flynn effect" shows that during the twentieth century, IQs rose, as society became more complex and people ate better. The Flynn effect probably surged during prior centuries (though we cannot prove this). However, your great-great-great-grandfather was more likely a guy who figured out how to use tools at a mill than a guy who shot another man to steal a horse.

After ten thousand years of Neolithic, near Stone Age living, people started to see startling changes in their living standards. Around 1800, incomes began a tenfold leap. People could afford breakfast, lunch, and dinner. They could imagine owning their own cottage. But did all this hurrying make people happier? That's hard to judge. We do not have good survey data on happiness for 1800, and even today's survey data is suspect. We do know that people "voted with their feet," and places that prospered attracted more wretched peasants hoping to breathe free. Hong Kong had just eight thousand inhabitants in 1840. We also know that their worries began to change in character. They began to fret about wearing the "right" clothes to church, and whether they could afford school for their children. Any parent knows these are questions that can steal a good night's sleep for weeks on end. But that is different from worrying whether your child has cholera or whether that last morsel in the cupboard will keep her from starving to death tomorrow. A seemingly chaotic system of trade and competition taught people that they could cooperate with and learn from strangers, who would make them healthier and wealthier.

FREE TRADE MAKES YOU TALLER

I once heard an American wit say that the English have given us nothing. Except, he said, muffins. They also gave the world a free trade policy that brought lower prices to consumers. Free trade brought new opportunities to far-off places like Bombay and Shanghai. Free trade inspired young people to leave the farm and pursue new careers that did not require backbreaking manual labor. Inspiration could replace perspiration.

Though Anglophiles and moviegoers enjoy books and shows glorifying the Tudors, Tudor England was remote, weak, and small compared to France, for example. (And, of course, there was that English weather.) England had one-third the population of France and a lot less gold in 1500. England's population seemed stagnant. Shakespeare wielded a mighty pen, but the Tudor treasure chest was often empty (as a result of foolish wars and miserable fiscal management). Nonetheless, the Industrial Revolution quickly catapulted England ahead of its rivals. Beyond creating wealth, the revolution created more people, as population tripled from the 1700s to the 1800s.

Edenists seem to think the Industrial Revolution was a big mistake. They imagine Oliver Twist in the arms of Fagin, covered with soot and desperate for a crust of bread. Of course, London had orphans, thieves, prostitutes, and suffering. But it always did. Edenists claim that disruptive competition ignited terrible inequalities. But Gregory Clark argues effectively that the most vital economic inequalities actually narrowed. Before our era of heated competition, poor people had fewer children and fewer of their children survived. Poor people were one-third less likely to be literate. Moreover, nutrition was so bad that wealthy people were significantly taller than poor people. When Hobbes said that life was short in a state of nature, he was right in two ways: for poor people life expectancy was just thirty-three years, and they would stand several inches shorter than rich people. In 1800, cadets who attended the prestigious Sandhurst Academy towered over the grunts. These differences have collapsed. The Edenists might prefer family gardens to modern farms, where "sustainable" growth means picking your own apples rather than shopping at a grocery store. But if the world had followed their vision over the past two hundred years, fewer people would be tall enough to pick those apples off their trees.

THE VIRTUE OF IGNORANCE

Nobody likes know-it-alls. It must have been hell to live in ancient and medieval times, when lots of people could know virtually everything. There wasn't so much to master. Before Newton, math and science were pretty easy. Even a boob would score high on *Jeopardy AD 1000*. Then things got jumbled up. A more competitive economic system created more cooperation, more children, more literacy, and a bit of a frenzy. By the 1800s, life had become super-complicated and specialized. With so much rushing about and dealing with strangers, it became impossible to know everything. Despite increasing literacy, each year a smart person would know a smaller and smaller proportion of facts about the world. What a disaster! Or maybe not. In a brilliant article destroying communitarianism and socialism, Friedrich von Hayek explained why only a competitive system can allow society to handle information that is dispersed and disorganized.

In an autocratic or communal or socialistic system, so-called experts, wise men, shamans, and bureaucrats must set the correct price for goods and services. But what happens if there is a drought? A bumper crop? Or what if people just decide they want more of a product? How can the experts figure out the cause of dislocations? How can they set a communal price? No one is smart enough. In contrast, a competitive system is not paralyzed, because it does not require know-it-alls. As long as prices can fluctuate, prices can send signals of shortages and surpluses, and the changing demands of consumers. People do not need to know why a good is in short supply; all they need to know is that prices have gone up. That gives consumers incentives to use less and businesses incentives to produce more. Hayek's article uses a striking quotation from Alfred North Whitehead: "It is a profoundly erroneous truism, repeated by all copybooks and by eminent people when they are making speeches, that we should cultivate the habit of thinking about what we are doing. The precise opposite is the case. Civilization advances by extending the number of important operations which we can perform without thinking about them." Here's another way to look at it: Suppose every time you bought a new car you had to read the engineering specifications and the user's manual, and that before turning the key you had to understand the chemistry and physics of the internal combustion engine. You would probably be stuck in your driveway the rest of your life. Instead, we rely on a bunch of strangers. All we need to do is figure out how to slide the key into the ignition.

Ignorance is bliss. Not because it's good to be stupid, but because it's stupid to waste your time trying to get to the bottom of everything. Better for the economy and for your own happiness to learn what you need to, take action, and then move forward. As I said in an earlier chapter, the overexamined life is not worth living.

CONFUSION IS GOOD FOR OUR BRAINS

In our competitive environment a dizzying whirl of choices can make us irritable and confused. How do you choose which brand of salt to buy at the supermarket? Should you pay more for Morton's? Are all salts created equal? How do you choose which brand of laundry detergent to use? While social critics tell us to junk all the brands, and tell us that branding is a waste of time, our brains grow by encountering choices. Advice columns on mental health in magazines like *Men's Health* and *Cosmopolitan* are filled with suggestions, like brushing our teeth with the opposite hand, since this could rewire our brains and keep our neurons agile. This same constructive process goes on whenever we walk into a market and wade into a competitive economic environment. Our brains like variety. Variety is not just the spice of life. Variety is a higher form of living life. And most of us like contrasts, too. Many get bored of the same foods and the same routine, which helps explain why even good restaurants tend to die young. Entrepreneurs enjoy working more hours because they relish a new challenge. Even our vacations seek out new terrain. Last year Costa Rica was hot, now Belize is the sexy destination. Miami Beach was so 1960s, until the 1990s, when it became SOBE and cool again. Our frontal cortexes want us to try different things. Researchers showed that we perceive tastes and smells more strongly when they are contrasted. We like them better. Here, try this swordfish. You might rate it a 7 on a scale of 1 to 10. Now, eat this banana. Now, go back to the swordfish. Suddenly, the swordfish will taste better. What had seemed bland is magically deemed delightful. Is this because we are irrational or stupid? No, it's because we are wired to appreciate variety.

Edenists believe that we should attempt to equalize income because more income does not provide much more happiness. The economic term is "diminishing marginal utility." They cite psychological studies to show this. For a guy making $150,000 who already owns a BMW, another car won't make him much happier. But here is the flaw: Diminishing marginal utility reverses when we are presented with new choices. Not only that, it restores and revivifies what has been diminished by overuse. The "communal" system of an Edenist would more likely snuff out pleasure and happiness because it provides no incentive for entrepreneurs to develop new choices. Our brain waves would dampen in amplitude and frequency. A flat economy flatlines our brains.

CALVIN COOLIDGE'S SEX LIFE

There's one glitch in my paean to variety. It messes up a lot of marriages. Psychologists and biologists know the story of Calvin Coolidge, whose visit to a poultry farm gave name to the phenomenon known as the Coolidge effect. The president and his wife were touring the farm, when Mrs. Coolidge asked about rooster virility. She wondered how a small number of roosters could lead to so many dozens of fertilized eggs. The farmer boasted that his roosters perform their task dozens of times each day. "Would you please tell that to Mr. Coolidge," Mrs. Coolidge replied. So the farmer did. The president responded: "Does the rooster do his business with the same hen each time?" "No," said the farmer. "Would you please tell that to Mrs. Coolidge," the president gloated.

Sure enough, it's not just roosters who seek variety among mates, nor is it presidents in the 1990s. Researchers have tested and teased rats, squirrels, and snails, too. Put a male rat in a cage with a bunch of girl rats. His dopamine level surges, doubling, in fact. Watch him initiate intercourse with all of them. After each climax his dopamine level drifts downward. Finally, he will fall asleep, exhausted and disinterested. But wait, throw another female into the cage at the last minute, and he will suddenly perk up for one more round of rodent sex. Merely seeing a new female will perk up his dopamine by nearly 50 percent. The Coolidge effect has some pull in human males as well. That is why societies need moral codes to buttress our nobler impulses.

The Coolidge effect seems to attack the Rule of Repeats: a civil war inside our own heads. The Rule of Repeats says we should deal with the same people; but the Coolidge effect suggests we do not want to. Here's a simple way to reconcile the two, when we think about the economy. We want to deal with people we have learned to trust, but we do not want to make the same deal with the same person on the same terms every time we see him. If we learn to trust a merchant, we would like him to show us new wares next time we see him. And that's pretty much how I feel about walking into Costco, I must admit.

WILLIE MAYS AND YOUR BRAIN

During the best years of his career in the 1950s, Willie Mays would have made almost as much washing cars in the New York Polo Grounds parking lot as he did playing center field for the Giants. He always said he would've played for free. He played with a contagious joy. He'd take a big lead off first to rattle pitchers, swing for the fences, and then chase down fly balls that mere mortals would have waved good-bye to. His ferocious competitiveness combined with his gleaming smile symbolized the love of sport. All cultures honor sports, whether sumo wrestling, Ping-Pong, or that disturbing Afghani version of soccer played with the head of a sheep. With about a hundred countries vying in the Olympics, there may be something universal and aboriginal about human beings chasing each other around on grass or bouncing a ball on hardwood. Simply put, our bodies get a charge—a surge of dopamine, endorphins, and testosterone—from play. Snobs might disdain sports as just another example of "bread and circuses," diversions for the masses to divert their attention from the rat race or the economic fleecing they are suffering from at the office. But the truth is, human beings enjoy turning physical activity into competition. Moving muscles makes us happier. But we form teams to cooperate in sports only *after* first seeing the competitive gleam. Teamwork follows the competitive urge. Rooting for teams comes next. Watching others play releases neurotransmitters and enhances our mood. It would be difficult to gauge who got more joy from Willie Mays catching Vic Wertz's line drive in 1954—Willie or a random Giants fan. Animals enjoy play, too.

Let's face it: Chasing down fly balls, spiking volleyballs, and running a 5K race does not get us very far. It does not feed the hungry or clothe the naked. Working out in a gym can be called self-indulgent. In the logic of the Edenist, running on a literal treadmill in a gym is no more admirable than running on a figurative one. The goal in both cases is egotistical and self-centered. But the Edenist misunderstands the role of competition in the workplace, and the role of competition in our leisure space. To be happy, we need to move, and we need to know that we are moving relative to other human beings.

Competitive sports spark another aspect of our human character: the desire for camaraderie among teammates. The slap on the back, on the butt, and the high five release opioids and oxytocin. *Here again we see an example where competition begets cooperation and the neurotransmitters that make us feel better about ourselves.* Even teasing makes us feel better. "Your mama" jokes and fraternity pledge dares are competitive games that bring people closer. Of course, teasing can turn into bullying, but track a bunch of boys or girls at the mall or on the soccer field and you'll mostly hear the teasing that builds character, self-confidence, and social bonds.

How can you stretch your life span by two and a half years? We all know the usual (and probably accurate) answers, including eating fish and exercising. But a careful statistical study in the *Journal of Death and Dying* presents a new and nifty prescription: engage in competition and earn a nickname! For example, baseball players with nicknames live several years longer than teammates without nicknames. A study of hundreds of British dairy farms showed that when farmers give names to their cows, milk output jumps 6 percent. Cows with names get more affection. Now, why would a nickname help a baseball player live longer? Because you have to earn a nickname by convincing your peers and competitors to use it. You are fighting not just to win baseball games, but fighting to stand out on the field. Even bad nicknames can extend life. The baseball legend Fred "Bonehead" Merkle, whose infamous blunder (failing to touch second base) cost his New York Giants the 1908 National League pennant, outlived most of his team. And Willie "Say Hey!" Mays still looks strong at seventy-nine. All that tearing about in center field, all that swinging for the fences, all those years sitting on the dugout bench plotting his next turn at bat turned out to be a lot healthier than lazing on a park bench.

CHAPTER 9

Forget Utopia: Necessity Is the Mother of Happiness

What's the Big Idea? You can't get the good things in life without stress.

An ambulance carrying my father is weaving through traffic to a hospital in Phoenix. My father, on vacation, is short of breath, his lungs compromised by a sudden, dangerous bout of pneumonia. My mother is panicked. My brother and I are flying in from California. We don't know anyone in Phoenix. My father needs surgery. Two surgeons emerge. One is a mild-mannered gentleman, the sort you'd like to play golf with because you know he wouldn't nudge the ball with his shoe. The other, a brash *Top Gun* type, is the kind who'd wear a leather jacket under his scrubs. I didn't like this guy. But like a top gun, he had spent more training time under intense pressure and had performed more lung procedures. Who did we choose? Well, if you were lying on the operating table, an anesthesiologist about to connect your vein to a bag of liquid tethered to a pole, would you care more about golf manners or waking up after the operation?

Do we want competitive people in our lives? Would we be better off if we burned the A-list of type A personalities? Probably not. Thomas Edison famously said that genius is "1% inspiration, 99% perspiration." They couldn't pull Jonas Salk from his laboratory to take a break. And I bet Gutenberg stayed up many nights working on his printing press. Some people gravitate toward stressful jobs, whether as policemen, soldiers, airline pilots, or chaperones for rappers. But what of the rest of us, who do not feel compelled by an unstoppable drive to show up early, stay late, and jump to the front of any line? Is the stress of modern life killing us? Is it unnatural? Can we do anything about it? Surely, a faster pace is spreading throughout the world. Think about the last time you flew on an airplane. Flight attendants beg passengers to turn off their cell phones as they close the cabin door. Then, as soon as the plane lands, what happens? Everyone turns on his cell phone and begins yapping. It's never important, usually something like, "Yeah, we just landed and I'm going to get my luggage. . . ." A friend of mine noted that she has never heard anyone urgently say, "Okay, I'm here with the kidney."

Once upon a time, life was slower. But was slower better? On January 8, 1815, in darkness and fog, British soldiers crossed the Mississippi River and began firing howitzers and rifles at Andrew Jackson's troops in the Battle of New Orleans. Jackson's troops ducked into canals and into swamps, but began returning fire. As the fog lifted, their aim became more lethal, killing almost three hundred British soldiers. The Americans lost seventy-one. The British turned to Biloxi and were poised to attack Mobile. Then the commanders of the British and American troops got the message. That bloody firefight of January 8 was not needed. It turned out that on December 24, England and the United States had signed a peace treaty in Ghent. So, six weeks after the treaty was signed, and leaving hundreds of corpses behind, the English retreated back across the Atlantic. Meanwhile, Andrew Jackson's glory paved the way to the White House. Six weeks of bloodshed because the world was a slower place.

I admit that modern life creates new forms of stress, but I will argue that our minds and bodies need some stress, that dismantling the modern economy or encouraging individuals to drop out is naïve and hazardous to our mental health. Back in the 1960s Dr. Timothy Leary, the Harvard psychedelic psychologist, urged students to "turn on, tune in, drop out." I spent a day with Leary later in his career, while he was making bundles of cash on the lecture circuit debating the hard-nosed Watergate burglar G. Gordon Liddy. Leary came off as an affable airhead, a space cadet, we would say. I wasn't surprised that when he died in 1996, some grams of his cremated ashes were sent in a rocket to outer space. But oh, what a legacy! How many smart kids burnt out their minds tripping on LSD in order to tune out the hazards and stresses of the 1960s and 1970s. Some tripped out over window ledges and committed suicide. Leary confessed to me that he felt bad about how some of the experiments turned out. Leary began his drug research with scientific rigor and rectitude. The problem came when his experiments met an ideology that said "drop out." The social successes of past decades did not come through dropping out of the fray; they came through people like Martin Luther King Jr., who refused to go away. What if Nelson Mandela had retreated to a commune? What if Ronald Reagan had declared, "Mr. Gorbachev, that's a nice wall"?

STAND UP WHILE READING THIS

We hear that a competitive society creates stress, which kills us by allegedly destroying neurons, inviting Alzheimer's and heart attacks. (Doctors used to list ulcers among the "stress maladies," until scientists recently showed that bacteria, not nagging bosses or nosy neighbors, create ulcers.) But recently, some more balanced studies on stress have taken on conventional wisdom. The phrase "Take it easy" may be a quicker route to depression and illness than the admonition to "Keep it up." Studies at Johns Hopkins found that pregnant women under moderate stress gave birth to babies who proved more developmentally advanced, and scored higher on cognitive tests. Could stress be good for you, by toughening you up, so you are in top condition to face the real awful trials in life—for example, disease or the death of a loved one? Such a hypothesis would send those Zen monks into cardiac arrest.

We really need to be turning some questions and assumptions upside down and inside out. Perform those yoga moves in reverse. Let me give you an example. A number of years ago I was watching an obese man waddle down the aisle of the supermarket. I resisted the temptation to look into his shopping cart in order to count the Twinkies and judge his eating habits. I do believe that for some people genetics pose terrible obstacles to weight control. So I simply watched him waddle and assumed that he was waddling slowly because he was fat. Then it occurred to me: maybe he is fat *because* he waddles! In other words, maybe he has spent his lifetime walking slowly and moving methodically. How many more calories would he have burned if he had sprinted or darted or dashed across the store, across his office, or his kitchen? In the years since overturning my conventional assumption, I have noticed the gaits, weights, and walking speeds of people. I suspect that slow walking causes obesity almost as much as obesity causes slow walking. In fact, research has shown that fidgety people tend to weigh less. Likewise, a lifestyle or an economy that avoids speed and stress will trend toward illness, psychological and physical.

Stand up while reading this chapter. Relaxing by the fire or by the television can kill you. Okay, I'm exaggerating, and some relaxation is good for us. But how much? Few things are more relaxing than sprawling out on a sofa and channel surfing on a television. But a six-year Australian study asked about nine thousand men and women how many hours they spent watching television. Those who spent more than four hours a day "de-stressing" scored an 80 percent higher chance of cardiovascular disease than those who spent less than two hours. Americans average about five hours reclining in front of the television, basically slowing down their metabolism. In your bloodstream is an enzyme called lipoprotein lipase. It's a friendly enzyme because it draws fat to your muscles, where it can be burned as fuel. But sitting on your fanny relaxing leaves fat in your bloodstream, where it might as well clog into formations that spell out 9-1-1. Now, I tend to be skeptical of population survey studies. Too often there is a bias in the sample and self-selection. People who watch television for hours are probably more sedentary during the rest of the day, too. Maybe they are more willing to sit down and fill out a survey form. Or they are more likely to scarf down a bag of potato chips, for example. Nonetheless, the Australian study should warn us that the passive life may pose as many hazards as the "stressed" life.

A British study of 2,401 twins discovered that sitting around seems to age us. Every time our cells divide, the telomeres at the ends of chromosomes shorten. Under powerful microscopes, telomeres look and act like the caps of shoelaces, preventing chromosomes from fraying. When they become too short, the cells can no longer divide. Scientists showed that a lazy twin has shorter telomeres in white blood cells than an active twin, implying that the cells were losing their ability to continue dividing. Without more cell division, the body grows vulnerable to age-related diseases like Alzheimer's. Telomeres act like a countdown clock to a funeral, and while too much stress can speed up the clock, too little stress can also damage them.

MICHELANGELO AND YOUR STRESSED-OUT MIND

If we hate stress so much, why do we seem attracted to art that depicts it? Consider the *1812 Overture*. Does it charge you up? Now consider paintings from AD 1300. Do you get charged up by them? I don't. Giotto's early Renaissance paintings look staid and dull; you cannot find a furrowed brow on Mary or baby Jesus. Excuse my blasphemy, but Mary looks like an advertisement for Botox. Only in the era of Michelangelo do the paintings show humanity. Whenever I visit Rome, I make my way across town to the church called San Pietro in Vincoli (St. Peter in Chains), to stand before Michelangelo's magnificent *Moses*. Forget

Schwarzenegger, here are rippling forearms and a steely glare! Go to Florence to see *David*. Now, there is a furrowed brow, among other striking features. Even the Statue of Liberty's face shows stress. Why are these among the most popular sculptures/statues in the world? Precisely because they reveal the stress of human life, not some ethereal retreat suited for Walden Pond!

One day in 1506 Rome, Michelangelo heard a knock on his door. Swiss soldiers stood in front of him. They had just begun to guard the Vatican. They had a message from the pope. You must come right away. You must help us solve a mystery. It could bring great fortune. Michelangelo rushed to the scene. A dirty, twisted marble sculpture was being hauled from the ground, unearthed from a vineyard. Could it be? Impossible. It's been lost forever. Maybe it never existed. But there it was: the Laocoon! A stirring sculpture from Ancient Rome (now found at the Vatican Museum) that depicts a Trojan father and his two sons writhing in anguish as they wrestle snarling sea serpents. In 1500, the sculpture was considered mythic, not just because it illustrates a mythic event, but because it had been lost. By the 1500s Italian artists were not sure it had ever existed. But sure enough, the ancient sculpture had survived. Michelangelo called it "a singular miracle of art," and it began to play a powerful role in the mood and culture of Rome. With all the rapid change of the Renaissance and the political upheaval of popes and Medicis, Romans felt disconnected and rootless. Sound familiar? The discovery of the long-lost Laocoon helped connect fifteen hundred years of Roman history, giving stressed-out urban dwellers a connection to the past. "Renaissance" means, of course, *re*birth, and the tragic Laocoon sculpture inspired by illustrating the struggle of human life, and assuring Italians that the struggle was as old as human life. Romans, who triumphantly paraded the sculpture through the city streets, found their roots in an old but daring carving of marble that depicted, well, stress.

Which brings us to today. Sometimes relaxation and meditation make sense—for example, while waiting for a dentist to drill. I'd much rather stare at dull, pastel daisy field paintings than the Laocoon while waiting in the dentist's chair. But is that life? Or just a still life? Do you want to live a still life? What is good for the dentist's chair is not good in the office chair or at the kitchen table. Somehow, in the era of Google, when almost all human knowledge is available at a keystroke, happiness studies urge us to turn our backs on our most basic human drives and stresses. We must confront them as fully formed human beings, not still lives. There is no real escape, short of the sweat houses of charlatans or Tim Leary's old narcotic recipe book.

WHERE DOES STRESS COME FROM?

One of the loudest audience laugh interruptions came in 1953, during the filming of the *I Love Lucy* episode "Lucy Goes to the Hospital." Lucy is pregnant, very pregnant. Ricky, Fred, and Ethel have been rehearsing very methodically how to drive Lucy to the hospital—that is, who will carry the suitcase, help Lucy on with her overcoat, call the taxi, and so on. Suddenly, Lucy enters the room and says, "Ricky, this is it." All hell breaks loose. The suitcase crashes to the floor, clothes scatter, and Ricky ends up putting Lucy's fur-collared coat on Fred Mertz, as they barrel into each other and out the door. As the others race to the hospital, we see Lucy left alone, asking, "Hey, what about me?" Classic. A classic comedy scene and a classic example of stress. The good life is full of stress and angst. A new baby, a wedding, a job promotion, or even hosting a Thanksgiving dinner will pump our blood pressure. We all handle stress differently. My mother packs for a vacation one week ahead of time, yet my wife hurls balled-up socks at me as we back the car down the driveway. Who feels more stress? I can't tell you.

An ideology that repels stress leaves us unprepared for the good life, and does not allow us to escape the bad life. What is stress? What happens to our bodies when we feel the pressures of life? Let's return to the Stone Age for a moment and that saber-toothed tiger staring down at us from a rock. Or, if you prefer to keep things modern, the IRS agent driving up in his Ford to knock on your door. Your brain sends hormones pumping, as adrenaline and cortisol race around, channeling energy to your muscles so you can run away from the tiger, or hide from the IRS agent behind a file cabinet. Your heart rate quickens, your armpits dampen, your hearing and eyesight get sharper. You know the term "cold sweat." Your body sends blood away from the extremities so they can fuel your large muscles in what the psychologist Walter Cannon coined "a fight or flight" response.

In the 1950s, a clumsy Canadian scientist named Hans Selye kept dropping rats on his laboratory floor. In scenes recalling Woody Allen's scrambling among lobsters in *Annie Hall*, Selye's rats became stressed-out, and the fight-or-flight response directed body chemicals toward muscles and away from digestion, tissue repair, and immune response. He noticed their adrenal glands were enlarged, and their immune tissues were shrunken. They seemed to get sick. Life-threatening clumsiness can reshape our organs and neurons. Most people would be too embarrassed to admit to being a klutz. Not Selye. He published his findings and popularized the term "stress." But Selye admitted that life was full of good stress, too, which he called "the salt of life."

Now, no human being could live a happy life if constantly on the run from a predatory saber-toothed tiger, an IRS hit man, or a mad scientist dropping us on our heads. Our bodies are not made for continuous, life-threatening stress. Neurons can get exhausted and neural connections begin to fray. Our bodies may be more susceptible to disease. But how many Americans are really under the stress of a fugitive? More likely they are yanking at their hair because the cable man won't show up on time, the kids are acting up, or the car insurance bill just went up.

Happiness books describe the lethal impact of some super-extreme stressors and then cavalierly extend the diagnosis to every part of modern life. The psychoanalyst and social activist Erich Fromm wrote a book called *Escape from Freedom*, bemoaning our many life choices. He longed for the simplicity of medieval life, never mind the random acts of violence visited on huge swaths of the population during that era. We may feel paralyzed or traumatized in the supermarket, standing in front of rows of toothpaste brands. There are some studies that do show that too many jars of jam can cloud the mind. But it is going too far to claim that we can achieve happiness by taking away choices. Better studies show that it's a lack of control that incites stress. Remember Seligman's learned helplessness? So if choosing between Crest, Colgate, Tom's, or Aquafresh makes us tense, imagine how tense we would be if some authoritarian snatched our choices from us?

Though there is nothing pleasant in the stress of sickness, our bodies often do try to compensate, to offset the worry. Have you ever played an exhausting game of tennis or touch football? After the first set or quarter, you are sure you will die before the final whistle blows. But something happens. Opioids, endorphins, and enkephalins kick in, and somehow your arms and legs continue to move. We may feel tremendous pain the next morning and reach for a bottle of Advil, but we get through the stress. Hell, we might even feel a hint of euphoria. Some people who abhor aspirin and ibuprofen instead ask acupuncturists to poke needles into their aching bodies. Is acupuncture hocus-pocus? An Asian voodoo game? No; apparently those needles that prick the skin are themselves a kind of stressor, inciting your body to release opioids that will relieve the pain.

A HARDY MAN—OR WOMAN—IS GOOD TO FIND

There is a big difference between the stress of everyday life and the chronic, unrelenting chase of a predator. To handle modern stress, we need to get hardy. Our ability to handle stress is a bit like a muscle. A cushy life will kill you. An inadvertent, "natural" experiment was carried out in the 1980s. A federal court broke up Ma Bell (AT&T), leading to huge layoffs and the splintering of the company. In the confusion, some employees who kept their jobs complained that they had to report to ten different supervisors. Thousands of employees were fired, and not only that, they lost the mother figure in their daily lives. Who made it through the business disaster without resorting to drugs, suicide, or tumbling into prolonged depression? Who avoided strokes and heart attacks? Was it those privileged few who grew up with silver spoons in their mouths and country club caddies by their sides? No. In fact, the most resilient workers were those who had already experienced suffering, whether they were the children of alcoholics or army brats who had moved from town to town. They tended to hold on to jobs, hold on to their spouses, and hold on to their lives under searing stress. Salvatore Maddi, who conducted the research at the University of Chicago, developed the concept of hardiness, which is now employed by the Navy SEAL program. And when the marines say they "want a few good" men and women, they do not mean those without the scars of everyday life.

When Tom Brokaw created the concept of "the Greatest Generation," exalting Depression-era youngsters who fought in World War II, I took offense on behalf of every other human being who had ever lived. I was proud of my father, who as a teenage navy sailor helped liberate Shanghai, but the *greatest*? Isn't that presumptuous? But Maddi's research supports Brokaw—stress can make people stronger, more flexible, and more daring. These Depression babies had a deeper well of character to draw upon when they faced enemy fire shooting down on them from the cliffs of Normandy.

A long time ago, Ella Fitzgerald appeared in a catchy television commercial for a cassette audiotape, in which her high notes appeared to shatter a crystal goblet. The slogan: "Is it live . . . or is it Memorex?" Why did Ella Fitzgerald or Frank Sinatra ever perform live? They sold millions of albums without concerts. Besides, singing live before an audience is nerve-racking. Even Sinatra admitted he got butterflies in his stomach. Back in the 1950s, while singing at the Copacabana, his voice failed him and he had to flee the stage in shame like a deposed dictator. And yet, Sinatra came back, again and again. Why? Of course, money mattered. Pride, too. But Sinatra believed that the stress of performing live inspired him to sing better and ultimately brought him the happiness he couldn't find in a soundproof recording booth, at the craps table, or on a bar stool in the wee small hours of the morning.

Terrence McNally's play *Lisbon Traviata* is propelled by a character's desperate desire to hear a bootlegged recording of Maria Callas's 1958 live performance. Apparently, Callas's daring live performance creates an exhilarating rapture even for fans who hear it decades later.

I frequently lecture to business executives, and I have shared programs with everyone from Tony Blair to Terry Bradshaw to a motivational clown who finished his speech by doing a backflip onstage. Before going onstage I peek through the curtain at the audience. A big audience is best. Sure, there is stress, but a bigger audience revs me up. More important, the audience is more charged up. Lost in the anonymity of a crowd, they will more freely laugh, applaud, or even hiss if I annoy them.

A crowd of two thousand is an easy audience. You want a tough audience? Find an audience of one. When my mother was a girl in the 1950s, her family spent the summer at a resort, dining at the same table as Jerry Lewis's family. Jerry's father, Danny, was a moderately successful comedian. According to my mother, every night Danny would try too hard to entertain his dinner mates. My grandfather did not find him entertaining. Finally, Danny turned to my grandfather and said, "Why don't you laugh at my jokes?" Grandpa Sam responded, "Why don't you say something funny?" My point is no smart comedian will ever tell a joke to an audience of one. It is far too intimidating. What does that tell us about stress? Debilitating stress does not come from the complexity of modern life or from a seemingly manic free-enterprise economy. Complexity can enhance our lives. No, bad stress comes when you feel trapped, at the mercy of just a few grumpy people. And those grouches were more likely to poison your pleasure in the simple old days of 1611 or 611 than in 2011. In simpler days, a single boss, feudal lord, or warlord called the shots, rather than the clash of consumers in a busy marketplace.

WHO'S THE BOSS?

Thank goodness for rats. No one said that during the Black Death, but we can say it now, for rats have allowed researchers to do all sorts of tests without torturing people. You can go online today and order your own "Rat helplessness chamber." Model number 80010 will allow you to test two rats and make sure the "rat in the yoked chamber has no control over the delivery of tail-shock and is thus in an inescapable paradigm. The rat in the control chamber will not receive the tail-shock but will experience behavioral contingencies." The result of most rat-stress studies is this: Rats don't like to feel out of control, whether at the mercy of a capricious klutz (Selye), or even another rat. In one noted experiment, scientists put two rats on two different exercise wheels. Here was the trick: the second rat had no choice but to run whenever the first rat decided to go for a spin. The result: the free-choice rat got slimmer, smarter, and ended up with more lush hair. The "victim" rat got stupid. When rats or humans feel victimized by capricious dictators, they feel the stress of fear.

This raises a basic question: What kind of economic system most likely creates capricious dictatorships over workers? Are most of us really trapped in a helplessness chamber? For all the worries of American life, Americans seem to feel among the most free, the most able to "spring from our cages." During the twelve months of 2007, 12 percent of Americans voluntarily said "I quit," and moved on to other jobs. Men in their twenties and thirties are almost 40 percent more likely to voluntarily switch jobs than they were in the 1970s. The average American holds more than a dozen jobs over a lifetime, more than ten by age forty-two. Most of these job jumps are by choice. We are more mobile in geography, too. Every year about 50 million Americans move homes, 15 to 20 percent of the population. And they are not just moving across the street. Almost half of those moves are across county lines, state boundaries, or from overseas. We could make it even easier for people to be mobile by, for example, reforming restrictive licensing laws that impede workers from practicing their professions in other states, but in general, Americans in the twenty-first century are less yoked than virtually any people in history. This does not guarantee happiness, of course. We could still be miserable, but we shouldn't blame it on an imaginary locked cage.

HOME CREATES AS MUCH STRESS AS WORK

A friend of mine helps runs GE's MRI division. He's an engineer by training but now knows more than most doctors about medical diagnostics. I asked him about cholesterol. "Here's the best thing you can do to improve your cholesterol . . ." I leaned forward, awaiting his expert, lifesaving advice. "Change your parents," he said. When it comes to stress, we can't change our parents, but we can choose how much time we spend with our families. And we do choose our spouses, our friends, and to some extent our coworkers. Few things make people more unhappy than a lousy marriage. It can also make them sick. In fall 2009, Tiger Woods shocked his fans and sponsors when he showed up unconscious on the street, next to his wrecked Cadillac Escalade. His wife had apparently chased him with a golf club. Poor guy. Not only was he bruised and bleeding, but he was probably suffering from a surge in cortisol, and a crash in the number of antibodies that attack viruses. Pesky researchers named Janice Kiecolt and Robert Glaser actually provoked arguments between couples to measure any immune response (ironically, the researchers, Kiecolt and Glaser, are married!). Sure enough, when spouses hurl epithets or lamps at each other, their antibodies hide. And it's not just marriages that can fray your neurons and drive you crazy. A sour roommate can do so pretty easily. Close quarters and closed minds are a combustible setting. They make for great anxiety and great drama, whether we're trapped in a dorm room or a foxhole. *Twelve Angry Men* would describe nearly any sequestered jury, stripped of control and forced to look at each other's faces for too long.

But remember, these enraging, stressful settings don't have much to do with people rushing around in a free-wheeling economy. Quite the opposite. They come from being stuck in one place, not from darting around among destinations. Dangerous stress does not come from engaging in a free-ranging, flexible, and ever-changing economic system. Dangerous stress arises when you come home from work to a home vibrating with rage and disappointment. It is not the rushing that hurts your soul, it's the thud of a paralyzed situation.

LEARN TO LIKE THE LEAN AND HUNGRY LOOK

As a hedge fund manager, I was always asked the same question by the savviest investors: How much of your personal money is at stake? To mix metaphors, those investors always wanted portfolio managers to (a) be hungry and (b) have skin in the game. My mentor, Julian Robertson, justified the large incentives fees that hedge fund managers earn (usually 20 percent of the profits) by referring to ancient Phoenician sea captains, who would earn a similar cut on the cargo they delivered, as they crossed perilous seas and double-crossed pirates not nearly as charming as Johnny Depp. Smart investors want to make sure that if their portfolios plummet, their investment managers would go down with the ship and drown with them. Why? Because it gives the managers powerful incentives not to do something stupid and reckless! (When the Bernie Madoff scandal unfurled, it was surprising how little his investors demanded of him.) The fear of losing is incredibly strong—especially when people have their own cash at stake. If they had limitless oceans of free money available, they would be less careful.

In the first part of this chapter we saw how good stress can help individuals. Now let's talk about societies, for the stress created by scarcity—which seems like bad stress—can make the difference between a thriving country with a high standard of living and a meandering mess of a society where people may own televisions but cannot afford a cheap TV dinner. Jared Diamond's best-selling books point to ecological explanations for the thrill of victory and the agony of defeat. A big piece of land with big elephants might persuade people to create joint hunting expeditions. Eurasia was blessed with docile horses, but Africa got stuck with rambunctious zebras. Chile got alpacas, but the Andes were too tough a climb, so the Aztecs didn't get great wool and good packers.

Diamond's view fits with much conventional economics. In fact, economics textbooks are clear: scarcity is a bad thing. Abundance is good and purportedly makes us happier. The Italian word *abbondanza* was the title of a hit song in the 1950s musical *The Most Happy*

Fella. But now I'll flip conventional economics on its head. Scarcity can motivate and inspire. We can't produce abundance without first confronting scarcity, marshalling our resources and fighting to produce. Countries blessed with natural resources are often poorer than those bereft of them because they lack the fighting spirit.

Most people, including many professional economists, think about a country's economy the way a potential home buyer thinks about a model home. It's awfully hot in Panama! How lucky that Venezuela has oil! Too bad Australia is so far away from the action! The cliché "location, location, location" might work well for buying a three-bedroom colonial in Peoria, but it's hardly worth a hill of beans when analyzing a country. Take Mexico, please. Mexico has enjoyed a great location, right on the U.S. border. It hasn't moved. Yet America's wealth and technology has not rubbed off much. Now look at prosperous Australia—a twelve-hour flight even after you change planes at LAX! And settled by criminals who sailed on leaky boats!

Economic textbooks waste a lot of time focusing on "factor endowments," telling us that a country blessed with lots of minerals and natural resources has a big advantage. Really? Hong Kong is a pile of rocks. The Netherlands was a sinking Venice, but without the charming bridges or the spumoni, and yet in the seventeenth century she leapfrogged her better-endowed neighbors. And then there's Israel today. She may be settled by God's chosen people, but He chose not to give them a drop of oil, while gushers spout across Arabia. Did you ever read Mark Twain's description of this arid and empty land? Israel's terrain doesn't naturally grow enough green for a sprig of parsley on your dinner plate, and yet there she blooms. In the race for economic development, would you rather bet on a country with a million tons of endowed zinc or one with a couple of extra IQ points and a free flow of ideas? Israel, trapped between the Mediterranean and the nastiest neighborhood since Howard Cosell announced "the Bronx is burning," has more companies listed on the NASDAQ than any other but the United States. Sure, soldiers carry Uzis, but they also carry Intel chips that they designed and the dream of inventing even better versions.

A big endowment of riches may even be a curse. The earth under many parts of Africa bulges with metals. And yet the economies appear retarded, and warlords hang on to power. Think back to the schoolbook atlases that displayed the natural resources of each country. As a kid, I always thought it unfair that the evil Soviet Union seemed to have all the great stuff, even bauxite, which sounded like a mysterious, earthly version of kryptonite, a bad thing in an enemy's arsenal. But the Soviet system had a reverse Midas touch. It turned precious metals and rich soil into famine and poverty. Way back in 1500, when Ming dynasty vases were being baked, the Chinese had all the technology they needed to beat England to the Industrial Revolution. But the mandarins of the time stomped on trade and the competitive spirit. In the twentieth century, socialists made excuses for the Soviet Union's sorry agriculture, citing seventy years of bad weather. As Ronald Reagan put it, there are just four things wrong with communist farming: "spring, summer, winter and fall."

What counts most, then? *Attitude, not latitude.* Grit, not cash. If you grab some images of Panama City off the Internet, you might think you are looking at Vancouver, with gleaming towers and a quickly gentrifying old town called Casco Viejo jutting out into the Pacific with colonial architecture and hanging bougainvillea. Ships enter and exit the canal from Panama City. Now travel through the canal, or across a new highway, just forty-five minutes to the north. On the Caribbean side sits Colon. Hold on to your wallet and take off your rings. Colon, which generates plenty of money and job opportunities, is surrounded by slums. People from Panama City are afraid to go there and consider Colon dwellers to be lazy and lawless. Colon is a culture of dysfunction and failed government relief efforts. Another example: The horrific Haitian earthquake of January 2010 forced people to ask why Haiti could be so crime-ridden and desperate, while its neighbor, the Dominican Republic, prospers on the other side of the same island, with average incomes seven times as high. The Dominican Republic has thriving forests and raises major league shortstops. Haitian villages are often stripped of vegetation and raise the promise only of early death (life expectancy is forty-four). David Brooks in the *New York Times* observed that the voodoo religion "spreads the message that life is capricious and planning futile. . . . Child-rearing practices often involve neglect in the early years and harsh retribution when kids hit 9 or 10." If the Dominicans switched places with the Haitians, and the Panama City folk swapped with the Colon families, those same poor and hopeless populations would remain in despair.

THE DEVIL'S EXCREMENT

Venezuela is a troubled and troublesome place today. I was in Cartagena, Colombia, recently, and a taxi driver volunteered, without my inquiring, that the Venezuelan leader Hugo Chavez was "crazy," and that Cartagena now houses many people from Caracas trying to get away. Venezuela has raging inflation, miserable joblessness, and soaring crime rates. It has one other thing, too: oil. Even with oil prices bouncing around in record ranges from 2007 to 2010, Venezuela's economy is a shambles. It's not just because Chavez is an authoritarian, utopian Marxist. It's because the "blessing" of oil has distracted and distorted the country's economy for fifty years. Venezuela's per capita income has gone nowhere since the early 1960s. It suffers the boom and bust of oil prices. Compare this to South Korea, which lacks gooey black gold, or even the shiny 14-carat kind. It is the world's fifth biggest oil *importer* and mines less gold than Serbia. In the early 1960s South Korea was poorer than Venezuela, on par with Haiti! Now, it challenges parts of western Europe in the ranking of living standards. Because South Korea has little oil, it must rely on brainpower and hard work. South Korea pours its resources into educating its children; Venezuela watches the oil pour and squanders the money. Back in the 1970s, Venezuela's own oil minister called oil "the devil's excrement" and predicted that "oil will bring us ruin." When countries discover vast natural resources, it seems to dampen their competitive urges and turns the mind away from creating wealth. This is crucial for anyone trying to understand competition, greed, and happiness. The danger for mental health does not come from competition, which is so frequently and wrongly condemned as greed. The danger comes when governments try to fulfill the needs of the people, relieving them of the need to work, and draining their desire to move forward. There are few combinations more lethal to the mental health of the people than vast resources and an authoritarian, paternalistic government. In those cases, a land of plenty turns into a land of scarcity. It would have been far better to start with scarcity, and provide the incentives to weave scarcity into plenty. There are a number of ways that vast resources can hobble an economy and a people, some of them more technical. First, countries with rich resources usually enjoy a stronger exchange rate on their currency, which the elites in the cities particularly relish because it gives them access to Prada clothing and ski vacations in Chamonix. Second, when there are pots of gold or oil wells just sitting there, warlords will think about trying to capture them, feeding fear and instability. Remember that in the summer of 1990 Saddam Hussein of Iraq invaded Kuwait to take over oil wells. Third, when a country depends on a resource like oil, it becomes like the "family business," so that the smartest people go into that field, and the leading universities tend to cater to it, ignoring all else.

Rich resources are not always a curse, of course, but they require vigilance. Norway stands out because the country has been investing its oil proceeds into other businesses and other countries, creating one of the world's largest nest eggs. As for Venezuela, Iran, and others, there is no nest egg, just a deadly trap.

Similar reasons explain why foreign aid so frequently fails to generate strong economic growth and so often undermines democracy (I'm not talking about emergency relief from natural disasters and terror). A World Bank Report—and remember, the World Bank has spent sixty years doling out development aid—concluded that foreign aid provides a windfall to recipient governments, and generates frantic activity as players try to grab their share, and then some. It's like a fumble on a football field—everyone piles in a heap to steal the ball. More disappointing, the study showed that foreign aid undercuts freedom. The report looked at 108 countries between 1960 and 1999. The upshot: More foreign aid led to less voting, fewer elections, and more dictators.

The land of plenty is the land of looting unless people feel they are working for a better tomorrow.

The stress of scarcity forces us to prioritize and work harder. In the garages of Silicon Valley, start-ups burn the midnight oil—in the quest to invent new sources of energy. Fortune 500 companies funnel money to those garages. Why? Because those corporate bigwigs realize that small labs with scarce resources have a better chance of cracking scientific codes than their million-dollar counterparts festooned with gold-plated microscopes.

CARGO CULTS AND CRAZY GODS

In the 1980s cult movie *The Gods Must Be Crazy*, a Bushman named Xi is minding his own business in the Kalahari Desert when a Coca-Cola bottle falls from the sky, dropped from a passing airplane. The Bushmen had never before seen such a sparkling thing. It must be a gift from the gods! But the bottle, which lands unbroken, eventually breaks the harmony of the tribe, for there is only one bottle. Pretty soon, envy, anger, evil spirits, and all sorts of mania break out. Xi ends up racing across the Kalahari trying to throw the bottle off the end of the earth. The film, a noble savage fantasy, generated many laughs and four sequels. While the Bushmen seem naïve, soon they run into enough white men to describe them as "heavy people," who are "not very bright" and need their magical toys in order to get anything done.

It's almost never good news when a Coca-Cola bottle flies in unannounced and without charge. Far better for a vending machine to show up, which would at least tell people that drinking soda comes with a price. The Edenist view of the world seems to promise happiness and a pleasant level of prosperity without the price of stress, anxiety, envy, and risk. Moreover, this view often suggests that staunching our competitive juices would somehow repair environmental degradation. Tell that to the people of Haiti, foraging in stripped forests, or to rural Chinese, living astride rivers through which float human waste and even human bodies.

On planet Earth, nobody rides for free. And yet many people think that we can shower ourselves with better health and a high standard of living without relying on the drive to strive, to compete, and to feel the natural high of dopamine and endorphins. If gods blessed us with manna from heaven, it would be a nice thing. But what would wheat and soy farmers do? How reliable would manna be? Would the gods deliver it each year? What if they skipped a year to punish bad behavior? Manna might do more harm than good. It would turn the whole world into a cargo cult. Cargo cults are the fascinating bittersweet result when modern people, with all their toys and technology, encounter primitive people. For an illustration, let's go back to the 1940s. During World War II, Japanese and American soldiers land on remote islands. The unknowing villagers of Micronesia and New Guinea hear roaring noises and look up to the sky to see big metal birds swooping in for a landing. The alien soldiers might leave behind radios, jeeps, pinups of Betty Grable. Entranced, the villagers soon look at the visitors as gods, or their jeeps as "chariots of the gods" (to borrow a phrase from a best-seller in the 1970s that claimed Stonehenge was built by aliens from outer space). The villagers drop their own religions and begin worshipping the strange visitors. The toys they leave behind carry magic and mystery. On Pacific islands, cargo cults emerged and began to pray on airplane landing strips, hoping to wave down the magical metal birds. They carved from coconuts imitation radios and microphones, hoping to speak with their newfound gods. (If Amelia Earhart didn't crash, she could have lived out her life as queen of some remote isle.) In 2009 the Travel Channel featured a cult from the island of Tanna that worships "Tom Navy," a World War II navy sailor who helped settle some tribal disputes in Tanna. On the program, cult members got to meet Colin Powell and speak of the living spirit of Tom. All this sounds like an episode of *Star Trek* or that World War II spoof *McHale's Navy*. I find it sad to see innocents fooled by battery-operated gadgets. But here's the thing: Cargo cults ultimately end in sadness because the gods stop sending the cargo. Tom Navy may have been a saint, but now that he's dead he will not show up with medicine when some little kid gets sick. And those Coke bottles stop showing up, too. Pretty soon, if the villagers want radios, or Band-Aids or malaria vaccines, they will have to work for them. Likewise, we cannot expect our society to produce vaccines or laptops without recognizing that we need to work for them. And that requires harnessing our noblest motives, as well as those that are less lofty.

PROGRESS IS NOT GUARANTEED; SOCIETIES CAN BACKSLIDE

The frenzy of modern life takes a toll, of course. A couple raising a family may feel overworked, underpaid, and undersexed. But we should not follow those who stand in front of the waves and shout "Stop!" We compete, therefore we are. If we do not, we and our society slump back to a dulled state reminiscent of the Soviet Union, where everyone got a bed but no one had a reason to get out of it. Free to compete, free to win, free to lose, free to be happy. Today, people in still communist Belarus report they are miserable compared with now capitalist Slovakia, though Slovakians don't earn much more.

Competitive societies raise people up from poverty, allowing them a better chance to conquer misery. In the past ten years hundreds of millions of Chinese and Indians have figured out how to put food on their plates. *When I was a kid, we were told "finish what's on your plate; kids in China are starving." Now those kids are eating our lunch.* All because Deng Xiaoping nodded his head and allowed people to strive without losing face. After half a century of begging and borrowing from the World Bank, Asian peasants are eating. And it is because they are allowed to plant and hunt and toil for themselves. This is virtually the only War on Poverty that is being won.

But these "animal spirits," as John Maynard Keynes called them, can be dulled or even beaten out of a society by its political and social leaders. For example, prior to World War II, Germans had a reputation for punctuality, order, and hard work. After the war the communist system robbed East Germans of their incentives to compete and organize efficient firms. More surprising, though, is what happened in West Germany between the 1950s and 1990s. Social-democratic policies, providing free spa visits, nearly unlimited job leave, and barriers to firing employees, robbed even the West Germans of their historical trait as hard workers. In the 1990s alone, the German workweek fell by 6 percent and the typical German now works 16 percent fewer hours than Canadians, and 25 percent less than Americans. Today Germans themselves scoff at their own workforce's dedication and diligence. In their own eyes they have surrendered their edge. In corporate board-rooms in Germany executives are deciding whether to build their new factories and offices in Germany, or to migrate across the border so they can hire more aggressive, more motivated employees in the Czech Republic, Slovakia, and Slovenia.

What happens when paternalistic governments try to remove all the stress? They remove the incentives and the spark of life, too. I recently reread one of the greatest football memoirs ever written, *Instant Replay* by Jerry Kramer, an offensive guard for Vince Lombardi's legendary Green Bay Packers. I was visiting the Green Bay area and wanted to feel some inspiration, so I ducked into a Lombardi's Steakhouse and dipped into the memoir. Green Bay prides itself on being a working-class town, emphasis on *working*. When Kramer started playing professional football in the late 1950s, even star quarterbacks didn't get paid enough to feed their families in the off-season. Kramer earned $7,750 in his first pro season. Almost all players chased down summer jobs, selling cars, hawking sporting equipment, or even delivering mail. They created networks of employer contacts to help each other get jobs. By the late 1970s, football players got lucky, because television coverage exploded, carrying salaries skyward. Today's minimum is over $300,000. Now the players can relax in the off-season. But what if the government had come along in the 1960s and said, "Fellas, it's not fair for you to be unemployed every January through August, so we're going to pay you welfare and unemployment compensation." What would have happened? For the answer to this question, look at a map of Wisconsin and turn right to Newfoundland, Canada.

Fisherman in Newfoundland, who numbered around sixty thousand in the 1960s, have an on-season and an off-season. They traditionally made much of their income hauling in fish from the sea, but in the off-season they found alternate work, logging, farming, or weaving nets. Then the government decided that this was too big a burden for the men. Representatives for the fishermen persuaded the government that they were entitled to payments during the off-season. Newfoundland became depressed, and so did many of the fishermen. From 1963 to 1973, welfare caseloads in New Brunswick more than doubled, and they jumped 85 percent in Nova Scotia. Those networks of contacts that allowed the Newfoundland fishermen to find work in the off-season frayed and their alternate skills waned. Welfare became a perfectly acceptable lifestyle. Canada lost jobs in the process, but the number of fishing bureaucrats reached six thousand. Even fishing skills eroded. Newfoundland's sixty thousand fishermen catch fewer fish than Iceland's far smaller fleet. Worse, the Ottawa government has turned the fishermen into a kind of cargo cult, tearing apart their traditional way of life and replacing it with one that exalts pleading and praying to foreign ghosts, rather than slipping on boots and gloves and getting to work.

BEWARE OF PEOPLE WHO WANT TO SCRAP GDP

Edenists don't like gross domestic product. To them, it is a symbol of cold, calculating competition. Hugo Chavez in Venezuela doesn't like to admit his economy is a mess, so he attacks arithmetic, calling GDP a capitalist conspiracy. Now, I too can criticize GDP, which does not directly take into account variables like water quality and the crime rate. But alternatives to GDP can too easily be twisted like taffy to suit political goals. During the last days of the Soviet Union, Michael Boskin, the chairman of the president's Council of Economic Advisers, was sent to Moscow to help Mikhail Gorbachev with economic reforms. He discovered that they kept "two sets of books: those they published, and those they actually believed (plus another for Stalin when he was alive)." Take a look at something called the Happy Planet

Index, which ranks countries based not on GDP but on whether the people are happy and healthy. For 2009, Costa Rica ranked highest. I've recently been to Costa Rica, and I loved the lush landscapes and banana plantations. Now look a few spots down the list. Jamaica ranks third, which fits nicely with the ubiquitous Reggae beat in "Don't Worry, Be Happy." But Jamaica's got a lot to worry about, including one of the world's highest murder rates. Tourists enjoy its turquoise Caribbean waters, but see them from behind locked gates in all-inclusive compounds. On the Happy Planet Index, Cuba ranked seventh, and, in an astounding finding, people under the Palestinian Authority are apparently happier and healthier than Israeli citizens! Now, if a pro-Zionist spokesman argued that the Palestinians are happier and healthier, he'd be laughed at. Or stoned. Of course, the United States shows up number 114, safely ahead of Zimbabwe. If Cuba clobbers the United States and most of western Europe, ask yourself this: When was the last time you heard of an American, a Brit, or a German trying to fake a passport and sneak into Cuba in order to raise a happy family? Which way were those leaky rafts headed, anyway? There's no point in quibbling over such a ranking system. The point is that utopians have a hard time resisting the temptation to try to make people happier by making them less free.

If we shouldn't look at standard measures like GDP, how about looking at life expectancy, schooling, and the willingness to volunteer? What if it turned out that when GDP grows, people live longer, grow smarter, and help each other more? Would that redeem GDP a bit? A study by the OECD asked exactly those questions and found that countries with stronger per capita GDP end up with populations that live longer, become more educated, and volunteer more. Moreover, in countries with strong GDP, fewer citizens are victims of crime. So much for the argument that a growing GDP actually hurts more than it helps.

Here is another typical mistake in the happiness "literature." Numerous studies by economists and psychologists suggest that people hate to lose what they've got. Most are risk-averse. Losing $100 is more painful than winning $100 is joyous. Taking away money or prized possessions hurts. Agreed. If so, why do so many psychologists believe that heavy taxes would make a country better off? I'd call this the "loss aversion error," because it argues that confiscating income would add smiles. Yet almost all the studies show that losing ground is terribly painful.

THE PARADOX OF SHRINKING POPULATIONS

I was flying across the country last year and the airline showed a *60 Minutes* segment on Denmark. Why Denmark? Because *60 Minutes* had a study in hand showing that the Danes were the "happiest people on Earth." Apparently, they had shaken off the wallowing melancholy of Hamlet. In the segment, they interviewed sincere-looking young Danes. The Danes attributed the findings to the wide variety of social services, including free child care, paternity leave, and so on. I like Denmark very much. In my desk drawer I have tokens left over from rides at Tivoli Garden and photographs of my kids in front of the famous Copenhagen statue of Hans Christian Andersen (even though he was often despondent and repressed). Denmark has much to be proud of in its history. However, here's the paradox: Denmark's population has been nearly flat for the past fifty years. In fact, the birth replacement rate has been negative, according to the government: "The last 30 years of the 20th century show a far-reaching change in the demographical characteristics of the Danish population. The decline in fertility accelerated from 1967, and the lowest level so far was reached in 1983, when the average number of children born per woman was 1.4. As 2.1 births per woman are necessary to avoid a fall in the size of the population, fertility rates are thus below the level needed for reproduction." During much of the 1980s, when many of the *60 Minutes* interviewees were born, Denmark's population was actually shrinking. What's the point of hailing a people as happiest if their purported happiness does not inspire them to reproduce? That kind of happiness looks like a biological cul-de-sac or extinction. You might as well interview cocaine addicts while they're high and ask whether they're happy. A long-run view must be included. A further issue is life expectancy. If we prize life—and why would we care about happiness if we didn't—doesn't a longer life expectancy make a country more desirable? Here, too, Denmark seems to slip up. Although life expectancy rose in the last half of the twentieth century, the government admits "it is notable that there has not been the same rise in life expectancy in Denmark as in the countries with which Denmark is normally compared (the OECD countries). This stagnation applies particularly to women." Maybe it's the heavy drinking and smoking. By my analysis, fewer kids and relatively shorter lives should shake up the *60 Minutes* view of this happiness paradise of former Vikings. And for all the happiness *60 Minutes* lauded, reporters did not report finding overwhelming friendliness.

"People are not looking very happy in the street. They don't talk very much," said a Danish journalist on the program.

"So people don't just strike up casual conversations on the train?" the *60 Minutes* reporter Morley Safer asked.

"No. No, never. . . . When, if you are stuck on the window seat of a bus, and want to get out, and there's a person next to you on the aisle seat, then you don't say, 'Excuse me, could I please get off?' You start rattling your bags and make sort of a gesture saying, 'I'm about to get up so please get up so I don't have to talk to you,'" explained the journalist.

And what of the explanation of why Danes tell pollsters they are happy, that social welfare programs cheer them up? The Vanderbilt political scientist Benjamin Radcliff would nod vigorously, for he says that people have more "life satisfaction" as a country moves away from competitive states and closer to "social democratic welfare" ideals. Here's the smelly herring in that claim: Among various studies that show Danes the happiest people on Earth, hypercompetitive Americans often beat out the Swedes, Belgians, Germans, and French, who set the mark for social welfare guarantees.

BRING YOUR DOCTOR CANDY

If we got everything we wanted, we'd be happy for a little while. But then we'd start to ask, "What's next?" Social critics quote Gordon Gekko, "greed, for lack of a better word, is good." But it's not greed; it's motivation. It's our humanity speaking to us. We do best with a life of flux. Flux even makes us smarter. Surprises make us smarter. Even little surprises. Listen to this. A researcher named Alice Isen observed doctors diagnosing patient symptoms. Before the diagnoses, Isen arranged for some of the doctors to receive a surprise—free candy. They got four little chocolates and six hard candies. Then Isen watched the doctors work. Those who received the surprise thought more creatively and came up with sharper inferences. Why? Because giving them a surprise, shaking up their world, supercharged their dopamine levels and got them thinking with more energy, vigor, and rigor. The next time you visit a doctor, do you want him to think he has no surprises left in his life, or that his status will be equalized to create an immovable status quo? Do you want your doctor so relaxed and stress-free that he does not feel the stakes of a life-and-death matter? Not me. I like my doctors optimistic, looking forward, and feeling the healthy tension that comes when men and women play at the top of their game.

PART 3

LEARNING AND LIVING
IN THE REAL WORLD

CHAPTER 10

No Competition Without Motivation

What's the Big Idea? Soft CEOs doom their employees.

Let's now look at some corporate managers and explain that they can create good competition or bad competition. I've seen this in the business world and in politics, and I will share some of my experiences. Winning is not everything. Winning at any price is losing. There's surely a difference between winning a chess game on wits and winning it by poking your pawn into the eyeball of your opponent. That can make it tough to get invited back for another game. As we learned earlier, it is the Rule of Repeats and the anticipation of success that make human progress possible. Just remember, after Mike Tyson bit off the top of Evander Holyfield's ear in 1997, no one was willing to step in the ring with him for a long time. And, of course, Tyson lost that fight anyway.

THE WORKPLACE: GOOD AND BAD COMPETITION

I'll never forget the provocative preview advertisement for David Mamet's witty but disturbing 1992 movie (based on the play) *Glengarry Glen Ross*. A dirty sales office with army-surplus metal desks. The sharklike real estate sales manager in an undertaker's suit and slicked-back hair cradles a pair of brass balls on a string. He's instructing his sales team, no, berating the men, emasculating them with his management threats: "We're adding a little something to this month's sales contest. . . . First prize is a Cadillac Eldorado. . . . Second prize a set of steak knives. Third prize is you're fired." The manager sets up a feeding frenzy. He won't even tell them his name. Why should he? "You drove a Hyundai," he yells, "and I drove an $80,000 BMW to get here . . . you can't play in a man's game." It's a depressing, demeaning, and riveting monologue. It's also no way to motivate. Though in this book I have lauded competition and argued that it is vital to the history of our species and the mechanics of our mind, and plays a role in allowing us to feel waves and tinges of happiness, nothing in this book condones or recommends rhetorical or physical brutality.

There's a big difference between constructive competition and destructive competition. There is a big difference between meeting healthy, productive challenges and plundering your coworker's ego. It is true that some managers succeed and others turn their employees into snake pits. In the business world, how can a manager best motivate his troops?

A BRIEF HISTORY OF GM

Let me show you some institutions that have spurred internal competition in order to motivate their employees and generate the best ideas and outcomes. Let's start with General Motors. What a wild hundred-year trip in history! Recently, GM has been notable for plummeting into bankruptcy and for begging the U.S. taxpayers for a bailout. By 2008, the market capitalization of GM—the value of all outstanding shares—was worth less than the shares of the Hot Wheels toy franchise. That's right, Mattel's Hot Wheels cars, which sell for $1.07 at Target and are roughly 1/100th to scale, were more valuable than GM's business. Of course, GM was not always enfeebled. In fact, in the 1960s GM's market share and profitability were awe-inspiring.

But such dominance eventually resulted in a sense of complacency, and the competitive spark fizzled out. In the 1970s, GM, Ford, and Chrysler started to slump and their cars often began to resemble rust buckets. Car dealers began to tuck their service departments out of sight, so that prospective new car buyers would not hear customers screaming about their breakdowns. When the oil crises of 1973 and 1979 hit, the Big Three had little to offer except the famously exploding Ford Pinto and the better-forgotten Chevy Vega. At the end of the 1970s my older brother owned a green Pinto with green shag carpeting. When stopped at a traffic light on the way to high school, he would stomp on the accelerator, and the cars behind would honk furiously. Because the car didn't move. It would take a few seconds for the poor little engine to putter things forward, even after flooring the pedal. When I was a kid, it seemed to me that my parents, and everyone else's parents, spent hundreds if not thousands of dollars each year at mechanic shops repairing their Big Three automobiles.

But how the world has changed. Cars are far more reliable now. Many cars come with 100,000-mile warranties, and some throw in free oil changes. *Consumer Reports* used to grade a vehicle on whether it started promptly when the ignition was turned on. The magazine gave up testing that feature, because by the 1990s every car they tested started flawlessly. Which raises a question: Why did car quality begin to rise? Why did GM's market share begin to plummet? A simple answer: The car market became more competitive. Foreign car makers, especially Japanese and later Korean, entered the market and left skid marks on GM's balance sheet. GM's market share went into freefall, dropping from 50 percent in the 1960s to 35 percent in 1991 and 25 percent in 2006, with Toyota, Nissan, and Honda grabbing most of the losses. The Japanese cars were peppier, more sophisticated, and more reliable. One hardly ever saw a Toyota owner stopped on the side of the road trying to wave for help (something that made the 2010 Toyota Prius braking scandal so stunning). The point is that *more competition* broke any stranglehold that GM had on consumers. Fluid, free-wheeling trade returned power to consumers, and probably made them happier. With rising quality they wouldn't have to spend as much time yelling at service mechanics.

WHAT CAN GM TEACH US ABOUT INTERNAL COMPETITION?

The real story about motivation and healthy competition comes from GM's glory years in the 1930s. GM's triumphs came through constructive, internal competition launched by Alfred Sloan in the 1920s, pitting Chevrolet against Pontiac, for example. A graduate of MIT (hence the Sloan School for Business at MIT), Sloan was given the presidency of GM because he figured out how to create a corporate structure that maintained a hierarchy but still got the competitive juices sluicing about. Each of the major divisions (Chevrolet, Pontiac, Oldsmobile, Buick, and Cadillac) had its own engineering team and styling studio. Sloan pictured the divisions as "ladders" for Americans to climb as their incomes rose, and he spoke of "a car for every pocketbook." Chevys were for the young, or less wealthy, while Cadillacs were the crown of the empire. But there were no delineating walls. A successful doctor might very well choose among Oldsmobiles and Buicks, depending on whether he liked the more powerful Oldsmobile engine or the more regal Buick styling. Each division competed against the other. Sure, there was teamwork at headquarters, but GM motivated each team to try to outscore the other teams.

But by the 1970s the system began to splinter and the competition was replaced by confusion and egalitarian nonsense. In the 1970s, Cadillac owners were scandalized to discover that when they lifted up their hoods they saw engines stamped with Oldsmobile. Oldsmobile buyers who thought they owned a legendary Rocket V8 opened their hoods to find a mere Chevrolet. Americans filed a 1977 class action lawsuit against dispirited management. GM loyalists tossed in the towel on their fealty. Eventually, GM began to warn consumers that "Oldsmobiles are equipped with engines produced by various GM divisions." By then it did not matter, because even the exterior styling made the cars almost impossible to tell apart. Internal competition was dead. Ford suffered here, too. You could hardly tell a Lincoln from a Mercury without opening up the glove compartment and reading the manual. It took thirty years for Cadillac to recover by breaking free in the 2000s, though the rest of GM continued to decay.

Through all this mess, GM also allowed its labor force to get less competitive. Management did not have the guts to take on unions, so as the company's market share unraveled and GM needed fewer workers on the assembly line, it agreed in 1984 to a bizarre "job bank" concept. The job bank would pay laid-off workers 95 percent of their usual wage. In 2005, twelve thousand workers were enrolled in the bank, with each costing the company $100,000 to $130,000 annually. According to many reports, "nonworking workers" were resigned to sitting on their duffs playing cards at nearly full pay. There was no limit to how long the union workers could stay in the job bank; they did not have to search for alternative work, and even if GM called them back they could turn down the offer if the offer came from a plant more than fifty miles away. One laid-off electrician used his time for good purpose. An intense man named Tom Adams was profiled in the *Wall Street Journal* while working away on a Ph.D. in history, writing a three-hundred-page dissertation on GM's dime. Between 2001 and 2005 he'd been in the bank, except for an eighteen-month stint working on a truck project. His dissertation topic: GM, the UAW, and the city of Flint. Mr. Adams is exceptional. Few have ginned up the motivation to study in such circumstances. But what about the other twelve thousand job bank "workers"? As we learned early in this book, people without real jobs tend to eventually lose their spark, and find happiness ever more elusive.

The job bank led to a perverse system of "reverse seniority" and "reverse layoffs." Here's how it operated. In a typical labor situation, when the economy weakens, junior workers get thrown out first. Those with seniority stay on the job. But the job bank was such an attractive alternative that the more experienced workers wanted to prolong the job bank experience, and so it was the junior workers who stayed on the job. The result? A less skilled, less experienced force on the assembly line, and of course multibillion-dollar bills that the American and Canadian taxpayers would partly absorb.

So what do we take away from the GM saga? First and most obvious, *consumers do best when companies have to compete for their business.* Therefore, we should not be deceived by any communitarian quest to calm down competition by blocking new entrants. If not for Toyota, we could all be stuck on the side of the road, sitting on the hoods of overheating Chevy Vegas. Second, *business management must instill competition within organizations.* It need not be one man struggling against another. But within a corporation teams should compete. Alfred Sloan succeeded for GM in the 1930s because every time a prospective buyer strolled into a Chevy dealer, the Pontiac team tried to wave a flag to get that customer's attention. Third and most important, *management should feel an obligation to motivate their employees, even when the employees don't want to be motivated.* Giving in to union demands for nonwork is a recipe for bankruptcy and for frustration. When I lecture to managers, I recommend they divide their staffs into three groups: First, the great employees who are pulling the company forward. Give them bonuses, plaques, and free trips! Pull aside their spouses, parents, and children, and let their relatives know how much you value them. Second, those who are doing a decent job but could improve. Mentor them, spend time with them, and let them see how better, smarter work would help their careers and the firm. Third, the laggards, who cannot be saved, who don't want to work for you and don't care whether you succeed. Send them far away and pray that your competitors hire them.

LIFE IN COMMODITY HELL

My wife, who has helped run nonprofits, including the Kennedy Center for the Performing Arts, has taught me that few places are scratched with the claws of envy so much as nonprofits. When I worked at the White House and she served as counsel at the Kennedy Center, she used to joke that she might quit in order to do work someplace less political—like Capitol Hill. Another lesson she taught me was that board members seldom want to stir up trouble for the chief executives. Board members don't come on a board to fight; they come to share the glory. With the comfort of a burled walnut office suite, many corporate executives fall into the same trap. By the time they get to the top, they have lost the fire in their bellies. They see the corner suite not as an incentive to push harder, but as a reward for what they have already done in the past. They cease to enjoy the thorns that prick them to compete. They grow too timid to draw on the competitive drives of their employees. And so they drive their companies into what I call "commodity hell." Who pays the price? The employees and the shareholders. What is commodity hell? Commodity hell is when you have a product or a service and you cannot honestly tell clients that your product or service is better, faster, or more reliable. When a client asks how your product compares to others, all you can say is, "We got what they got." That means you have no pricing power, no profit margin, and frankly, no reason to be in business. Such an executive might think he has in a genteel way alleviated the high pressure and rat-race nature of his business, creating a cushier place for his workers. But the truth is any executive who leads his company into commodity hell might as well lead his employees right to the state department of unemployment insurance claims.

Look at Michael Dell for a moment. A brilliant inventory manager, Michael Dell built from his off-campus dorm room at the University of Texas, Austin, a computer company that once trounced Hewlett-Packard, IBM, Gateway, and others. He dropped out of school and designed a lean, just-in-time inventory system that delivered reliable customizable computers to the doors of his customers. They were delighted. As a customer I was so impressed, I visited the Dell factory in Austin to marvel at his system. Dell insisted that UPS have an airport close by so he didn't have to worry about airport delays. But then Michael Dell slipped out of the picture as CEO in 2004, and other managers moved in. Hewlett-Packard, Toshiba, and others started to copy Dell's inventory techniques, and by 2005 Dell was dropping into commodity hell. The company struggled to explain why customers should buy a Dell. In 2006, Dell's market share in PCs slipped from about 19 percent to 14 percent. Pricing and profit margins collapsed. A popular advertising campaign based on a mischievous slacker's catchphrase, "Dude, you got a Dell," started to symbolize a laid-back, ineffective strategy. To add insult, the young actor in the commercials got arrested for attempting to buy a bag of marijuana in New York. Today, Dell is still fighting its way out of commodity hell. But it's a tough fight, a fight the company could have avoided if it had vigorously pursued a competitive edge, instead of rounding off the edges and getting too comfortable.

Dell has other partners in commodity hell. Sony is still kicking itself for not coming up with the iPod, the iPhone, or the iPad. Co-founder Akio Morita would have been devastated a few years ago when Sony CEO Howard Stringer sounded downright resigned to never again owning the portable music market, even though Sony had invented the Walkman back in the 1980s. In the 1960s Morita wanted to penetrate the American market. He knew he needed to attract competitive souls to his company. What did he do? He took out advertisements in Japanese newspapers: "Wanted: Japanese men up to 30 years of age who can PICK A FIGHT—in English!" He wasn't looking for salesmen who would strangle each other; he wanted spirited employees who would not take guff from naysayers. When faced with obstacles, Morita could develop new tactics. In 1956, he promised the world the first "pocketable" transistor radio. Then a glitch occurred. The radio started rolling off the assembly lines and Morita tried to put it in his pocket. It was a smidge too big. So what did Morita do? He called up the tailor who made the clothing for his sales force and ordered a new batch of men's shirts—all with pockets exactly a smidge bigger than the standard size. He would not delay the pocketable radio!

Finally, Morita knew he had to keep his employees on their toes. Laziness would only hurt them in the long run. He had a wild imagination, but he would never dream of a job bank like GM's. In the 1970s, Sony was opening a plant in Rancho Bernardo, California, which today makes Vaio laptops and is an engineering center. Morita was worried that American workers might be sloppy. He probably had rented a Vega or Pinto at some point. At first, Sony ordered the American workers merely to reassemble television sets that had already been assembled, adjusted, and disassembled back in Japan. Management was nervous that even this simple trick would stump the coddled Americans. To prove to the workers the importance of quality, Sony rigged many of the sets on the Rancho Bernardo assembly line to come out defective. This would teach employees how potential mistakes could ruin the product. Back in Japan, Morita had been requiring any new engineer—no matter how senior—to work on the assembly line so he would learn the risks inherent in any manufacturing operation.

COMPETING TO BE ON THE TEAM

In the 1980s and 1990s Julian Robertson was a legendary investor, whose returns averaged over 30 percent annually. He didn't follow the pack; packs tried to follow him, but were always many steps behind. I served as an adviser to Julian and then as a managing director of his Tiger hedge fund during the 1990s. He prided himself on hiring the smartest people, but he also liked team players. Many of my colleagues were varsity athletes (and I'm not talking about high school!). Julian built a great gym and supplied us with uniforms and trainers. But Julian's success was not just teamwork, a bunch of smart people sitting around a table trying to jointly calculate a solid estimate of S&P earnings growth. He liked competition, too, and set up a lively dynamic among his directors and analysts. We were not trying to clobber each other on the heads or on the ankles, like Tonya Harding did to Nancy Kerrigan right before the 1994 Olympics. Of course not. We were all competing to get our best ideas into the $15 billion portfolio. By getting our ideas into the portfolio, we would feel a burst of pride, a validation of our membership in the club. Yes, we might make an extra bonus, but that was speculative. After all, the idea might fail, and the fund might lose money if our idea soured. *The most heated competition was to get in the game.*

How would Julian set up this competition? With grace and charm. If I were not in the Park Avenue office on a particular day, Julian would call me on the telephone. In his honey-coated North Carolina drawl he would say, "Oh, powerful Todd, now what were you saying about buying Canadian bonds?" This was key. He wasn't buttering me up to sell me something; I was the one who would have to persuade him to buy more bonds. But he wanted me to go into the match feeling wanted. Before I could make my case, though, he'd apologize for interrupting, put me on hold, and then tell me that he called three guys into the room, and had two more on the telephone from London to debate me. We would have a verbal wrestling match over Canadian bonds. Sometimes I won; sometimes I lost. If I lost, next time I would come back with better data and arguments. Or maybe I would admit the others had a keener view of the world. In the end, Julian's investors were the real winners. In semiretirement, Julian designed and built golf course resorts in New Zealand. When I visited him recently, his resort managers took me aside and assured me that the tools he used to build competitive teams on Park Avenue worked just as well building golf courses on the other side of the world.

DESTRUCTIVE COMPETITION

The world of portfolio managers is swirling with money, testosterone, and risk. Money managers typically toil in tiny workstations. If you ever visit the trading floor of Citibank or Goldman Sachs you would be surprised at how many highly paid employees are squeezed into spaces a few feet across, roughly the same width as the front bucket seat of a Cadillac. A beauty salon worker cutting hair for $30,000 a year has much more elbow room than a trader earning a million dollars. A trading floor is a stressful place, too, with people jumping up with news, screaming across the floor, and banging their fists on tables when an investment goes the wrong way. It's hardly a game. Julian Robertson teaches us how to keep our cool amid the chaos and high-stakes world of money. Now, let's look at a counterexample, in an industry far less important than retirement savings and 401(k) plans. Let's look at a game, and we'll see how bad management can come about even in a pastime.

Billy Martin was not a firecracker for the New York Yankees; he was a short-fused ton of dynamite. After a clutch-hitting career as a second baseman, he took on thirteen managing stints in nineteen years. Television shows like *Seinfeld* and *Saturday Night Live* made fun of Martin's celebrated firings—for example, "In Calgary tonight, Katarina Witt won the gold medal in figure skating, prompting Yankees owner George Steinbrenner to fire manager Billy Martin," announced Dennis Miller in 1988 on *Saturday Night Live*. Martin never shrank from a challenge, and in the 1950s he may have gotten in more bar fights than Rocky Marciano and Frank Sinatra combined. He was famous for kicking dirt on umpires and once got into a bloody fistfight with a marshmallow salesman.

As a baseball manager, Martin was like a shot of jet fuel in a Pinto. He would take over teams wallowing in last place and goad them into winning games. With a lunatic manager calling risky plays like stealing home plate, the players suddenly felt aggressive urges that had long left them. They would start winning games, and he would teach them that every night was the final battle to the death. Martin did not play to win. He "came to castrate.... Animals who mark their territory by urination were subtler than Martin." He would force pitchers to stay on the mound until their arms hung down like twisted licorice sticks. He didn't care about next week's game. Nothing was left in reserve. But baseball has a 162-game season so Martin's comebacks seldom lasted long. After a while, berating players for errors led to backbiting, and beating each other with bats turned the dugout into a war zone. Teams would burn out, and Martin would seek solace in Jack Daniel's. Martin would first excite the fans and then exhaust his welcome. If you wanted one manager to win one game once, you would call Martin; if you wanted someone to build something that would last, you'd do better dressing Martin up as a team mascot and having him rave on the sidelines.

Billy Martin and Julian Robertson show us two different styles, two different ways of creating a competitive climate in an organization. They both realized they had to kindle primal energies. Robertson was not interested in one single winning trade; he wanted to build a track record of trust and achievement, which stood for about twenty years. Investors begged to be allowed into his funds. Martin was fascinating and possessed all the energy of an electrical storm. But sometimes an institution needs a 100-watt bulb, not a jagged dagger of lightning.

CHAPTER 11

Everybody Play Nice

*What's the Big Idea? If you let every kid go home
with a prize, every kid loses.*

Back in 1986, an American minister named Robert Fulghum
wrote a best-selling self-help book called *All I Really Need to Know I
Learned in Kindergarten.* The book was a series of entertaining essays
about sharing and cleaning up, punctuated by stories about Mother
Teresa and others. Fulghum busted some myths—for example, that
merely possessing Y chromosomes gives a man the knowledge to connect jumper cables. I thought back to my kindergarten class at the
Shark River Hills Elementary School, a pretty scary name for a school.
What I remember most is a kid named Chuck hitting me on the head
with a wooden truck. (He's probably a laid-off truck worker in Detroit

right now.) Around the time Fulghum enjoyed his breakthrough literary hit, schools around the country began to focus on self-esteem and emotional intelligence. Who cared whether a kid could do algebra if he felt bad about himself? Who cared if a kid understood how electricity flowed through wires if he did not have a knack for the feelings of others? What was to blame for our children's failed egos and blustery dispositions? According to many experts, it was competition. The solution: call in an exorcist and free the schools of competitive demons. No more spelling bees. No more class ranks. No more bright red slashes on test papers marking wrong answers. No more keeping score at soccer. A school in Massachusetts encouraged jumping rope—but banned the rope. Not all schools adopted all of these techniques, of course, but the trend was real.

My children are being educated in this milieu. When my middle daughter was in kindergarten and playing on a soccer team, my mother made the terrible mistake of asking her the score. She replied, "Grandma, we don't keep score. But if we did, we're winning three to two." You really can't fool the kids, but you can waste their time and frustrate them.

Now, I'm not an angry, interfering Little League parent who screams at the coaches or at my child. My priority for sport is fun. But there's a downside to the noncompetitive, pro–self-esteem environment. First of all, it doesn't make kids happier when they know their efforts are unscored, as if the game didn't matter. Second, and more important, it robs them of the natural pleasures that come from excelling and improving. I asked a former roommate who is a Harvard Law professor how things have changed since his days as a student. He said, "I'm confronted with twenty years of self-esteem training. I can't use the Socratic method or cross-examine a student's logic without hurting their feelings." Hurt feelings? These are budding lawyers! And they better learn that they will sometimes lose a case.

LEAVE IT TO MRS. CLARK

I had a wonderful teacher in fourth grade named Mrs. Clark. She was a tough-talking black lady who broke all the rules. Rule #1: There are no bad questions, just bad answers. Mrs. Clark: "Lori, that is a *dumb* question." Rule #2: Never say anything bad about a student. Mrs. Clark: "Tyrone, you're nutty as a fruitcake!" Rule #3: Don't discuss a child's family. Mrs. Clark: "Michael, why are you talking to yourself? Only two kinds of people talk to themselves. People who are crazy, and people with money in the bank. Now, I know your mama, and I know there's no money in the bank. You're crazy."

I don't recommend Mrs. Clark's methods. But we loved her, and we strove to get her approval. How did we get her approval? Not with shiny apples. By learning to do long division! She was the toughest grader I ever had and refused to give straight As to nine-year-olds. She enjoyed presiding over spelling bees and was quite happy to see competition break out in her classroom. Many of the students in Mrs. Clark's class were from lower-income families in Neptune, New Jersey. Mrs. Clark knew they faced struggles at home. But she must have known that coddling the kids would merely set them up for a nasty fall.

Mrs. Clark might have learned some of her lessons from Beaver Cleaver, the Tom Sawyer of early television. Today the show can easily be mocked for being too staid, too stilted, and too white. No doubt "the Beav" ate his sandwiches on white bread. But let us see what lessons we can learn from this Beaver and his upbringing, as he and his family try to figure out what level of freedom is suitable for a seven-year-old boy facing the temptations of life. Young toothy Beaver is learning that his parents are neither omnipotent nor omniscient. They cannot protect him from his misjudgments, and they make mistakes themselves. Among other challenges, Beaver must face television's embodiment of Eden's snake: Eddie Haskell. Eddie is malicious, cunning, and devious, doing all he can to undermine the basic ethics that June and Ward try to nurture in their sons. The parents know that Eddie brings trouble, but they realize he cannot be eliminated. In one episode Beaver's older brother, Wally, tells his mother that he is going over to "slug Eddie." She replies, "That's no way to talk on a Sunday." Wally: "You're right. I'll wait till tomorrow and slug him in the cafeteria."

Though the Beaver will face innumerable hazards and temptations, his parents do not swaddle him in foam rubber, or escort him each day to school. If the Beaver is ever going to grow beyond the mental age of seven, he will have to fight some fights himself. He will win, and he will lose. If he experienced only winning, he would grow to be both a boring character and a dysfunctional person. Indeed, when Beaver comes home with a black eye, Ward stomps into the garage, straps on boxing gloves, and teaches his son to throw a left hook. Naturally, Beaver is then knocked down by the swinging punching bag. (Then Ward learns that it was a girl who gave Beaver the black eye.) The father's first instinct is not to call a lawyer but to better equip his child, and to let the Beav know that life is not fair, and cannot be contorted into fairness.

Leave It to Beaver ended its original run in 1963. Coincidentally, that same year a psychiatrist named Julius E. Heuscher published a book called *A Psychiatric Study of Myths and Fairy Tales* (from which Bruno Bettelheim seems to have plagiarized in *The Uses of Enchantment*). Heuscher and Bettelheim argued that children need to face anxieties, uncertainty, and fear. Bloody folktales like "Hansel and Gretel" give children an opportunity to live out their nightmares. While early Freudians warned that wicked fairy tales conjured neuroses, Bettelheim saw them as vehicles on which children could travel to a more mature emotional state. Heuscher points to lessons that can be learned from the differences in how the heroes behave—for example: "Not wishing to deprive anyone too much, [Snow White] eats just a little from each of the seven plates and drinks just a drop from each glass (how different from Hansel and Gretel who, rather disrespectfully, start eating the gingerbread house)." The point here is that evil, temptation, and allure cannot be wholly avoided. They must be dealt with. We cannot utterly control them, but we can use the tools we have to confront them. People have the capacity to do so. The human species has dealt with famine, vermin, and predatory wolves. It's remarkable and silly that Edenists think that our species cannot now handle the stress of too many choices of laundry detergents at the supermarket.

The Cleaver clan and my teacher Mrs. Clark did not have the statistics to back up their methods, but they were right to be less focused on self-esteem. Now the studies have come in. The American Psychological Society asked the Florida State psychologist Roy Baumeister to read through hundreds of studies on self-esteem and children. Despite all the posters telling kids that "everyone is special," the studies showed that high self-esteem did not bring higher grades in the classroom or less violence on the blacktop. Kids with high self-esteem were just as likely to get drunk and smoke. Other studies showed an intriguing connection between self-esteem and grades. Getting higher grades and actually learning stuff in the classroom delivered greater self-esteem. In other words, the kids felt good about themselves only after learning things and proving that they could compete. Merely boosting their egos did nothing except give them bigger egos and less reason to study. Physical danger may also result from sapping the world of comparisons. The Lake Wobegon effect (where nearly everyone believes he's above average) has been enhanced in recent years. Now most automobile drivers are convinced they are more skillful than the guy in the next lane, and should therefore be allowed to drive faster.

I reject the old saw "spare the rod, spoil the child." But parents (and teachers) do owe a duty to children that goes beyond food, shelter, and hand-holding. They should help their kids learn persistence, another enemy of the self-esteem movement. Persistence is not fun. But kids who can't stick to a task for a few minutes will not show up on time for a job as adults. There's a biological story behind persistence. Po Bronson and Ashley Merryman's *NurtureShock* does a nice job explaining in layman's terms the research of C. Robert Cloninger of Washington University, St. Louis, who has been a leader in the search to figure out which part of our personality comes from genetics and which part from the environment. Some people (and mice) seem more genetically predisposed to show persistence in doing tasks. Yet by monitoring a neural network running through the prefrontal cortex and the ventral striatum, Cloninger has been able to train mice to be more persistent in finding their way through mazes. The prospect of a release of dopamine stirs mice to stick to the task and overcome frustrations. But there's a lesson here: If the mice get too much dopamine and get it too dependably without showing effort, they will lose their drive to win. What does this study mean for our children? If we lavish unearned praise, whether through ribbons, automatic promotion to higher grade levels, or easy As, we will rob them of their spirit to try harder when the going gets tougher. This helps explain why so many college kids need remedial training in math and writing, even though they received glowing letters of recommendation.

EMOTIONAL FOOLISHNESS

As self-esteem training tried to knock competition from the classroom, the term "emotional intelligence" gained momentum, pushing aside old-fashioned IQ. No doubt, the concept of IQ has a cloudy and controversial reputation. In contrast, EQ seemed rather benign. Some people are better at gauging the emotions of others and handling their own feelings. The theory posits that even if these people do not score as highly on IQ or SAT tests, they may turn out to be the best managers of other people. However, only sparse data support EQ as a good predictor of managerial ability. That's not the surprising thing. The surprise is that in the schools it's not necessarily the class presidents or team captains who display superior EQs. Schoolyard bullies also have strong EQ. So do felons. Bullies and felons often have the skills to read the emotions of other people and to figure out how to best intimidate and manipulate them. I raise these examples only to suggest that schools should be focused on teaching children skills and ideas; we know too little about how to shape their self-esteem in productive ways.

How did younger people get such a distorted view of themselves? We can look at generational changes, and the impact of over-nurturing parents and an overprotecting "Nanny government." Every generation tends to believe it travels the roughest road, from the Greatest Generation to the Boomers, to the Xers, Yers, and young Gamers of today. The "matures" growing up amid World War II prize teamwork, "paying your dues," and respecting seniority. Younger workers want to be treated not as cogs but as special individuals.

Look in the back of a mature person's garage. He might have won a single trophy as a child. Look at any twenty-year-old's closet today and you will find a stack of trophies piled up like a massive car crash. In the movie *Meet the Fockers*, Robert De Niro's character teases Dustin Hoffman's and Ben Stiller's, "I didn't know they made ninth-place ribbons."

Jean Twenge of San Diego State University examined the surveys of over sixteen thousand college students completed from 1982 to 2006. The survey tested for narcissism, by asking students to react to such statements as, "If I ruled the world, it would be a better place," or "I can live my life any way I want to." Guess what? American kids scored high, with narcissism jumping by 30 percent since the 1980s. Twenge, the author of *Generation Me: Why Today's Young Americans Are More Confident, Assertive, Entitled—and More Miserable Than Ever Before*, updated the study with new data in 2009 and found even worse results. She blames the self-esteem movement for sabotaging healthy egos and replacing them with uncontainable nerve and unattainable expectations. Apparently, preschool teachers around the country have literally replaced the lyrics to "Frère Jacques" with the lyrics "I am special, I am special, look at me." Think about that. First of all, "Frère Jacques" taught a little bit of a foreign language, nudging kids to look beyond their borders. Second, in "Frère Jacques" the singer is asking about someone else. "I am special" is all about the ego, including the command, "look at me."

Surely, the drive to be special can yield wonderful results, including new music, art, math theorems, and innovations. But "specialness" should be achieved, not doled out willy-nilly.

Gather a group of sixty-five-year-old men around a table, point to one of them, and say, with a smile, "Oh, he's a 'regular Joe.'" Will the chosen chum take that as a compliment? Probably. Now try it with twenty-year-olds. It will spark a revolt: "Whaddayamean, a regular Joe?! Every twenty-something is special and can be anything he wants!"

Consider this contrast: Younger people have been told since birth that they are "special." They were raised to see their parents as friends, not authority figures. However, a man coming of age in the 1940s who stepped out of line would have been slapped on the head by his father, coach, or teacher and asked in a biting tone, "What do you think—that you're *special*?"

Jean Twenge's research points exactly to these differences. In the 1950s only 12 percent of teens agreed with the statement "I am an important person." By the 1980s almost seven times as many (80 percent) claimed they were important. Similar studies show more young people than ever before agreeing with this stunner: "If I were on the *Titanic*, I would deserve to be on the first lifeboat." No doubt, these narcissists would imagine themselves luxuriating in the first-class cabins, rather than locked in steerage with the unwashed masses, who looked nothing like Leonardo DiCaprio.

Facebook, MySpace, and all the other places where a young person can replace his own anxieties with a flashy avatar would seem to reinforce narcissism. There's no better cure for narcissism, and no better cure for the doldrums, than to shut off the escapist route and learn how to compete in the real world. How will this avatar generation fare in the workplace? While living in Washington, D.C., in the 1990s, I noticed something missing on snowy days. Where were the kids holding shovels offering to clear my driveway? They never knocked on my door. Were parents blocking budding entrepreneurs from picking up shovels? Was there too much good stuff on television during snow days? Were the kids too spoiled to care about making $10 or $20 for fifteen minutes' work? (Now, I must admit I did once see this poster on a telephone pole: "Will design website. Josh. Age 12.") Shoveling driveways may not tell us much, but disturbing reports are coming from offices around the country. According to a survey for careerbuilder .com, 85 percent of hiring managers report that twenty-somethings have a much stronger sense of entitlement than their coworkers, typically expecting a promotion within a year. And, of course, many expect great jobs right at the start.

A disgruntled young Yale grad, feeling rather entitled, wrote a book about the troubles faced by the millennial generation in the workplace. It was subtitled, "Why Now Is a Terrible Time to Be Young." Really? Would you prefer a different era? How does Vietnam sound? Or the Great Depression? Anyone for the Great Cholera Epidemic of 1832? The author bemoans "crap jobs" that do not provide lavish health care and vacation benefits. She profiles struggling young workers, who seem to have unrealistic expectations. Take Lagusta, who can't seem to pay off her debts, though she works hard at her business. What's her line, you ask? She is a vegan caterer. I bet she'd be rolling in dough if she threw a juicy steak on the barbie. Then there's Nita, who works in a dollar store and blew "ten grand she didn't have on restaurant meals and new CDs"—*in one summer!* The next time Nita feels like bingeing, she should call Lagusta and support the vegan trade. Brandon got a job "presenting" sex education in schools but then gave up a graduate-school fellowship because Orange County was too conservative. And these are the smart kids. How can you march in support of Dan, a thirty-three-year-old living with his parents, who says: "I'm perfectly willing to go through my life as a sort of half-assed bohemian, with no steady job. That freaks my parents out, because they don't understand how the job market has changed." I don't understand why his parents don't roll him off the sofa onto the front lawn. These individuals seem paralyzed, unwilling to consider fresh opportunities. Chris wants a high-paying job as a librarian. He'll do anything, as long as he doesn't have to leave Minnesota. I wanted to shout: "Chris, move! Those gray-haired Minnesota librarians are going to live a long time—unless, of course, they're forced to shovel snow off the walk."

In the 1940s, as a teenager pinched between the Depression and World War II, my father snagged a job offer from the Capitol Theater in Times Square. There was one catch. The uniform required black shoes. My father owned only brown. So he painted them black and showed up early for work. Soon after, he climbed aboard a navy ship and sailed off to help liberate Shanghai from imperial Japan. Members of the millennial workforce would have waited for someone else to hand-deliver a new pair of Pradas. In truth, there are no "crap jobs" when times are really tough.

FRAMING THE ISSUE

In 2004 leaders in Monza, Italy, decided that goldfish were living in too frantic a world. Those poor fish swimming in round bowls keep rushing past each other. "A fish kept in a bowl has a distorted view of reality . . . and suffers because of this," said a high official. So the city council passed a law requiring all goldfish to be placed in rectangular tanks. It would allow them a calmer frame of mind and a slower, less competitive frame of reference. This from Monza, a city best known for hosting the Formula 1 Grand Prix race, where Ferraris whip past McLarens at 200 miles per hour.

Modern societies have become too protective of goldfish and of children. A kid reaches for a glass of whole milk and her mother rushes to stop her. It could pump up her cholesterol. Put down that lollipop or you'll get diabetes in forty years! Once I made the mistake of bringing a few six-packs of yogurt to my daughter's end-of-school party. I didn't notice that the yogurt used aspartame as a sweetener. You'd think I was Dr. Jekyll trying to pour an evil potion down their throats. We might as well swathe ourselves in bubble wrap and hire food testers from the CIA. Were Americans always so jittery? When I was a kid, we played in a sandbox. I don't know where the sand came from, but I doubt my parents lugged bags of sterilized sand from Toys "R" Us. Ironically, some doctors now think that peanut allergies may be traced to kids not ingesting enough germs. So eat dirt, little kiddie!

To be truthful, I'm very careful about what I eat and what my kids ingest, but our risk aversion has gone too far, too broadly. It's one thing to protect kids from salmonella poisoning; it's another to protect them from a D on a report card and automatically promote them to the next grade, for fear we'll damage their confidence. We cannot place everybody in a lockbox.

Now, despite my critique of the self-esteem charade, I don't think we should whip our backs or even deny ourselves scrumptious Thin Mints Girl Scout Cookies after lunch. The good life is not best lived in pain, and I believe in hugging my children. But we should be careful about the expectations we create for our loved ones and for ourselves.

Among the most dangerous things we can do to children is teach them that every challenge, every instance of adversity, should be considered unusually, dangerously stressful. I jokingly tell my kids about my high school coach, who, when faced with a teenager writhing on the ground, wincing, would shout, "Walk it off!" Mr. H. gave no sympathy. Of course, when I tell the story I exaggerate a bit, suggesting that the coach yelled "Walk if off!" even after the kid was hit by a locomotive, one arm lying on one side of the railroad tracks, the other hanging off the train's caboose. There is a line separating "building character" from "callousness," and I'm not exactly sure where that line rests, but it should not condone "helicopter parents" who do their kids' homework for them. I've seen parent sports boosters in baseball bleachers who look like they'd drive their kid to first base rather than make the kid run. Here's what they do not realize: By defining stress as some alien creature that invades our space and attacks us, we create even more anxiety. Kids will see stress as unrelenting and unforgivable; as constant as gravity, but as lethal as the black dust in a Chinese coal mine. If everything in life can be defined as stress, the only thing to do is "turn on, tune in, drop out." That cannot be the answer. How we "frame" the issue counts tremendously. Self-help columns in magazines incessantly tell older people to do crossword puzzles (an excuse to keep magazine circulation alive?) because they force the brain to work and stay lively. But from a biological point of view, this is really just a way to place some stress on some neurons. Everyone seems to accept that this advice is productive. In the same way, working in an office, reporting to a boss, and shopping for dinner in a supermarket can be productive—unless we persuade ourselves that any stress is to be avoided and cursed.

Woody Allen teaches us about stress because his persona finds it everywhere. His persona is not a prescription for living, but that is how we would end up in a world ruled by Edenists. Back to *Annie Hall*, cowritten by my friend Marshall Brickman. Young Alvy is taken to a cigarette-smoking doctor by his mother. Alvy is depressed. He can't do anything. Something he's read has paralyzed him. Tell the doctor, his mother hollers.

Alvy: (*His head still down*) The universe is expanding.

Doctor: The universe is expanding?

Alvy: (*Looking up at the doctor*) Well, the universe is everything, and if it's expanding, someday it will break apart and that would be the end of everything! (*Disgusted, his mother looks at him.*)

Mother: (*Shouting*) What is that your business? (*She turns back to the doctor*) He stopped doing his homework.

Alvy: What's the point?

Mother: (*Excited, gesturing with her hands*) What has the universe got to do with it? You're here in Brooklyn! Brooklyn is not expanding!

If you are convinced the world is out to get you, pretty soon it will.

CHAPTER 12

Repair Yourself; Repair the World

What's the Big Idea? Competition is good
for work, play, and charity.

It's a jungle out there. True, the thorns are different from the ones our ancestors encountered when they beat their way out of Africa fifty thousand years ago. They had to worry about snakes, crocodiles, and poisonous daffodils. We have to worry about the guy sitting at the next desk or swerving across the next lane of traffic. In this book I have argued that retreating to the old jungle is not an option, even if it kindles our romantic fancies. I've poured buckets of cold water on the concept of a modern Eden, based on the entrancing power of meditation, spa visits, and high income taxes. At the same time, I have argued that our brains and our bodies actually need some stress, some tension, some competitive urges in order to feel alive and see glimmers of happiness.

Finally, I have claimed that we would suffer a much lower standard of living and shorter life span if we actually turned the United States into Walden Pond.

So where does that leave us? Do I now just tell you to get out there and beat your brains out, cut off the other guy in traffic, and steal the mouse pad from your nearest coworker? No. But I do think you can improve your basic moods and catch a few more rays of happiness than perhaps you do today. In this chapter I will discuss where to find those rays and how to orient yourself to see them. Figuring out where you stand today is the first and most challenging step.

I've said that rather than shrinking from the world and condemning it as a hellhole dominated by manic strivers, we are far better off if we recognize the inherent flaws and dangers in our species and in the world. In many cases the answer is more forward movement, more energy, and more competition. These principles also apply to our personal lives and our participation in matters of charity, romance, and friendship. Trust me, the world is not going to suddenly decide to make you happy. You are far more likely to feel some happiness if you first recognize that life is more than a bit of a struggle. Always has been. But oh, what great things that struggle can bring! The wise Dr. Seuss wrote of the "waiting place," where everyone waits for a better place. But that never works out. Better to hop along for the bumpy, frustrating, and exhilarating ride, and see "Oh, the places you'll go!"

FIND THE ESCAPE ROUTE

There was an offbeat movie in the 1980s called *The Adventures of Buckaroo Banzai*. Buckaroo was a neuroscientist, a physicist, a rock star, and an action hero in this bizarre tale. Frankly, I didn't get it. But I did get one line in which Buckaroo utters, "Wherever you go, there you are." That's not just witty and tautological, it's also good economics (and, ironically, the title of a Buddhist-themed book). We economists don't care how much time or money you have already spent on something. Those are sunk costs. We just want to know what choices you have in

front of you today. I don't care if you just spent five years getting seniority in your job. If you get a better offer from a different employer who
will treat you better, you should probably say good-bye. Economists
always ask what is the *marginal* (or extra) cost and benefit of doing
something. If the marginal benefit exceeds the marginal cost, take that
step. Don't worry about the proverbial water under the bridge.

When you think about your happiness and the competitive world
we live in, it's best to first get a grip on where you stand today. This is
extraordinarily tough. Most of us have trouble judging our place in
comparison to others. To make things worse, we seem to have an even
tougher time prodding ourselves to make big moves. That's why people
feel stuck in dead-end jobs and dead-end marriages. Are they really
stuck? Or have they lost the will to improve their lot? Didn't their forefathers pull up stakes? The United States is a nation of immigrants.
Some were pushed away from their homelands by despots. Others
crossed the Atlantic and Pacific because they heard the streets were
paved with gold. They wanted to pursue a better life. How many people
today who complain of being trapped are trapped in a way similar to
those who faced stark choices in the early 1900s or any period before?
It's surely not physical worries that enmesh them, it's psychological.

Why do so many people feel trapped, even amid a prosperous
life? For one, we are trained to be risk-averse too early in life. A coddling culture dampens spirits and dulls our native drives. Since the
1960s, we've lost a little nerve and gained another bureaucrat to purportedly protect us against life's uncertainties. If people are severely
discontent, perhaps it is because they have been falsely promised safety
and contentment. In truth, our brains and bodies were not designed to
stay in one place. We evolved roaming the savanna, not sitting on a sofa
in a knitting circle for seventy years. No wonder we end up being discontent when we anchor ourselves and turn down the opportunity to
go elsewhere.

I've heard even young workers in their twenties bemoaning their
"golden handcuffs." Our forefathers did not know this term, which entered business parlance in the 1970s. Golden handcuffs originally
meant lavish financial promises that kept a top executive from switch-

ing to another firm. But now even twenty-five-year-olds may use the phrase as an excuse to avoid looking for a better job. What are those handcuffs? A gym membership? A parking space? Maybe there are a few twenty-five-year-old investment bankers waiting for their million-dollar pension plan to vest, but that's pretty rare.

Wrongheaded government policies tend to reinforce psychological shackles. Almost 20 percent of the jobs in the United States require a government license, and many of these prevent people from moving to another state. Here's a real-life example from a few years ago. Ms. Essence Farmer spent three years performing African-style hair braid- ing in Maryland. When the twenty-three-year-old decided to move closer to her parents in Phoenix and open up her own shop, she learned about Arizona's twisted hair-braiding rules. The state demanded that she take sixteen hundred hours of classroom instruction at a cosmetol- ogy school sanctioned by the state of Arizona. How much would this cost? About $10,000. Never mind that Ms. Farmer had already trained extensively. Then the news got more absurd. Not one hour of the sixteen hundred would be devoted to African hair braiding. How many train- ing hours did Phoenix demand of a policeman? Six hundred. Appar- ently, it takes almost three times as much training to pick up a blow-dryer as a Glock 22. A licensing epidemic limits mobility and opportunity. In New York, you'd need a license to fix a DVD player, to work as a Broad- way usher, or even to sell tickets to a professional wrestling match, even if the wrestlers are total frauds pretending to pummel each other. All of these rules, under the guise of "protecting the public," discourage indi- viduals from taking up new professions or from moving to more attrac- tive venues. I have no gripe against government licenses for cardiac surgeons. But hair braiding and tearing ticket stubs at a theater are hardly done with a scalpel for people under general anesthetics.

Even if the laws encouraged Essence Farmer to pursue her dream, most people would not have demonstrated her courage (under pressure from Ms. Farmer's allies, the Arizona legislature eventually passed an exemption for hair braiders).

Neuroscientists, psychologists, and economists have conducted numerous experiments showing how difficult it is to assess our own circumstances. Most of the experiments were conducted on students, and most of them showed that it's pretty easy to trick them. Give a student a mug of hot coffee and then ask him about some fictitious character. He'll find the character more likable than will a student who has held a cup of iced coffee. Numbers confuse us, too. The behavioral economist Daniel Ariely asks students to write down the last two digits of their Social Security numbers. Then he asks them to bid for a bottle of wine and computer equipment. Sure enough, those with high Social Security numbers bid more. Behavioral economists and psychologists call this "framing" and "anchoring." Our view of things, and our perception of value, may rest on the frame of reference and on some initial anchor. That's why Realtors will often take you to a luxurious home first—so you will find it difficult to settle for a handyman special.

There are two ways to respond to these sorts of experiments. The first is to throw up your hands and say, "What's the point? The whole world is crazy! Since we can be so easily manipulated, the economic system is a total mirage." Supply and demand curves are just tracing the mesmerizing waves of a magician's hands. Many people interpret behavioral economics in this way and pronounce the death of economics and capitalism. Here's what they're missing: A market-based, competitive economic system will eventually adjust to such manipulation. Word will get out. You can get away with Ariely's Social Security trick once, but then people will catch on and figure out how to ignore the trick. The boy who cried wolf would have been a great behavioral psychologist—the first few times. But people do catch on.

Former chef Anthony Bourdain revealed restaurant secrets in his salty and jarring book *Kitchen Confidential*. Bourdain warned readers never to eat fish on Mondays, because that dried up fillet was probably delivered on Friday. To get rid of old fish, Bourdain says that chefs would dress it up in frittatas or plunge it into a pungent stew. They might try to trick customers with alluring names like Bouillabaisse and Poisson St. Jacques. Or throw it into a blender with Jell-O and call it a terrine. With hit books and popular shows on the Travel Channel, Bourdain has made it more difficult for chefs to get away with fobbing off smelly mackerel on Mondays.

Here's the better way to use these tests of framing and anchoring: We should admit that we may not have a good grip on our personal standing at home and at work. We have trace elements of paranoia floating around our brains. We think everyone is staring at us when we notice toilet paper stuck to our shoe. It's called the "spotlight effect." In 1998 an experimenter sent students into a classroom wearing T-shirts bearing Barry Manilow's face. The wearers were mortified. What could be worse than being a walking symbol of Muzak? It turned out the other students hardly noticed the terrible lapse of taste (Manilow got the last laugh; he now sells out in Las Vegas and made a star appearance on *American Idol*). When T-shirt wearers donned images of Martin Luther King Jr., Bob Marley, and Jerry Seinfeld, the audience still did not take much notice. If you think people are staring at you, more likely they are simply zoning out with their heads coincidentally facing in your direction.

OTHERS WILL HELP YOU, SAYS BEN FRANKLIN

Because we have trouble seeing ourselves, we should talk to friends, mentors, and family members who will give us a more objective assessment. You might consider forming your own little board of directors who can help you assess your standing and your progress in reaching your professional and personal goals. They may tell you that you are not, indeed, trapped in a job, in an apartment, or in a gloomy relationship. When I speak with young people who have told me they feel handcuffed, I ask some questions. Is your spouse dependent on you? "I'm not married." How much is your mortgage? "I rent." Do your kids go to day care? "I don't have kids." Then why in the world do you sound as if you are shackled to your desk chair! Let your competitive juices flow, don't be anchored by some false impression of stability and security. Our brains want us to take some risks, and it seldom helps to become too risk-averse too early in life.

Will people be willing to help you? Probably. We empower and validate others by asking for their guidance. Will successful people be willing to help you? Even more so. I was a graduate student writing my first book on the history of economics when I decided to send a few chapters to Milton Friedman, who, along with Keynes, is considered to be the most influential economist of the twentieth century. I mentioned it to some friends, who scoffed, "You really think a super-famous Nobel laureate is going to bother reading your stuff?" Not only did Friedman read it, he sent me a long critique and then put me in touch with another super-famous Nobel laureate, Ronald Coase, who also delved into my manuscript. Coase disagreed with some of Friedman's analysis, and it was thrilling to mediate between two giants. They gave me more attention than numerous economists who had hardly made a scratch on their profession. The fact is, most people enjoy being wanted. Outside of J. D. Salinger and Greta Garbo, most people don't want to be left alone.

Just as important, once someone has helped you, that person feels an emotional tug to help you succeed. It's the Ben Franklin Effect. In his autobiography, Franklin recalls a political opponent. How to win him over? A bribe? A threat? No. Franklin writes a note to the man asking whether he may borrow a rare book from the man's library. The man agrees. Franklin returns the book with a courteous note. From then onward, the irascible opponent is friendly and shows "a readiness to serve." Franklin stated a general principle: "He that has once done you a Kindness will be more ready to do you another, than he whom you yourself have obliged." Why does this work? Once someone has done a favor for you, he feels "invested" in your success. He doesn't want to feel as if he has made a mistake in choosing you as a worthy person to bestow kindness on. Second, subconsciously the person doing the favor tells himself that he must like you in order to do you a favor. So it becomes easier the next time.

Can this go too far? Of course. Entertaining dramas like *The Man Who Came to Dinner* are built on guests who stay too long or ask too many favors. My point here is not to urge you to manipulate or make outrageous demands. But you should feel more confident when looking for mentors and advisers. You're not looking for a handout or an inheritance. You're looking for a better sense of how you are doing at work and whether you are marching in the right direction to reach your goals.

DON'T BORROW OR LEND ALONE

Money can cause undue stress. So why not just do away with it, or come up with schemes to equalize it? That's silly. Better to home in on the aspects of money that create the most trouble—namely, borrowing and lending too hastily. The comedian Chris Rock has promulgated the following tenet: Once someone borrows money from you, you must collect it back right away. If you wait, he'll get used to owing you money and make you feel guilty for asking. It becomes a "character trait: you have a fat friend, you have a bald friend, you have a friend who owes you about fifty dollars." Before you know it, he starts boasting about what he's going to buy. "*Friend*: 'Next week we going to buy a house.' *You*: 'I guess you're going to be fifty dollars short, huh?'"

Borrowing and lending are treacherous activities for us. But we also know that countries cannot prosper unless they allow, even encourage, borrowing and lending. Our prefrontal cortex makes us forward-looking creatures. Capital markets allow us to invest and to begin to create our future today. Entrepreneurs can borrow to start new ventures. Families can live in homes they could not buy with a single lump sum. A few years ago, I visited Crete and saw neighborhoods of homes only partially built. Some were just foundations. I asked my host why there were so many abandoned projects. The answer: Those homes aren't abandoned; it just takes many years to build a house. Because Crete did not have mortgages, people would save a bit each year for the cement, stone, tiles, and so on. They would add to the home what they could afford. In countries with modern mortgage markets, families can move in much sooner. This is mostly a good thing,

The housing meltdown of 2007–2010 tells us, though, that human beings are prone to get a little reckless when it comes to borrowing. In Florida and Southern California people moved into homes without putting any money down, and in some cases without even showing their tax return to a bank. Politicians and government agencies like Fannie Mae goaded bankers into propping up the home ownership rate, regardless of credit quality. Many professional bankers fell asleep at the wheel—and the vehicle was hurtling ahead at 100 miles per hour. I spoke with FDIC officials in Arizona, who told me that in 2005 the bankers reported that about 200,000 people had moved into the state. So they lent money for thousands of new homes to be built. It turned out that number was way off; only half as many actually moved to Arizona. How could the bankers get that estimate so wrong? They looked out their windows and saw carpenters holding buckets of nails and two-by-fours. The bankers assumed people would move into those new homes. They never asked the builders, "How many of these houses are being built on spec?" The bankers and the borrowers figured that if things went sour, they would be bailed out by the government. So why not ride the wave? As an economist, I believe that speculation can play a very useful role in the economy. But, my Lord, you better know whether you are speculating or not! I hope when you go to Las Vegas and play the slot machines you don't think they're ATMs.

Critics of a market system blame competition and envy: "Everybody's greedy and grabbing everything because everyone is jealous of their neighbor." That's wrong. Instead, I'd blame a coddling culture that discourages work and suggests to people that they can have things for free, that they might as well borrow big, since society will bail them out if they fail. The real estate bubble was not incited by the competitive juices of the borrower—it was incited by borrowers thinking there was an easy way to a five-bedroom home and a BMW.

Regardless of the cause, the point is we shouldn't borrow or lend on impulse. Sitting in front of a loan application is not the time to blink your way onto the signature page. We should be asking our personal "board of directors" to throw up cautionary flags. This is especially true for young people. I was asked by an audience of high school students for one piece of advice on personal finance. I replied: "Don't open up an envelope from a credit card company until you're at least twenty-five." People who use cash spend 14 percent less than those wielding credit cards because it hurts us emotionally when we have to physically pull bills from our wallets. Only 40 percent of Generation Y (born after 1980) pay their bills on time. Why do young people tend to fail at finance? Young brains generally can't assess risks until they're in their twenties. Two parts of the brain are at war: the socio-emotional processor and the cognitive control system. The former tells a teenager to scream, jump off a roof, and bang his head against a wall. It also tells a teenager to jump onto his teammates with joy after winning a game. The socio-emotional processor goes into overdrive when peers are present. The results of peer pressure can be a glorious push over the football goal line, a harmless snowball fight, or a terrible car crash after the prom. The cognitive controller says, hold on, maybe it's not such a good idea to blast through that red light, while texting, and hiding an open bottle of beer. As parents discover, the cognitive controller does not mature until the mid-twenties. When you combine a slower-growing cognitive controller with a shiny new credit card, the results can be terribly disappointing.

Once again, the solution is not to ban borrowing and lending, but for individuals, especially young people, to seek advice, financial mentors, and cosigners for loans. Chris Rock provides some further profound thoughts on the topic of spending money and cognitive control: "ATM machines are open twenty-four hours a day. Twenty-four hours a day. For who? Who . . . is it open for? Have you ever taken out three hundred dollars at four o'clock in the morning for something positive . . . when you press that machine at four o'clock in the morning, I think a psychiatrist should pop up on the screen and go, 'C'mon, man, save your money, man. Don't buy drugs; buy some rims [for your car]. . . .'"

COMPETITIVE SHOPPING

We've all heard the phrase "shopping therapy," and at first blush it doesn't sound like a healthful prescription from a psychologist or from a debt counselor. The idea of going shopping in order to make yourself feel better doesn't, frankly, resonate with me. But I'm not a shopper. Nonetheless, spending time with friends prowling Neiman Marcus or the overflowing tables at Filene's Basement for bargains could be a fun social outing, for many. I applaud what I call "competitive shopping." What is it? It's the surge you feel when you compare prices, check circulars, and go online and offline to get good deals. I've seen friends come home from Nordstrom Rack gleeful, not because they accumulated a lot of new stuff but because they nabbed a great bargain. There's nothing wrong with this! Incidentally, by "competitive shopping" I don't mean stealing a sweater from the cart of a distracted shopper. You're not trying to compete against other consumers—you're competing against yourself and against the retailer. And it's not a zero-sum game. If you buy a sweater for $20, presumably you value the sweater more than the seller does. Both sides gain. But you do benefit more than you would if you bought it across town for $30.

Back to Willie Mays for a moment. At seventy-nine, suffering from glaucoma, Mays has had to give up golf, driving, and, of course, baseball. But according to his biographer, "shopping satisfies his competitive spirit. If a friend has bought a new television, he'll try to buy the same one for less money. A common ploy: he'll tell the salesperson that he plans on buying two televisions and he expects a discount. When he receives it, he says he's changed his mind and wants only one—at the discounted price." We may not cheer all of Mays's methods, but pitchers never liked when he stole second base, either.

Don't feel guilty about competitive shopping. Chances are the shopkeeper has his own tricks, too. For example, if he hands you the item to feel, your brain will begin to feel an attachment. You've heard the phrase "you break it, you buy it." Well, studies show that if you hold it for more than thirty seconds you'll pay more for it. Atmospherics count, too. On Fifth Avenue in New York, the scent of Abercrombie & Fitch's cologne seems to grab anyone under the age of thirty by the collar and yank him/her to the checkout counter. Martin Lindstrom, the CEO of a brand marketing company that bears his name, makes the following suggestion to avoid enticement: Always eat right before walking into a "scented store." It'll keep you focused on finding deals. The more pungent the snack, the better (since it will mute the allure of the store). So just before turning into the Abercrombie store, hit the falafel stand at 56th and Fifth.

Despite all the stress and dread of modern life, it is easier to competitively shop than anytime in human history. Silk and spice routes connected Asia to the Middle East a thousand years ago, and later entranced Marco Polo. In parts of Europe, markets from medieval times still exist in town squares. I've bought reindeer jerky in Finland, peddled next to DVDs of Hollywood hits. A hundred years ago, townsfolk across America waited anxiously for the Wells Fargo wagon to roll in with their shopping orders, and of course the Sears catalog was the national "wish book" for a good part of the twentieth century.

But today, there is no limit to access, and no limit to the ability to compare goods, prices, and quality. The Internet brings Chinese silk to our fingertips, and tripadvisor.com will suggest what hotel to stay in if you decide to go to Shanghai for yourself. Yes, there is much misinformation, but it is far easier than ever before to call upon the experiences of your fellow shoppers. This is the era of competitive shopping. Apple's iTunes brought us the 99-cent song. Does shopping have to end in a deluge of debt? Not necessarily. Remember, the biggest debt explosions facing the United States and much of the rest of the world do not derive from competitive shopping by individuals; they derive from government bureaucrats and politicians promising lavish retirement plans to themselves and to voters. Those promises were engraved in stone prior to the spread of the Internet and the era of competitive shopping. I'm not telling you the key to happiness is shopping. I don't believe that. I will say, though, that first, shopping involves a primal hunting and gathering impulse. Second, there's no point in denying it and trying to transcend it. Third, the best way to live with this impulse is to embrace our competitive urges, use all of our tools, and thereby get the best bargains we can.

It's also worth noting that necessities are cheaper than anytime in human history. Frank Sinatra (and Otis Redding and the Donkey from *Shrek*) sang a somber song called "Try a Little Tenderness." Okay, today it sounds chauvinistic, but the lyric from 1932 warns that a woman may get weary wearing "the same shabby dress." So in those weary moments, "try a little tenderness." Hearing that lyric today, I think: "Show her a *lot* of tenderness, and Frank, get out there and bring her a new dress!" Back in the 1930s, it was not far-fetched to imagine an American woman who owned just one shabby dress. Almost all products have fallen in price. In 1958 the Sears catalog boasted of a two-slice automatic toaster that would cost the average worker about 6.5 hours of wages. Today's online catalog lists a fine Sears toaster for the equivalent of about 1.5 hours of work. In the early 1970s, less than one-third of all American homes enjoyed air-conditioning. By 2005, nearly 80 percent of poor households (income below $19,350 for a family of four) had air-conditioning.

Shopping is not necessarily about material objects, dresses, and appliances. We derive more happiness from experiences than from hunks of metal. It's the music that we can listen to with our friends, the refrigerated drinks that make it pleasant to invite family over for a barbecue, the cheap Southwest airline flight that allows students to visit their grandparents—these are also the results of competition, and the experiences that imprint the happiest memories in our minds.

GIVE IT AWAY

Giving makes us feel better, and it makes other people feel better, too. It is almost impossible not to feel better when you are helping others. Even a prune-face like John D. Rockefeller couldn't stop a smile when he doled out dimes to children. People who give their time or their money to charity are 40 to 45 percent more likely to say they are very happy. Please, I'm not telling you to help people because of your own self-centered motivation. A selfish misanthrope would look at an old lady at the curb and say: "I'm going to help her cross the street so I feel good about myself. After she crosses, I don't care if she gets hit by a runaway bus on the sidewalk." I'm saying that regardless of motivation, helping others will release oxytocin and give you a warmer glow. And that glow does not discriminate by income. A study of 115 lower-income senior citizens who served as Foster Grandparents and Senior Companions (to older and disabled adults) showed a sunnier state of mind in those who volunteered than those who turned down the opportunity.

There is a caveat here. Charity brings happiness when it's voluntary. If an authoritarian government required you to come to everyone's aid, and to hand over your hard-earned savings, that glow would fizzle out.

The glow, the buzz, the warm fuzzy feelings from good acts come when we volunteer, not when we follow commands. Remember, our search for happiness is thrown off course when we lose control. When governments levy very high taxes—even when those revenues are used to promote social welfare—they tend to discourage charitable acts by individuals. Public charity crowds out private charity. Policymakers have a choice: they can (1) encourage individuals and families to donate their time and money; or (2) force people to donate their time and money, which will discourage (1), because it depletes their levels of happiness. Unhappy people will volunteer less, which means people who need help will get less help.

Compare countries that squeeze citizens with high taxes in order to promote social welfare spending to countries that encourage private individual giving by, for example, giving generous tax breaks for generosity. In the United States in 2005, with a marginal tax rate of 27 percent for the average worker, Americans gave away 1.67 percent of GDP. This sounds like a small number, but not when compared with other countries. Germans, with a marginal tax rate of 53 percent, gave away .22; and Frenchmen facing a rate of 40 percent contributed .14 percent. The Charities Aid Foundation concluded that "giving tends to represent a lower proportion of GDP in countries with higher levels of personal taxation, particularly social insurance; if social insurance payments were to rise in the future . . . this could represent a threat to voluntary income." For these reasons, I became concerned in 2009, when President Obama urged Congress to slash the tax incentives for individuals to contribute money to worthy groups. Instead, the government would raise taxes and then directly distribute funds to charities. A government clearinghouse is no recipe for happiness, and a pretty quick route to discouraging charitable efforts.

I have noticed another phenomenon when it comes to charitable giving. When people suspect that a charitable cause has a "sugar daddy" in the government, individuals shy away from sending that charity their own money. The Kennedy Center for the Performing Arts in Washington, D.C., has a difficult time raising money. That sounds odd. After all, it's a national monument for a popular president, and it puts on wonderful concerts, plays, opera, and ballet. Each December CBS broadcasts a spectacular event in which the president bestows awards to legendary performers. At those shows I got to meet everyone from Mary Poppins (Julie Andrews) to 007 (Sean Connery) to Oprah. So what's the problem? Taxpayers look at the gleaming white structure on the Potomac and figure, "Oh, well, they must get my money anyway through taxes, so why should I bother reaching into my own pocket?" Truth is, the Kennedy Center receives support for its building infrastructure because it is a national presidential memorial. But the operas, ballets, concerts, and plays rely on selling tickets and attracting charitable gifts.

Let's take a look at two periods in U.S. history to see how individuals can be discouraged from helping others. During the 1930s, the Great Depression drove up the jobless rate to 25 percent and sent many to wait in lines for soup and cheap grub. It would've been a perfect time for churches to open their purses. But churches dramatically slashed their charitable giving. You might think this was simply a matter of fewer people putting money on the church plate, and therefore the churches having fewer resources. But even when one takes into account the high jobless rate and lower incomes, the churches cut back. A careful study by Jonathan Gruber and Daniel Hungerman concluded that "benevolent church spending fell by 30% in response to the New Deal, and that government relief spending can explain virtually all of the decline in charitable church activity observed between 1933 and 1939."

In 1986 Oliver Stone directed a movie called *Wall Street*, which did a brilliant job portraying the 1980s as an alleged "decade of greed." With slicked-back hair and fine pinstripes, Gordon Gekko struts to a microphone and declares to shareholders, many of whom were detested yuppies: "The point is, ladies and gentlemen, that greed, for lack of a better word, is good. Greed is right. Greed works. . . . And greed, you mark my words, will not only save Teldar Paper, but that other malfunctioning corporation called the USA."

Sure enough, during the 1980s lots of people got rich, as 17 million net new jobs were created. New companies with names like Apple and Microsoft went public, after bursting out of garages. The unemployment rate dropped in half, from 10.8 percent in 1983 to 5.3 percent in 1989, on its way to under 4 percent in the 1990s. But what happened to charitable giving in a "decade of greed" when marginal tax rates dropped sharply (at the top end from 70 percent to 30 percent)? Charitable giving soared. Individual giving was growing at a 3.1 percent pace from 1955 to 1980. During the "decade of greed," individuals gave at a 5.2 percent pace, a 67 percent jump over the prior twenty-five years. For all the talk of Rolex watches and diamonds, people spent more on charity than they did on jewelry and health club visits. Corporations, too, reached into their pockets (or their shareholders' pockets), contributing a greater share of their profits.

The truth is Oliver Stone and/or Gordon Gekko misunderstand what competition is and what an economy is. Gekko is not a lizard, he's a dirty rat, and such rodents show up in every culture and economic system. At one point, the hero, Bud Fox, asks: "How much is enough?" Gekko replies: "It's not a question of enough, pal. It's a zero-sum game, somebody wins, somebody loses. Money itself isn't lost or made, it's simply transferred from one perception to another." If that were the story of the world, we'd all be sitting in our caves, scratching our caveman beards, hoping to take down a meaty mammoth.

COMPETING TO GIVE

Several times a year, when my kids come home from school, they hand me forms to fill out for charitable activities. They typically involve readathons, walkathons, jumpathons, and so on. I remember doing laps with my high school swim team in a swimathon. They are channeling energy and a competitive spirit for good works. They are moving forward in order to conquer diseases, afflictions, and the results of natural disasters. The results are astounding for the beneficiaries and for the kids who do the fund-raising. And let's not forget the Susan G.

Komen Race for the Cure, which has generated over a billion dollars for breast cancer research and to help victims. Notice: it's a *race*, not a sit-in! Both a race to cure cancer and a race to get fund-raising participants to cross the finish line. You might take a moment to go to the Web site both to contribute and to read the heartbreaking story of Susan Komen's sister, who watched as Susan's cancer spread and her original family physician seemed too relaxed: "The truth of the matter is that growing up in the small town of Peoria, our family had been treated our whole lives by one doctor. Suzy trusted him with her cancer the same way she did with her measles. Mistake number one. None of us knew enough to inquire about seeking information from a major cancer center or from a group of physicians associated with one in Peoria. He was our doctor. Period." The family eventually brought in a surgeon, who did not seem to recognize that they were fighting a fast-moving biological enemy.

Sometimes speed, aggressiveness, and competitiveness are vital. Now, with support from all those men and women who have been running and walking the race for twenty-five years, the survival rate for breast cancer victims whose cancer had not yet spread has climbed from 74 percent to 98 percent. It is a story about calling on primal urges for survival and for progress. Neither the race nor the stunning improvement in survival rates would have come if Susan's sister had decided to step back, sit down, and try to de-stress her life.

One more note on competition and charities deserves mention. Ever since the "decade of greed," charities have felt themselves under pressure from contributors. This is a good thing. Back in the "non-greedy" days of the 1950s–1970s, charities could hide behind thick-pillared facades and dole out largesse without anyone questioning their methods or their efficiency. I'm not impugning anyone's motivation. However, in the past twenty-five years a revolution has come to non-profits. Many of those purportedly greedy yuppies in the 1980s began to demand more scrutiny and more involvement in the charities they support. As a result, charities are now required to explain exactly how much of their budget goes to, for example, overhead, as opposed to the needy families they serve. A competitive spirit has been injected into charities—they compete to raise funds, but they also have to compete to demonstrate they are spending the money effectively. The result: more money is going to the needy. I've attended meetings of foundations that distribute millions of dollars each year to worthy causes. But before the foundations write a check, managers sit down with the administrators of the charities to make sure that in fact the check is going to good use, not just to pay for fund-raising parties.

Before the advent of competitive charitable giving, I don't believe that inefficient administrators were knowingly dining on shrimp rolls while beneficiaries starved. But I do believe that many were simply unaware of how they spent the money they worked so hard to attract. Naturally, when contributors give money with strings attached, it can create discomfort. Eli Broad, a billionaire philanthropist in California, likes to see results. Large gifts to museums should inspire more people to visit and elicit greater generosity from trustees, for example. As Jane Nathanson, a longtime trustee of the Los Angeles Museum of Contemporary Art, explained, "I happen to think you need strings . . . there is a new type of philanthropist now. With old family wealth, people gave money because it was the chic thing to do. New wealth is earned, and if you can get it, there is going to be a great deal of control."

In 1992, the American Institute of Philanthropy began to rank charitable groups for their efficiency and on the basis of whether they actually worked toward achieving stated goals. The institute revealed that in 2007 a group called the National Veterans Services Fund distributed just 2 percent of the $6 million it took in. Another group paid its founder and wife over half a million dollars and distributed only about one-third of its contributions. I do not cite these examples to spread cynicism. Quite the opposite. I cite them to show they have been caught, and that the world of nonprofits has become a more competitive place. In 2002, another nonprofit, Charity Navigator, began evaluating charitable groups to assess their efficiency. By 2006, *Time* named the Charity Navigator Web site one of the "coolest" fifty on the Internet. Today, it is far more likely that your contribution to one of the United States' 1.4 million charities will fulfill your wishes because there is more scrutiny. A laid-back system produced more layabouts and more abuse. So here's the upshot: You should research, give, and feel good about it. Now give more.

ROMANCE AND BROMANCE: COMPETITIVE THINGS

What is an ideal date? Since the 1930s the classic American date has been dinner and a movie. Before movies came along it might have been dinner and a rodeo. Here are the two factors that matter most: the buildup and the bonding that can take place. Dating and falling in love are not just a matter of finding a person to hold hands with. To understand ideal dates, forget the bars and nightclubs. Instead, go to any high school or college or to any senior citizens' development. A boy and girl plot to meet at some locker in between periods. A date is planned. The girl picks out her clothing, fixes her hair, asks her roommates which style looks best. The boy showers and, these days, spritzes himself with one of the thousand colognes and body sprays advertised in *Sports Illustrated* and *Men's Fitness*. As they anticipate meeting, opioids, dopamine, adrenaline, testosterone, and estrogen flow. Thomas Loving (his real name) at the University of Texas, Austin, found that merely thinking about a fun date raises the cortisol level in saliva. The couple feels a little nervous, and a bit out of sorts. Stress hormones make them literally and metaphorically weak at the knees. It is hard to "be yourself" when your body is turning the spigots on all your neurotransmitters and hormones. You are not yourself; you're almost a different person under the influence of natural drugs. (If this were a deserted island and only two of you were left, there would be no surge, because part of the thrill comes from competitive excitement. If you were alone, there would be no competitors to beat.) The excitement and chemical stimulation come from the possibility of love, romance, and mating.

The ideal date also involves bonding. Bonding generally involves a shared experience, but often a movie does not do the trick. Unless the movie is a heart-stopping affair, watching can be a kind of passive experience, leaving the two individuals to enjoy the event as individuals, instead of as a couple. Better to share an experience that tests the couple, and makes those hormones and neurotransmitters keep pumping. I do not pretend to be a dating coach, and so I don't cite the following with the authority of Dr. Ruth, Dr. Phil, or even Dr. Strangelove. Nonetheless, an extra dose of risk and competition usually adds to the excitement and romance: kayaking, tennis, bowling, playing a Nintendo Wii game, or even tossing whipped cream pies at each other's faces might be better choices than a movie. A recent article in *Men's Health* recommended zip-lining, horse racing, and even skinny-dipping, reminding readers to "bring a lantern to place on shore so you can find your clothes."

Romantic bonding comes, then, not from sitting in the lotus pose, but in the forward-looking excitement at what might be discovered next. That tingle of stress one feels inside is a friendly tingle, a good stress. And the flutter in the stomach and the heart that hopes to find love and romance comes from competitive, primal vibes. They add sweet mystery to life. Rodgers and Hart wrote a wonderful song called "Manhattan," with the lyric "the city's clamor can never spoil, the dreams of a boy and goil." Indeed, clamor, not quiet, is the underscore for the skipping heart of lovers.

Romantic bonding is not the only kind of bonding that makes us more merry. Happy people tend to have friends. It's a two-way, reinforcing street: because they seem happy, happy people attract more friends. And because they have friends, these people grow even happier. Studies show that having friends is more important to happiness than having children. Like romance and dating, friendship deepens with shared experiences. Two guys owning an identical large-screen TV gives them something in common. For those same guys, sitting in the stands at a Bears game in thirty-two-degree sleet and spilling beer on each other also gives them a bond. Friends are not collectibles or dollar bills, where "the more the better." It's the quality of the experiences and conversations we share that count, not the sheer number of people we can call "friend." Men and women seem to worry more these days about loneliness and a lack of friendship. A study in the *American Sociological Review* reported that in 1985, Americans had an average of three confidants. By 2004, the number dropped to two. Twenty-five percent reported no friends. While people report they have grown more dependent on their spouses for companionship, they know fewer people outside of the home. "If something happens to that spouse or partner, you may have lost your safety net," stated one of the coauthors.

A bawdy but interesting 2009 movie called *I Love You, Man* depicted a young man with a beautiful fiancée who thought he was happy until he realized he did not have a best man for the wedding. Then he goes on "man dates" in order to find some friends. The *American Sociological Review* survey suggests this is a more common issue these days than it used to be. Is it the rush of life, the stress of work? Would we have more friends if we just slowed down? I'm not convinced. Perhaps Americans have fewer friends precisely because life provides fewer truly stressful, life-and-death moments to share. The guys in the trenches in World War I made lifelong friends—if they made it out alive. In a small town in 1900, virtually every man was part of the fire brigade, or manned sandbags when the rivers overflowed. These are tasks that save lives and also call forth powerful biological drives. Now we mostly leave such toiling to professionals. But the opportunity for bonding is lost. Earlier I mentioned Robert Putnam's classic *Bowling Alone*, lamenting the erosion of athletic activities for community members. I bring up these examples to show that friendship itself emerges best in a forward-looking, hardworking, hard-playing climate. Once again, the Edenist ideal of kicking back under the palms has it backward. If we lack deep friendships today, it's more likely a result of human beings doing too little, not too much. We should not aim to gather friends like some collection of baseball or Pokemon cards to be filed. We should be looking to share experiences with them. This search may explain why in the past few years millions of women have bonded while rolling dice at Bunco parties.

Parents are probably not helping when they organize "parallel playdates" for their children. These seem to evolve into dysfunctional events. I have friends who threw a big party at a hotel for junior high school kids. The parents rented a battalion of gleaming, vibrating video consoles. Each teenager played his own individual video game, not together but side by side. It would be far better to yank out their electrical cords and have them play a game together, even if it's something as juvenile as popping balloons with their backsides. Even spin the bottle might be better than having eight kids sitting next to each other playing computer solitaire.

Whether speaking of male friends, female friends, coed friendships, or your relationship with your whippet dog, scientists have shown that a touch, a hug, and an arm on the shoulder reinforce good feelings. Premature babies who get massaged gain more weight; waiters who touch patrons get better tips; and doctors who touch patients generate more goodwill and fewer malpractice lawsuits. This can be manipulative, of course. In Hollywood they say people always greet you with a big touch because they want to see how soft you are before they eat you. Cynics aside, touch is powerful. It brings us together to share personal space. The football team crushed together in a huddle is not just leaning in to keep secrets; the players are leaning in to pledge to each other their lives and sacred trust. It gives them strength and makes them play better. They can feel each other's pulses. Perhaps that's why Andre Agassi in his remarkable memoir admits to hating tennis. He calls it the loneliest sport.

At his home near Walden pond, Henry David Thoreau spoke of "masses of men leading lives of quiet desperation." But it's no longer quiet. The din of blaring televisions and radios is loud now, with interviews, articles, books, and speeches blaming our perceived unhappiness on too much competition and on a too-long to-do list. I have argued throughout this book that competition is not what's driving us to bowl alone. Our best chance to regain a spirit of community and friendship is to embrace our selves as competitive spirits, embrace each other as comrades in all sorts of struggles, and get on with the hard work of living. This task is best met by getting a grip on where we stand, keeping out of terrible debt, giving to charity, and trying to create shared experiences that can turn a passing acquaintance into a friend who would save your house in a fire and drape his arm on your shoulder if your dog ran away.

CONCLUDING THOUGHTS

Your Most Important Competitor—You

Maybe you agree that prosperous societies need competition. Does this mean we have no choice but to unleash the most ruthless competition possible, a Roman coliseum's duel to the death? In fact, competition needn't destroy our souls or society. Early on, I stated that our ability to imagine the future is an extraordinary evolutionary gift. We don't know whether kittens go into deep REM sleep, but we're pretty sure they do not dream about innovative plans for the future. Kittens, cute as they are, don't wake up and say, "I think I'd like to be an astronaut when I grow up," or "Could we cure dandruff by adding pyrithione zinc to shampoo?" For those who just cannot abide the stress of shopping, the job market, the real estate market, and the stock market, let me now reveal a second evolutionary gift, a relatively new route to happiness: A human being can set out a personal goal and consciously compete against himself. *We can and should be setting personal goals that do not require us to root for the defeat of others.* Learning Italian from the Rosetta Stone company and then saving up to buy an airline ticket to Florence to see Michelangelo's *David* is a fulfilling form of competition—with yourself. When you learn the Italian word for David's slingshot (or his body parts), you are not snatching the word from someone else's mouth.

None of the Iditarod dogs that race the grueling twelve hundred miles across Alaska care much whether they beat last year's time. Their driver yelling "Mush!" does. We can set personal goals and consciously try to reach them. Our drive to compete does not force us, therefore, only into zero-sum games against other people. Nor is happiness a zero-sum game. You don't steal joy from other people, any more than you steal good health. You share your blessings.

We should set ambitious goals, not settle for a Zen-like state of calm. The nice thing about competing with ourselves is that we seldom get jealous of the winner.

WHEN DO WE SAY ENOUGH?

Whether or not we are competing against ourselves or others, we all feel tired and annoyed from time to time. Why don't we just call a truce, an end to consumerism, materialism, and struggling for more? The problem is, the struggle for more is impossibly intertwined with every other aspect of our lives. At what point in time in the past should people have declared, "Stop! Enough progress. Let's keep things simple"? Would 1 BC have been a good time to hit "pause"? Or July 3, 1776? Or on the eve of the 1964 Civil Rights vote? It's a good thing Teddy Roosevelt did not lock us into the standard of living of 1904, or we would never fly on airplanes, get a polio vaccination, or expect to live past the age of fifty. With all due respect to medicine men, who sometimes come across valuable herbal tonics, it was daring science, not the jungle, that produced Jonas Salk. Grants from the Mellon Foundation helped, too.

Without the twentieth century's progress, Milton Berle said we'd all be watching television by candlelight. We cannot know what we could be missing if we halted our climb toward affluence and greater possibility.

And there is something unfair about decrying consumption and prosperity at this stage in the game. Even if we simplify our lives and forswear "extra income," we will still be benefiting from centuries of innovation and wealth creation that others have yet to enjoy. Make no mistake: To embrace a small-is-beautiful ethos is to crank up the draw-bridge and leave a crocodile-infested moat between elites who already own Viking ranges and the world's "slumdogs" yearning to gain access to indoor plumbing.

As Albert O. Hirschman noted in his book *The Passions and the Interests*, traditional societies in the Middle Ages believed that the kings, lords, and dukes living in their castles were fundamentally different kinds of people from the rest of us. Kings and queens, it was thought, should pursue their passions, whereas the rest of us should just tend our sheep, drink ale, and forget about the mannered and manored life. But all that changed with the rise of democracy and modern economies—and the arrival of broad affluence. Now is no time to send ourselves back to the life of simple serfdom.

Does the flurry and pursuit of affluence make us happy? It's tough to say. Human beings are finely tuned for surviving. For happiness seeking, we are neither finely tuned nor pitch-perfect. We are more like a broken-down piano in the basement of the old elementary school down the block, but still we try to pluck out a tune. Happiness is elusive almost by design. Yet we try.

WE CAN'T SHARE PARADISE

We can share hugs, handshakes, and ice cream sundaes. The one thing we cannot share is paradise and perfection. We don't have it to share.

Yogi Berra said that "even if the world were perfect, it wouldn't be." The world keeps spinning, keeps evolving, and so do we. Even if historians, theologians, and botanists got together, crossed the Tigris in rafts, macheted their way through the forests of Babylon, and actually discovered the real Eden, we wouldn't find it very comfortable. No doubt, some vines would be overgrown. We'd have to do some pruning. And then we would disagree where to cut. Or where to plant a new fig tree. Or what to do with that devilish snake. Before you know it, we would have a human society all over again—full of tears, clamor, competition, and yes, just enough slivers of happiness to encourage us to live another day.

ACKNOWLEDGMENTS

This book takes a long view through history and refers to some great minds. Many of them, including Charles Darwin, Alfred Marshall, Thomas Malthus, and Ludwig Wittgenstein, were closely tied to Cambridge University. I would like to thank St. John's College, Cambridge, for its support and for a fellowship that allowed me to pursue this study. I wrote my first book as a graduate student in Cambridge, and it was thrilling to pursue another while walking through, not Tudor-*style* archways but actual Tudor gates endowed by Henry VIII's grandmother. It's easier to get a handle on history when you can point to a window and say, "Oh, there's Isaac Newton's room."

My lovely and loving wife, Debby, not only encouraged my writing but helped secure permission to quote lyrics from *West Side Story*. I'm married to someone who knows someone who knows Stephen Sondheim. Debby still beams when I walk into a room. Who could ask for anything more? My dazzling daughters, Victoria, Katherine, and Alexia, inspire me, correct me, and make me laugh. I suggest you leave room on your bookshelf, Kindle, and iPad for their future achievements. My witty mother, Joan, is always willing to read drafts and return them with insightful comments. I don't know how she finds the time with all those e-mail jokes, stories, and urban myths she's busy forwarding. My father, Alvin, who loved trains and ships, showed us the capacity for happiness while rushing around, ready to check his wristwatch for the next station stop. He had hobbies and passions but hated to be late. As Groucho Marx sang, "Hello, I must be going."

Thank you to Dr. Denis Burdakov of Cambridge University and Dr. William Anapoell of Scripps Health for carefully reviewing sections on physiology. Thanks also to my editor, Caroline Sutton, for her patience and advice. This is not a fat book, but without skillful editing, it might have turned out clunky. My agent, Susan Ginsburg, stood by my side, always prudent and enthusiastic—a rare combination. Finally, I'm grateful for people who read books, for they keep authors going when lonely hours and blank pages give plenty of reason to call the whole thing off.

NOTES

---

xi. **a story about yoga:** Sara Eckel, "Is the Spirit of Competition in the Soul of Yoga?" *New York Times*, November 19, 2009, p. E1.

4. **A *Journal of Happiness Studies* compiles empirical and philosophical research:** Ed Diener and Robert Biswas-Diener, *Happiness: Unlocking the Mysteries of Psychological Wealth* (Malden, Mass.: Blackwell, 2008).

6. **wrote one visitor:** Steve Burgess, "Seeking Happiness in Bhutan," *Tyee*, March 9, 2009.

7. **these Edenists claim:** Philip Brickman and Don Campbell, "Hedonic Relativism and Planning the Good Society" (1971), in M. H. Apley,

ed., *Adaptation Level Theory: A Symposium* (New York: Academic Press, 1971), pp. 287–302.

9. **The FAA is trying to block nature's unselfish pathway in the brain:** I am indebted to my daughter Victoria for this observation.

10. **as the psychologist Martin Seligman calls it:** See Martin E. Seligman, *Authentic Happiness* (New York: Free Press, 2002).

11. **A British economist actually titled an article:** Andrew Oswald, "The Hippies Were Right All Along About Happiness," *Financial Times*, January 19, 2006.

11. **the noble savage:** The "noble savage" phrase comes from the poet John Dryden's tragic 1670 play *The Conquest of Granada*.

12. **Steven Pinker points to surveys of art:** Steven Pinker, *The Blank Slate* (New York: Penguin, 2002), p. 405.

13. **The British scholar Ashley Montagu, another Boas protégé, argued:** Ashley Montagu, *Man and Aggression* (New York: Oxford University Press, 1973), p. 9.

13. **A psychologist named Zing-Yang Kuo asserted:** See Zing-Yang Kuo, "A Psychology without Heredity," *Psychological Review* 31 (November 1924); and Zing-Yang Kuo, "How Are Our Instincts Acquired?" *Psychological Review* 29 (September 1922).

15. **George Bernard Shaw, identified as a Fabian socialist, was gung ho for eugenics:** George Watson, *The Lost Literature of Socialism* (Cambridge: Lutterworth Press, 2010), p. 81.

16. **Thorstein Veblen and John Kenneth Galbraith published screeds on conspicuous consumption:** For a treatment, please consult my *New Ideas from Dead Economists*, 3rd rev. ed. (New York: Penguin, 2007), chap. 8.

16. **Andrew Oswald further argues:** Oswald, "The Hippies Were Right All Along."

17. **A well-published behavioral economist opined:** Jon Gertner, "The Futile Pursuit of Happiness," *New York Times Magazine*, September 7, 2003. The prominent economist is George Loewenstein of Carnegie Mellon.

17. **Another happiness psychologist urges:** Tim Kasser, "A Revolution of Values: Psychological Research on Materialism & Its Alterna-

tives"; available at www.surrey.ac.uk/resolve/seminars/Tim%20Kasser%20 Slides.pdf.

17. **Coined by Philip Brickman and Donald T. Campbell:** Brickman and Campbell, "Hedonic Relativism."

17. **Adam Smith, the father of economics, observed:** Adam Smith, *The Wealth of Nations*, Bk. 1, chap. XI [1776] (New York: Collier, 1911), p. 267.

17. **Over the course of a sixteen-year survey:** See Richard Easterlin, "Explaining Happiness," *Proceedings of the National Academy of Sciences* 100, no. 19 (September 16, 2003), pp. 11176–83.

18. **A measure of happiness did not budge:** Richard A. Easterlin, "The Worldwide Standard of Living Since 1800," *Journal of Economic Perspectives* 14, no. 1 (Winter 2000), pp. 7–26.

18. **Mexicans are happier than the French, and wealthy San Franciscans are more dour than Chattanoogans:** Arthur C. Brooks, *Gross National Happiness* (New York: Basic Books, 2008), pp. 115–16.

18. **Most people choose the latter:** See Amos Tversky and Dale Griffin, "Endowment and Contrast in Judgments of Well-Being," in Richard Zeckhauser, ed., *Strategy and Choice* (Cambridge, Mass.: MIT Press, 1991), pp. 313–14.

19. **Rush recorded a song:** Thanks to James Carter of the U.S. Senate Budget Committee for recommending the Rush song.

20. **studies show that their happiness quotient will likely exceed that of someone who earns more money but considers himself unsuccessful:** Vicente Navarro, "Inequalities Are Unhealthy," *Monthly Review* 56, no. 2 (June 2004). Navarro suggests he'd rather be a middle-class person in Ghana than a poor American.

20. **homes are 50 percent larger:** Steve Brown, "Ever Bigger House Finally Stops Growing," *House & Home* (April 1, 2007).

21. **Edenists move on to argue:** Vincente Navarro, ed., *Political Economy of Social Inequalities* (Amityville, N.Y.: Baywood, 2000).

21. **Schumacher . . . argued for "enoughness,":** E. F. Schumacher, *Small Is Beautiful: Economics as If People Mattered* (New York: Harper & Row, 1973), p. 125.

25. **writes John Pomfret:** John Pomfret, *Chinese Lessons* (New York: Holt, 2006), p. 75.

27. **with good data, Patz was able to unveil stunning results:** William Tasman, Arnall Patz, et al., "Retinopathy of Prematurity: The Life of a Lifetime Disease," *American Journal of Ophthalmology* 41, no. 1 (January 2006), pp. 167–74.

28. **The study suggests:** James H. Fowler and Nicholas A. Christakis, "Dynamic Spread of Happiness in a Large Social Network: Longitudinal Analysis over 20 Years in the Framingham Heart Study," *British Medical Journal* 337 (2008), pp. 1–9.

28. **Happy fans of word puzzles solve 20 percent more puzzles than cranky ones:** Jonah Lehrer, *How We Decide* (Boston: Houghton Mifflin Harcourt, 2009), p. 246.

28. **An Australian researcher has shown:** Jessica Hamzelou, "Happiness Ain't All It's Cracked Up to Be," *New Scientist* (February 26, 2010).

29. **Such people also send out more seek-out-and-destroy cells:** Stefan Klein, *The Science of Happiness*, trans. Stephen Lehmann (New York: Marlowe and Company), pp. 43–44.

32. **Most everyone turns down the theoretical bargain:** Incidentally, Nozick's concept came out years after the novelette that inspired Arnold Schwarzenegger's movie *Total Recall*, in which workers do not take vacations but just have the memory of such vacations implanted in their brains. Of course, the Nozick version does not include a muscleman hurling dead bodies across a movie screen.

33. **The German physicist Werner Heisenberg could get lost in beautiful equations:** Michael Frayn's Tony Award–winning play *Copenhagen* portrays a 1941 meeting between the sophisticated Heisenberg and the Danish physicist Niels Bohr. With Sean Cunningham, I've penned a play about Heisenberg and baseball player Moe Berg called *The Greatest Game.*

33. **we are left with a third kind of happiness, *fulfillment*, which the psychologist Martin Seligman calls "the meaningful life.":** See Martin E. Seligman, *Authentic Happiness* (New York: Free Press, 2002).

33. **the meaningful life would follow Viktor Frankl:** Viktor E. Frankl, *Man's Search for Meaning*, trans. Ilse Lasch (Boston: Beacon Press, 2006).

34. **"Where is my faith? Even deep down . . . there is nothing but emptiness & darkness.":** Mother Teresa, *Mother Teresa: Come Be My Light,* Brian Kolodiejchuk, ed. (New York: Doubleday, 2007), p. 187.

36. **"Tell them I've had a wonderful life.":** Peter C. John, "Wittgenstein's 'Wonderful Life,'" *Journal of the History of Ideas* (July–September 1988), pp. 495–519.

36. **Solon replies, "So I may learn it and then die.":** Incidentally, Solon was not against bodily or material pleasures. In fact, he is often credited with setting up legalized brothels to democratize all sorts of social intercourse. His views recall the line in Peter Weiss's play *Marat/Sade* that there is no freedom "without general copulation."

36. **From 1991 to 1995 only four economics papers were published . . . from 2001 to 2005, there were over one hundred:** Daniel Kahneman and Alan B. Krueger, "Developments in the Measurement of Subjective Well-Being," *Journal of Economic Perspectives* 20, no. 1 (Winter 2006), pp. 3–24.

37. **But a unit of happiness is more flimsy and faulty:** See Will Wilkinson, "In Pursuit of Happiness Research," *Policy Analysis* no. 590 (April 11, 2007).

37. **those who found a dime reported a greater sense of satisfaction in life:** Short-term weather changes affect one's general life satisfaction, as does whether your favorite team wins a championship. See Norbert Schwarz and Gerald L. Clore, "Mood, Misattribution, and Judgment of Well-Being: Informative and Directive Functions of Affective States," *Journal of Personality and Social Psychology* 45 (September 1983), pp. 513–23.

37. **People who report being happy have an easier time coming up with pleasant synonyms:** See Gregory P. Strauss and Daniel N. Allen, "The Experience of Positive Emotion Is Associated with the Automatic Processing of Positive Emotional Words," *Journal of Positive Psychology* 1, no. 3 (July 2006), pp. 150–59.

39. **fMRI, DTI, and MEG:** Functional magnetic resonance imaging, diffusion tensor imaging, and magneto-encephalography.

40. **A woman who lost her amygdala through surgery could no longer detect the difference:** S. K. Scott, A. W. Young, A. J. Caldera, D. J. Hellawell, J. P. Aggleton, M. Johndon, "Impaired Auditory Recognition of

Fear and Anger Following Bilateral Amygdala Lesions," *Nature* 385 (1997), pp. 254–57; and Heinrich Kluver and Paul Bucy, "Preliminary Analysis of Function of the Temporal Lobe in Monkeys," *Archives of Neurology* 42 (1939), pp. 979–1000.

41. **". . . I'll hurt you if you stay.":** *The Fly*, written by George Langelaan, Charles Edward Pogue, and David Cronenberg, directed by David Cronenberg (1986).

42. **Bill Bryson has pointed out:** Bill Bryson, *A Short History of Nearly Everything* (New York: Broadway, 2003), p. 415.

42. **surgeons didn't even know they should wash their hands:** Not until Joseph Lister came around in the 1860s did cleanliness and disinfection seem to matter much. His predecessor, a Hungarian named Ignaz Semmelweiss, literally went insane trying to persuade doctors to change their ways. Thomas Eakins's famous painting *The Gross Clinic* (1875) depicts ungloved surgeons operating in their street clothes. His 1889 work *The Agnew Clinic* looked much more hygienic.

43. **that untrod road *was taken*:** Interesting that some cosmologists believe we literally take all alternative steps in multiple universes. See work by Max Tegmark and David Lewis, e.g., Max Tegmark, "Parallel Universes," *Scientific American* (May 2003), pp. 41–51.

43. **He placed a marshmallow in front of them:** See Jonah Lehrer's excellent, "Don't!" *New Yorker* (May 18, 2009), p. 26.

44. **as the great Victorian economist Alfred Marshall explained:** Alfred Marshall, *Principles of Economics*, vol. 1 (London: Macmillan, 1890), pp. 613–14.

44. **species were stuck in what Daniel Gilbert calls a "permanent present.":** Daniel Gilbert, *Stumbling on Happiness* (New York: Knopf, 2006), p. 16.

44. ***Homo sapiens* spend about 12 percent of their lives thinking about the future:** Gilbert, *Stumbling on Happiness*, p. 17. The function of our frontal lobe, our future machine, also tends to decline with old age, which might explain why older people seem to lose patience more easily. Not only do they have fewer years left, but their appreciation for that remaining time diminishes. Perhaps this phenomenon is a kindness performed by evolution. As people grow elderly, they tend to fear death less

and resign themselves to the inevitable. If the brain can imagine fewer opportunities in the future, it would seem to ease the elderly into accepting death. In contrast, depressed people will think about the future, but believe that the future will bring only more dread.

45. **his frontal lobe is too modest:** Eliot C. Bush and John M. Allman, "The Scaling of Frontal Cortex in Primates and Carnivores," *Proceedings of the National Academy of Sciences* 101, no. 11 (March 16, 2004), pp. 3962–66.

46. **A study of poor adults:** Robert Carroll, David Joulfaian, and Mark Rider, "Income Mobility: The Recent American Experience," Andrew Young School of Policy Studies Research Paper Series Nos. 07-18 (April 2006).

47. **Eadweard Muybridge:** Arthur P. Shimamura, "Muybridge in Motion: Travels in Art, Psychology, and Neurology," *History of Photography* 26, no. 4 (Winter 2002), pp. 341–50.

47. **According to the *San Francisco Daily Evening Bulletin*:** Ibid., p. 343.

48. **His business associate testified:** Ibid., p. 348.

49. **David Mamet has suggested:** David Mamet, *Bambi vs. Godzilla: On the Nature, Purpose, and Practice of the Movie Business* (New York: Random House, 2007), p. 19.

51. **he even argued on behalf of trees:** *Sierra Club v. Morton*, 405 U.S. 727 (1972).

51. **Douglas confided:** James Shreeve, "The Brain That Misplaced Its Body," *Discover* (March 1995), pp. 82–91.

52. **". . . It's certainly not mine.":** Ibid.

52. **The left makes up its own story:** See Michael S. Gazzaniga, *The Mind's Past* (Berkeley: University of California Press, 1998).

53. **brains of severe introverts and neurotics gleam right:** See Richard Davidson, "Anxiety and Affective Style: Role of Prefrontal Cortex and Amygdala," *Biological Psychiatry* 51, no. 1 (2002), pp. 68–80.

53. **P. G. Wodehouse describes:** P. G. Wodehouse, "Code of the Woosters" (1938) in *The Best of Wodehouse: An Anthology* (New York: Knopf, 2007), p. 4.

54. **In Plato's world we are like charioteers:** Plato, *Phaedrus* in *The*

Dialogues of Plato, vol. 1, translated by Benjamin Jowett (London: Macmillan, 1892).

54. **Antonio Damasio points to numerous examples:** Antonio R. Damasio, *Descartes' Error* (New York: Putnam, 1994).

55. **Babe Ruth was known:** In fact, Ruth was amblyopic and never had more than 20/200 vision in his left eye. G. B. Kara, "Lost Vision, Babe Ruth's Legend," *Argus* 13, no. 7 (1990), p. 6.

55. **Malcolm Gladwell's book *Blink* argues:** Malcolm Gladwell, *Blink* (Boston: Little, Brown, 2005).

56. **they used the emotional firepower to psych up their energy level and transmit more impulses:** A. Lo, D. Repin, and B. Steenbarger, "Fear and Greed in Financial Markets: A Clinical Study of Day-Traders," *American Economic Review* 95, no. 2 (2005), pp. 352–59.

58. **James argued:** William James, "What Is an Emotion?" *Mind* 9 (1884), pp. 188–205; for a fine biography, see Robert D. Richardson, *William James* (New York: Mariner Books, 2006).

59. **Ekman was pilloried:** Pinker, *The Blank Slate*, pp. 107–8.

59. **Ekman brings a different message:** Dacher Keltner, *Born to Be Good* (New York: Norton, 2009), p. 43.

59. **According to one of Ekman's students:** Ibid., p. 44.

60. **they could rewire nerves back to front:** Colwyn Trevarthen, ed., *Brain Circuits and Functions of the Mind: Essays in Honor of Roger W. Sperry* (Cambridge: Cambridge University Press, 1990).

60. **I placed my first real monetary bet ($1) on Ali against Joe Frazier:** Feel free to read my boxing novel, *The Castro Gene* (Ipswich, Mass.: Oceanview, 2007).

62. **Ali's dopamine neurons would send up a flare:** This discussion is not to argue that Ali was a superior boxer because he had stronger, better, or more free-flowing dopamine, but simply to illustrate the role of a key neurotransmitter.

62. **Ali has been a victim of Parkinson's syndrome:** I will not enter the debate as to whether Ali's ailments stem from boxing. It does seem, though, that while many boxers become brain-damaged and "punch-drunk," few exhibit the classic signs of Parkinson's as does Ali. Ali was approximately the same age as the actor Michael J. Fox when he displayed

Parkinson's symptoms, but no one has asked Fox whether appearing on television could impair dopamine production.

62. **teaching the bee to skip this field on the next trip:** When a ship passenger feels motion sickness, it may come from a mix-up of crossed prediction signals and then confound dopamine levels. The inner ear feels motion, but the eye senses a different movement.

63. **Chief Financial Officer Richard Galanti says:** See the Zogby International survey at http://articles.moneycentral.msn.com/Smart Spending/ConsumerActionGuide/10-companies-that-treat-you-right .aspx?slide-number=2.

64. **neurotransmitter studies have been done on lobsters and crayfish:** E. A. Kravitz, "Hormonal Control of Behavior: Amines and the Biasing of Behavioral Output in Lobsters," *Science* 241, no. 4874 (September 1988), pp. 1775–81; and Shih-Rung Yeh, Russell A. Fricke, Donald H. Edwards, "The Effect of Social Experience on Serotonergic Modulation of the Escape Circuit of Crayfish," *Science* 271, no. 5247 (January 1996), pp. 366–69.

65. **the rats quickly "adopt" nearby babies:** C. Pedersen et al., "Oxytocin Induces Maternal Behavior in Virgin Female Rats," *Science* 216, no. 4546 (May 1982), pp. 648–50.

66. **A fascinating study of 132 students showed:** D. C. McClelland and C. Kirshnit, "The Effect of Motivational Arousal Through Films on Salivary Immunoglobulin A," *Psychology and Health* 2 (1988), pp. 31–52.

67. **the doctor Eryximachus . . . argued:** E. M. Craik, "Plato and Medical Texts," *Classical Quarterly* 51, no. 1 (July 2001), p. 109.

71. **A free society with a free-wheeling economy offers the best hope:** Now, this brings up thorny definitions of freedom. Am I free to live in Beverly Hills if I don't make a million dollars a year? Many of the sociologists and moralists I've encountered in universities would say no. To them economic freedom means actually being able to afford all that you want. They are wrong. Money does not define freedom. Laws, regulations, and dictates do. A black man in South Africa was not free, because no matter how hard he worked or how much money he attained, apartheid would encage him in townships and labor camps. The government basically guaranteed a separate destitute life.

71. **"literally puts the fear of God into us . . . unaccountable as parents are to infants.":** Ralph Ross and Ernest van den Haag, *The Fabric of Society* (New York: Harcourt Brace, 1957), p. 23.

73. **"Like a dog!":** Franz Kafka, *The Trial*, trans. Breon Mitchell (Oxford: Oxford University Press, 2009), p. 165.

73. **Could he demoralize mutts?:** Demoralizing dogs is not, of course, the end goal; it is to help people who are suffering grave mental depression and to avert suicidal tendencies and child abuse. While experimenting with the dogs seems cruel, it is not an example of sadism, for the sadist wishes to witness suffering (contra Michael Vick). According to his biography, Seligman owns a few dogs and is presumably very kind to them. See also D. W. Rajecki, ed., *Comparing Behavior: Studying Man, Studying Animals* (Hillsdale, N.J.: Lawrence Erlbaum, 1983), chap. 4, pp. 67–102.

74. **They lay down, whined, and resigned themselves:** See Martin Seligman, *Helplessness: On Depression, Development, and Death* (New York: W. H. Freeman, 1975).

75. **he said her research was not original enough for Harvard's standards!:** Judith Rich Harris, *The Nurture Assumption* (New York: Simon & Schuster, 1998).

75. **suffered through the noise in about 50 percent of the instances:** Donald S. Hiroto and Martin Seligman, "Generality of Learned Helplessness in Man," *Journal of Personality and Social Psychology* 31, no. 2 (1975), pp. 311–27.

75. **the hobbled group later stumbled when trying to solve simple word problems:** Some psychologists, e.g., Jay Weiss, believe the humans and animals in these tests are more physically exhausted than morally exhausted, which could also explain their pathetic performance. See Howard I. Glazer and Jay M. Weiss, "Long-Term Interference Effect: An Alternative to Learned Helplessness," *Journal of Experimental Psychology* 2, no. 3 (July 1976), pp. 202–13.

76. **"God, grant me the serenity . . .":** Laurie Goodstein, "Once in Doubt, Credit for Prayer Won't Change," *New York Times*, November 28, 2009, p. A1.

76. **we bet more money!:** See D. S. Dunn and T. D. Wilson, "When the Stakes Are High: A Limit to the Illusion of Control Effect," *Social Cog-*

nition 8 (1991), pp. 305–23; and E. J. Langer, "The Illusion of Control," *Journal of Personality and Social Psychology* 32 (1974), pp. 311–28.

77. **they finished just one spot above dead last:** Richard Cohen, "Self-Esteem: Sorry, No Extra Credit," *Washington Post*, June 12, 1991, p. A23.

77. **to create order out of chaos:** Like the God of Genesis, human beings behold chaos, take action to create, and then hope to look upon it and say, "it was good." Perhaps this is what the Bible means when it says man was created in God's image (Imago Dei) to dominate the fish of the sea, the birds of the sky, and every animal that walks the earth. And this is the concept that Shakespeare toys with, teases, and tweaks in Hamlet, "What a piece of work is man! . . . in apprehension, how like a God?" William Shakespeare, *Hamlet*, act II, scene ii.

77. **The easier life was an easier path to the grave:** Judith Rodin and Ellen J. Langer, "Long-Term Effects of a Control-Relevant Intervention with the Institutionalized Aged," *Journal of Personality and Social Psychology* 35, no. 12 (1977), pp. 897–902.

78. **Thorstein Veblen . . . suggested:** See my *New Ideas from Dead Economists*, pp. 177–86.

79. **In 1963, *Time* magazine paid tribute to his work ethic:** "Hotels, By Golly!" *Time*, June 19, 1963.

79. **When I was doing research for a book on legendary CEOs:** Todd G. Buchholz, *New Ideas from Dead CEOs* (New York: HarperCollins, 2007), pp. 177–85.

80. **Wide-ranging surveys show:** Peter Kuhn and Fernando Lozano, "The Expanding Workweek? Understanding Trends in Long Work Hours Among U.S. Men, 1979–2004," NBER Working Paper 11895 (December 2005).

80. **Those with postgraduate degrees work more hours than those with bachelor degrees, who work more than high school graduates:** Lymari Morales, "Self-Employed Workers Clock the Most Hours Each Week," *Gallup*, August 26, 2009.

80. **vacation time is among the least envied features in the workplace:** Sara J. Solnick and David M. Hemenway, "Is More Always Better? A Survey on Positional Concerns," *Journal of Economic Behavior and Organization* 37, no. 3 (November 30, 1998), pp. 373–83.

81. **Self-employed people are 29 percent more likely to work over forty-four hours a week than the average, and 63 percent more likely than those who work at nonprofit foundations:** Ibid.

81. **France threw in the towel on the thirty-five-hour cap, which neither created more jobs nor more happiness:** Associated Press, "French Bid Au Revoir to 35-Hour Workweek," March 22, 2005.

82. **A random sample of over twenty-seven thousand Americans between 1972 and 2006 showed:** Tom W. Smith, "Job Satisfaction in America: Trends and Socio-Demographic Correlates," General Social Survey, University of Chicago (2007).

82. **Looking at similar data, Syracuse University's Arthur Brooks concluded:** Brooks, *Gross National Happiness*, p. 157.

84. **For achieving flow, the workplace beats listening to our favorite music or hanging out in our free time:** See John Haworth, *Work, Leisure and Well-Being* (London: Routledge, 1997), pp. 94–95.

84. **Do you ever wonder why Norman Mailer . . . ?:** F. Post, "Creativity and Psychopathology: A Study of 291 World-famous Men," *British Journal of Psychiatry* 165 (1994), pp. 22–34.

85. **Daniel Gilbert has cleverly noted:** Gilbert, *Stumbling on Happiness*, p. 24.

86. **People who do not feel responsible for their own success feel sadder 25 percent of the time:** Brooks, *Gross National Happiness*, p. 142.

88. **Mother Nature gives most of us the willies:** This revulsion seems universal, not just cultural. See R. M. Nesse, "Evolutionary Explanations of Emotions," *Human Nature* 1, no. 3 (1990), pp. 261–89.

88. **Darwin's father himself told young Charles:** Charles Darwin, *The Autobiography of Charles Darwin 1809–1882*, Nora Barlow, ed. With the original omissions restored. Edited and with appendix and notes by his granddaughter (London: Collins, 1958), p. 28. During a stormy summer vacation in 1816 in Lake Geneva with Lord Byron, Mary Shelley composed *Frankenstein; or, the Modern Prometheus*. Prometheus gave man fire, stealing power from the gods. Coincidentally, in the first sentence of her introduction to *Frankenstein*, Shelley thanks Charles Darwin's grandfather Erasmus for inspiring the idea of a monster come to life. Of course, to many people, including utopians, fundamentalists, and communitarians,

Charles Darwin has been playing the role of monster ever since *On the Origin of Species* arrived in 1859.

89. **He penned a cost-benefit analysis:** Darwin Correspondence Project, "Darwin's Notes on Marriage"; available at www.darwinproject .ac.uk/darwins-notes-on-marriage.

89. **people will spend 50 percent of their income on food:** P. Rozin, "Towards a Psychology of Food and Eating," *Current Directions in Psychological Science* 5 (1996), pp. 18–24.

90. **a friend drew wonderful cartoons of Charles:** A traveling exhibit of Darwin materials has been touring the world since 2009, including .many of the letters and artifacts mentioned here.

91. **He surmised that the finches had adapted:** Darwin was not the first to see species adapt. The ideas of Jean-Baptiste Pierre Antoine de Monet de Lamarck (1744–1829) were well known. But Lamarck argued that a species could pass on acquired traits. For instance, if a giraffe stretches to reach a leaf, it might stretch his neck, and then give birth to longer-necked baby giraffes.

91. **Darwin had read *An Essay on Population* by the English economist Thomas Malthus:** See my *New Ideas from Dead Economists*, chap. 3.

92. **Ironically, the man . . . was fitted with fits and proved most unfit:** Coincidentally, around the same time Darwin suffered, another intellectual revolutionary, Karl Marx, sat in the British Museum scratching his own carbuncles. Marx turned out to be a fan of Darwin and sent an inscribed copy of *Das Kapital* to Down House, which was later found in Darwin's library.

92. **"explains everything. . . . But you must read it.":** Benjamin Disraeli, *Tancred* (1847), reprinted by Kessinger Publishing, 2004, p. 93.

92. **Darwin fretted:** Francis Darwin, ed., *The Life and Letters of Charles Darwin*, vol. II (London: John Murray, 1887), pp. 117–18; also available at www.darwin-online.org.uk.

93. **"Everybody is interested in pigeons,":** "Darwin's Pigeons"; available at www.darwinspigeons.com/#/john-murray/4535045590.

93. **Thomas Henry Huxley declared:** Letter of T. H. Huxley to Charles Darwin, November 23, 1859.

94. **Polly apparently had a very expressive face:** Francis Darwin,

ed., *The Life and Letters of Charles Darwin*, vol. I (New York: Appleton, 1887), p. 92.

95. **Steven Pinker has pointed out:** Pinker, *The Blank Slate*, p. 316.

95. **Studies on patriarchal and matrilineal societies show:** Uri Gneezy, Kenneth L. Leonard, and John A. List, "Gender Differences in Competition: Evidence from a Matrilineal and a Patriarchal Society," *Econometrica* 77, no. 5 (2009), pp. 1637–64.

96. **psychologists report:** See J. D. Duntley and D. M. Buss, "The Plausibility of Adaptations for Homicide," in P. Caruthers, S. Laurence, and S. Stitch, eds., *The Innate Mind; Structure and Contents* (New York: Oxford, 2005), pp. 291–304.

98. **"horrific pictures . . . from the legends of childhood.":** Quoted in David Livingstone Smith, *The Most Dangerous Animal: Human Nature and the Origins of War* (New York: St. Martin's Press, 2007), p. 163.

98. **Among these critics is . . . Frans de Waal:** Frans B. M. de Waal, "A Century of Getting to Know the Chimpanzee," *Nature* 427 (September 2005), p. 57: "Initially, skeptics attributed chimpanzee 'warfare' to competition over the food that researchers provided."

99. **The founder of a bonobo support group stood up at the yoga club and said:** Ian Parker, "Swingers," *New Yorker*, July 30, 2007.

99. **Leonard Bernstein served Roquefort cheese hors d'oeuvres to the Black Panthers:** Tom Wolfe, *Radical Chic and Mau-Mauing the Flak Catchers* (New York: Bantam, 1999), p. 2.

99. **He points out:** Frans de Waal, "Our Kinder, Gentler Ancestors," *Wall Street Journal*, October 3–4, 2009, p. W3.

100. **the MRIs showed a glow coming from the primitive limbic brain:** Shankar Vedantam, "If It Feels Good to Be Good, It Might Be Only Natural," *Washington Post*, May 28, 2007, p. A1.

100. **Several studies show:** Jorge Moll and Jay Schulkin, "Social Attachment and Aversion in Human Moral Cognition," *Neuroscience and Biobehavioral Reviews* 33, no. 3 (2009), pp. 456–65; Jorge Moll et al., "Human Fronto-Mesolimbic Networks Guide Decisions About Charitable Donation," *Proceedings of the National Academy of Sciences* 103, no. 42 (October 17, 2006), pp. 15623–28; and D. Tankersley et al., "Altruism Is

Associated with an Increased Response to Agency," *Nature Neuroscience* 10, no. 2 (February 2007), pp. 150–51.

101. **thirty-four volunteers were 80 percent more generous:** P. J. Zak, A. A. Stanton, and S. Ahmadi, "Oxytocin Increases Generosity in Humans," *PLoS ONE* 2, no. 11 (2007), e1128, doi:10.1371/journal .pone.0001128.

101. **"How many goodly creatures. . . . O brave new world! That has such people in't!":** William Shakespeare, *The Tempest*, act V, scene 1.

102. **Keltner asserts:** Keltner, *Born to Be Good*, p. 230.

102. **the research is somewhat mixed:** Though Keltner cites Eisenberg's research, in the *Handbook of Child Psychology*, Eisenberg cites children's studies showing a negative relationship between vagal activity and sympathetic behavior. Possibly, the vagal connection strengthens with age. N. Eisenberg, ed., *Handbook of Child Psychology*, vol. 3, 6th ed. (New York: Wiley, 2006), pp. 693–94.

102. **He concludes:** Keltner, *Born to Be Good*, p. x.

102. **"I had come here to shoot at 'Fascists,' but a man who is holding up his trousers isn't a 'fascist' . . . and you don't feel like shooting at him.":** George Orwell, *The Collected Essays, Journalism & Letters— Volume 2: My Country Right or Left 1940–1943*, Sonia Orwell and Ian Angus, eds. (New York: Harcourt, Brace & World, 1968), p. 254.

103. **Keltner writes:** Keltner, *Born to Be Good*, p. 24.

103. **He reported:** Charles Darwin, *The Voyage of the Beagle* (New York: P. F. Collier, 1909), p. 228.

104. **mothers and fathers owned small farms that served as family and business units:** See D. Brendan Nagle, *The Household as the Foundation of Aristotle's Polis* (Cambridge: Cambridge University Press, 2006).

104. **That's why he stated:** *The Politics of Aristotle*, VII, iv, 1326b.

104. **In Keltner's book:** Keltner, *Born to Be Good*, pp. 3–4.

107. **a twelfth-century AD burial ground revealed the remains of twelve humans:** Amelie A. Walker, "Anasazi Cannibalism?" *Archaeology* 50, no. 5 (September/October 1997).

107. **In New Guinea today:** Gilbert H. Herdt, *Secrecy and Cultural*

Reality: Utopian Ideologies of the New Guinea Men's House (Ann Arbor: University of Michigan Press, 2003).

108. **Chinese locals ground them up into medicines:** Noel Thomas Boaz and Russell Ciochon, *Dragon Bone Hill: An Ice-Age Saga of Homo Erectus* (New York: Oxford, 2004).

108. **In Alan Bennett's brilliant play *The History Boys*, the old schoolteacher recalls:** Alan Bennett, *The History Boys* (London: Faber and Faber, 2004), p. 55.

108. **modern scholars have a tendency to romanticize:** Napoleon A. Chagnon, "Chronic Problems in Understanding Tribal Violence and Warfare," in Gregory R. Bock and Jamie A. Goode, eds., *Genetics of Criminal and Antisocial Behavior* (New York: Wiley/Novartis, 2007).

109. **the murder rate among the Bushmen surpassed Baltimore's many times over:** Grant S. McCall and Nancy Shields, "Examining the Evidence from Small-scale Societies and Early Prehistory and Implications for Modern Theories of Aggression and Violence," *Aggression and Violent Behavior* 13, no. 1 (January–February 2008), pp. 1–9.

114. **The Book of Ecclesiastes states:** Ecclesiastes 10:18.

115. **Do you want to take the *risk* of working only four hours?:** I recognize that the book's author, Timothy Ferriss, emphasizes clever ways to reduce the wasted time at work, which sounds prudent.

116. **authors of an international study on cognitive ability point out:** Susann Rohwedder and Robert J. Willis, "Mental Retirement," *Journal of Economic Perspectives* 24, no. 1 (Winter 2010), p. 137.

117. **Eric Hoffer observed:** Eric Hoffer, *The True Believer: Thoughts on the Nature of Mass Movements* (New York: Harper and Row, 1951).

117. **some hated the work and others loved it:** See A. Wrzesniewski, C. R. McCauley, P. Rozin, and B. Schwartz, "Jobs, Careers, and Callings: People's Relations to Their Work," *Journal of Research in Personality* 31 (1997), pp. 21–33.

118. **a UK study showed:** City & Guilds (UK) Happiness Index, 2007; available at www.cityandguilds.com/2342.html.

118. **A W. H. Auden poem states:** W. H. Auden, *Horae Canonicae*, sext.

118. **In a celebrated scene:** Mark Twain, *The Adventures of Tom Sawyer*, chap. 2.

119. **Marie Jahoda and her new husband, Paul Lazarsfeld, began regular visits to a depressed community:** Marie Jahoda, Paul F. Lazarsfeld, Hans Zeisel, and Christian Fleck, *Marienthal*, 4th ed. (New Brunswick: Transaction Publishers, 2002); and C. H. Feinstein, Peter Temin, and Gianni Toniolo, *The World Economy Between the World Wars* (New York: Oxford, 2008), p. 118.

120. **Support for the Nazi Party closely tracked the rising unemployment rate:** See Christian Stogbauer, "The Radicalization of the German Electorate," *European Review of Economic History* 5, no. 2 (2001), pp. 251–80.

120. **Arthur Brooks cites data:** Brooks, *Gross National Happiness*, p. 167.

121. **"Hurray for Herbert Hoover!":** Though I recommend a satirical musical called *Hoover Comes Alive!*, written by Sean Cunningham, music by Michael Friedman, directed by Alex Timbers.

123. **story of young Estée Lauder:** Buchholz, *New Ideas from Dead CEOs*, pp. 85–86.

124. **St. Augustine assured believers:** Augustine, *City of God*, Book XX, chap. 19.

124. **"the mills of the gods grind slowly but exceedingly small.":** From ancient Greek to a seventeenth-century German poem by Friedrich von Logau, later translated by Longfellow.

125. **Bertrand Russell . . . said:** Bertrand Russell, *Power: A New Social Analysis* (London: George Allen & Unwin Ltd., 1938).

128. **People stop trusting and trading:** Todd G. Buchholz, "Revolution, Reputation Effects, and Time Horizons," *Cato Journal* 8, no. 1 (Spring/ Summer 1988), pp. 185–97.

128. **Older children and girls score higher than boys:** Eric Bettinger and Robert Slonim, "Patience Among Children," *Journal of Public Economics* 91, no. 1–2 (February 2007), pp. 343–63.

129. **Because a better axe or a second axe will be surrendered to the chief, deleting any incentive to improve:** Tim Ingold, David Riches,

and James Woodburn, eds., *Hunters and Gatherers* (Oxford: Berg, 1997), p. 16.

129. **Amanda Wingfield from *The Glass Menagerie*, who warns:** Tennessee Williams, *The Glass Menagerie*, act 3, scene 5.

129. **the Mikea cite proverbs:** Bram Tucker, Daniel Steck, and Jaovola Tombo, "Experimental Evidence for Time Preference Among Mikea Forager-Farmers" (working paper, 2004).

130. **This solves the puzzle of the Great Depression:** See my *New Ideas from Dead Economists*, p. 200.

130. **comparing interest rates from Bronze Age Sumer to ancient Greece shows:** Michael Hudson, "How Interest Rates Were Set, 2500 BC–1000 AD," *Journal of the Economic and Social History of the Orient* 43 (Spring 2000), pp. 132–61.

130. **the temple could attach the property:** John Day, *An Economic History of Athens Under Roman Domination* (New York: Columbia University, 1942), pp. 57–61.

131. **Shakespeare set the bitter money-lending of *The Merchant of Venice* in Italy:** Of course, Shylock could not have been in London because England had banished Jews in 1290. For data, see Sidney Homer and Richard Sylla, *A History of Interest Rates*, 3rd ed. (New Brunswick, N.J.: Rutgers, 1996), pp. 119–21.

132. **Robert Wright correctly argues:** Robert Axelrod, *The Evolution of Cooperation* (New York: Basic Books, 1984).

132. **Thucydides, the great historian of the Peloponnesian War, spelled out his case:** Thucydides, *History of the Peloponnesian War*, trans. Richard Crawley (London: J. M. Dent & Sons, 1914), p. 2.

134. **humans can identify a sibling by scent:** G. E. Weisfeld, T. Czilli, K. A. Phillips, J. A. Gall, and C. M. Lichtman, "Possible Olfaction-based Mechanism in Human Kin Recognition and Inbreeding Avoidance," *Journal of Experimental Child Psychology* 85, no. 3 (July 2003), pp. 279–95.

135. **Hamilton's idea can be stated in a simple equation:** William D. Hamilton, "The Genetical Evolution of Social Behavior," *Journal of Theoretical Biology* 7, no. 1 (1964), pp. 1–52.

136. **we sometimes snip that wire:** In *Oedipus*, a young man unknowingly kills his father. There is, of course, great rivalry among siblings

among animals and men. Baby hyenas have large, deadly teeth and often demonstrate their use on weaker siblings.

136. **According to Plutarch:** Plutarch, *On the Fortune or the Virtue of Alexander*, vol. IV (Loeb Classical Library, 1936), p. 6. Alexander did not take Aristotle's nationalistic advice and instead tried to follow the more universalist precepts of Zeno the Stoic.

136. **The Old Testament sounds more kindly:** Genesis 15:13; Deuteronomy 1:16; Leviticus 19:10. The stranger must be given food and shelter, and must be allowed to harvest crops from the corner of the fields. And yet, there is a difference. The Bible specifically forbids lending money at interest to neighbors: "If thou lend money to any of My people, even to the poor with thee, thou shalt not be to him a creditor; neither shall ye lay upon him interest." Nor may Israelites lend at interest to non-Jews. However, Deuteronomy gives one exception: Israelites may lend to itinerant merchants. This division led to a bizarre result: the Israelite could legally finance the economic development of others, but not the economic development of his brothers. The Old and New Testaments recognized a basic human impulse to treat relatives and neighbors best. That's probably why it included so many passages reminding people to care for the stranger, too. In the Gospel of Luke, Simon fails to welcome Jesus and to provide water for Jesus to wash his feet, his omission of hospitality a terrible act in the desert. To ancient Greeks, hospitality was so important, Zeus himself oversaw the industry (a precursor to Caesars Palace in Las Vegas), and Zeno the Stoic expressed enthusiastic feelings about it.

137. **they have exalted shared characteristics—blood, history, culture, language:** Go to a baseball game. When a Red Sox slugger comes to the plate, fans jump to their feet, but not because of a logical calculation. Neural scans show that the emotional part of their brain is humming. But if the same Red Sox fans watch, say, the Orioles and the Angels, their brains are basically idling. See Mina Cikara, Matthew Botvinick, and Susan Fiske, "Neural Responses to Rival Group's Pleasures and Pains" (paper presented at the Behavioral Decision Research in Management Conference, Carnegie Mellon University, June 11, 2010).

137. **Henry V's rallying cry at Agincourt:** Shakespeare, *Henry V*, act 4, scene 3.

139. **estimates Paul Zak and Stephen Knack:** Stephen Knack and Paul J. Zak, "Building Trust: Public Policy, Interpersonal Trust and Economic Development," *Supreme Court Economic Review* 10 (2003), p. 92.

139. **that would raise the present value of family wealth by roughly $20,000:** I calculate the present value of a 1 percent increase in family income at a discount rate of 3 percent.

142. **An exhaustive study of indigenous peoples asked:** Lawrence H. Keeley, *War Before Civilization* (New York: Oxford, 1996).

143. **The one who had killed sired more children:** Napoleon Chagnon, "Life Histories, Blood Revenge, and Warfare in a Tribal Population," *Science* 239 (1988), pp. 985–92. Robert Wright's cogent and entertaining *Nonzero* describes how war spread innovation.

143. **Pepys famously wrote:** Robert Latham and William Matthews, eds., *The Diary of Samuel Pepys*, Volume I: Introduction and 1660 (London: Bell & Hyman, 1970).

144. **top-rated television program in the United States, France, and Australia is the same:** Amy Chozick, "Deconstructing TV's No. 1 Show," *Wall Street Journal*, December 11, 2009, p. W1.

144. **Homicide rates in Europe today are perhaps one-tenth the rate of the year AD 1300:** See, e.g., Barbara A. Hanawalt, *Crime and Conflict in English Communities, 1300–1348* (Cambridge, Mass.: Harvard University Press, 1979).

145. **The Hiwi of Venezuela work . . . achieving just 1,705 calories per day:** See Kim R. Hill, A. Magdalena Hurtado, and R. S. Walker, "High Adult Mortality Among Hiwi Hunter-Gathers: Implications for Human Evolution," *Journal of Human Evolution* 52, no. 4 (April 2007), pp. 443–54; and A. Magdalena Hurtado and Kim R. Hill, "Early Dry Season Subsistence Ecology of Cuiva (Hiwi) Foragers of Venezuela," *Human Ecology* 15, no. 2 (1987), pp. 163–87.

147. **Lewis notes:** *The Journals of the Lewis and Clark Expedition*, Vol. 4, Gary E. Moulton, ed. (Lincoln, Neb.: Bison Books, 2002), Wednesday May 29, 1805.

147. *Science* **magazine reported a fascinating study:** Joseph Henrich et al., "Markets, Religion, Community Size, and the Evolution of

Fairness and Punishment," *Science* 327, no. 5972 (March 19, 2010), pp. 1480–84.

148. **The sandwich later fetched $28,000 on eBay:** BBC News, "Virgin Mary Toast Fetches $28,000," November 23, 2004.

149. **"hot hand" in basketball is really in the eye of the beholder:** Still, I suspect there is something to the "hot hand," but it is different from what Lehrer and others describe. When we say that, e.g., Kobe Bryant has a hot hand, we mean that he was more likely to score a third basket in a row after hitting two than someone else playing the game. We assume that the odds of a third basket go down, but less so for Kobe Bryant than for other players on the court. He has a relative hot hand, not an absolute hot hand. See Jonah Lehrer, "The Illusion of Streaks"; available at http://scienceblogs.com/cortex/2008/03/the_illusion_of_streaks.php.

150. **Zajonc discovered:** See Jennifer L. Monahan, Sheila T. Murphy, and R. B. Zajonc, "Subliminal Mere Exposure: Specific, General, and Diffuse Effects," *Psychological Science* 11, no. 6 (November 2000), p. 462.

151. **A University College, London, study showed:** Eleanor A. Maguire et al., "Navigation-Related Structural Change in the Hippocampi of Taxi Drivers," *Proceedings of the National Academy of Science* 97, no. 8 (April 11, 2000), pp. 4398–4403.

151. **When the head of Cab Drivers Club learned about the research, he said:** BBC News, "Taxi Drivers' Brains 'Grow' on the Job," March 14, 2000.

153. **He quoted Bama Athreya:** Randy Cohen, "The Ethicist," *New York Times Magazine*, July 10, 2007.

153. **Rivoli points out:** Pietra Rivoli, *The Travels of a T-Shirt in the Global Economy* (New York: Wiley, 2006), p. 240.

154. **historically it had been practiced whenever food was short:** James Z. Lee and Cameron Campbell, *Fate and Fortune in Rural China: Social Organization and Population Behavior in Liaoning: 1774–1873* (Cambridge: Cambridge University Press, 1997).

154. **the richer half of the population fathered 40 percent more children:** See Gregory Clark, *A Farewell to Alms* (Princeton: Princeton University Press, 2007), pp. 116–23.

154. **the hereafter became subsumed in the here and now:** See

Max Weber, *The Protestant Ethic and the Spirit of Capitalism*, trans. Talcott Parsons (New York: Scribner's, 1958). A recent empirical paper by David Cantoni at Harvard did not substantiate Weber's hypothesis, "The Economic Effects of the Protestant Reformation: Testing the Weber Hypothesis in the German Lands," November 2009.

155. **More people means more geniuses:** See the work of Michael Kremer, e.g., "Population Growth and Technological Changes: One Million B.C. to 1990," *Quarterly Journal of Economics* 108, no. 3 (August 1993), pp. 681–716.

156. **The "Flynn effect" shows:** James R. Flynn, "The Mean IQ of Americans: Massive Gains 1932 to 1978," *Psychological Bulletin* 95, no. 1 (1984), pp. 29–51.

158. **life expectancy was just thirty-three years, and they would stand several inches shorter:** See Clark, *A Farewell to Alms*, p. 283.

159. **Hayek's article uses a striking quotation from Alfred North Whitehead:** F. A. Hayek, "The Use of Knowledge in Society," *American Economic Review* 35 (September 1945), pp. 526–28.

160. **Researchers showed that we perceive tastes and smells more strongly when they are contrasted:** Edmund T. Rolls, "Brain Mechanisms Underlying Flavour and Appetite," *Philosophical Transactions of the Royal Society* 361 (2006), pp. 1123–36.

161. **he will suddenly perk up for one more round of rodent sex:** R. E Brown, "Sexual Arousal, the Coolidge Effect and Dominance in the Rat (Rattus norvegicus)," *Animal Behaviour* 22, no. 3 (1974), pp. 634–37.

163. **A study of hundreds of British dairy farms showed:** Catherine Bertenshaw and Peter Rowlinson, "Exploring Stock Managers' Perceptions of the Human-Animal Relationship on Dairy Farms and an Association with Milk Production," *Anthrozoos* 22, no. 1 (March 2009), pp. 59–69.

166. **type A personalities:** While the idea of a simple type A personality has been discredited in research, it still serves a useful purpose, since we all encounter extra-competitive types.

166. **The Americans lost seventy-one:** Walter R. Borneman, *1812: The War That Forged a Nation* (New York: HarperCollins, 2004).

168. **Studies at Johns Hopkins found:** Janet DiPietro, "Prenatal/

Perinatal Stress and Its Impact on Psychosocial Child Development," *Encyclopedia of Early Childhood Development* (June 3, 2002); available at www.enfant-encyclopedie.com/Pages/PDF/DiPietroANGxp.pdf.

168. **slow walking causes obesity almost as much as obesity causes slow walking:** This is not the right book in which to explore the physiological effects that cause slow walking, which causes obesity.

168. **research has shown that fidgety people tend to weigh less:** James A. Levine, Sara J. Schleusner, and Michael D. Jensen, "Energy Expenditure of Nonexercise Activity," *American Journal of Clinical Nutrition* 72, no. 6 (December 2000), pp. 1451–54.

168. **a six-year Australian study:** D. W. Dunstan, E. L. M. Barr, G. N. Healy, J. Salmon, J. E. Shaw, B. Balkau, D. J. Magliano, A. J. Cameron, P. Z. Zimmet, and N. Owen, "Television Viewing Time and Mortality: The Australian Diabetes, Obesity and Lifestyle Study," *Circulation* 121, no. 3 (January 2010), pp. 384–91.

169. **It's a friendly enzyme because it draws fat to your muscles, where it can be burned as fuel:** Ron Winslow, "Watching TV Linked to Higher Risk of Death," *Wall Street Journal* (January 12, 2010), p. D4.

169. **Scientists showed that a lazy twin has shorter telomeres:** Lynn F. Cherkas et al., "The Association Between Physical Activity in Leisure Time and Leukocyte Telomere Length," *Archives of Internal Medicine* 168, no. 2 (2008), pp. 154–58.

169. **Michelangelo's magnificent *Moses:*** To raise funds, the church has turned *Moses* into the world's classiest peep show, where you must deposit coins in order for a spotlight to shine on the statue.

172. **psychologist Walter Cannon coined:** Walter B. Cannon, *Bodily Changes in Pain, Hunger, Fear and Rage*, 2nd ed. (New York: Appleton-Century-Croft, 1929). As for the impact of stress on extremities, in Claudia Shear's play *Restoration*, the restorer of Michelangelo's *David* explains his modest genitalia by pointing out that the stress of confronting Goliath would do that to a man.

172. **He noticed their adrenal glands were enlarged:** Vinay Joshi, *Stress* (London: Sage Publications, 2005), p. 31.

172. **There are some studies that do show:** Sheena S. Iyengar and

Mark R. Lepper, "When Choice Is Demotivating: Can One Desire Too Much of a Good Thing?" *Journal of Personality and Social Psychology* 79, no. 6 (2000), pp. 995–1006.

174. **Salvatore Maddi, who conducted the research at the University of Chicago, developed the concept of hardiness:** Salvatore R. Maddi, "The Story of Hardiness: Twenty Years of Theorizing, Research and Practice," *Consulting Psychology Journal* 54, no. 3 (2002), pp. 173–85.

175. **I frequently lecture:** See Robert Zajonc, "Social Facilitation," *Science* 149, no. 3681 (1965), pp. 269–74.

175. **Grandpa Sam responded, "Why don't you say something funny?":** For years, I thought my grandpa Sam, who was very witty, must have been very impolite to Danny Lewis. Then I read Jerry Lewis's autobiography and figured that Danny got off lucky and deserved worse.

175. **You can go online today and order your own "Rat helplessness chamber.":** www.lafayetteneuroscience.com/product_detail.asp?ItemID=872.

176. **Men in their twenties and thirties are almost 40 percent more likely to voluntarily switch:** James Sherk, "Job-to-Job Transitions," Center for Data Analysis Report Nos. 08-06 (September 2008).

176. **The average American holds more than a dozen jobs over a lifetime, more than ten by age forty-two:** www.bls.gov/nls/y79r-22jobsbyedu.pdf.

176. **Every year about 50 million Americans move homes. . . . Almost half of those moves are across county lines, state boundaries, or from overseas:** See Jason Schachter, "Geographic Mobility," Current Population Reports (U.S. Department of Commerce, March 2001).

176. **We could make it even easier:** See my *Bringing the Jobs Home* (New York: Penguin, 2004), chap. 5.

177. **when spouses hurl epithets or lamps at each other, their antibodies hide:** See Robert Glaser and Janice Kiecolt-Glaser, eds., *Handbook of Human Stress and Immunity* (New York: Academic Press, 1994), pp. 321–39.

177. **A sour roommate can do so pretty easily:** Cameron Anderson, Dacher Keltner, and Oliver P. John, "Emotional Convergence Between People Over Time," *Journal of Personality and Social Psychology* 84, no. 5 (2003), pp. 1054–68.

178. **Jared Diamond's best-selling books point to ecological explanations:** Jared Diamond, *Guns, Germs, and Steel: The Fates of Human Societies* (New York: W. W. Norton & Company, 1997).

179. **Mark Twain's description of this arid and empty land:** In *Innocents Abroad*, Twain says about Palestine that "such dismal desolation cannot surely exist elsewhere on earth" (p. 361), calling it a "silent, mournful expanse" (p. 283). Mark Twain, *Innocents Abroad*, vol. 1, Lawrence Teacher, ed. (Philadelphia: Courage, 1997).

179. **Israel . . . has more companies listed on the NASDAQ than any other but for the United States:** See Dan Senor and Saul Singer, *Start-Up Nation* (New York: Twelve, 2009).

181. **David Brooks in the *New York Times* observed:** David Brooks, "The Underlying Tragedy," *New York Times*, January 15, 2010, p. A21.

181. **Venezuela's own oil minister called oil "the devil's excrement" and predicted that "oil will bring us ruin.":** Jerry Useem, "The Devil's Excrement," *Fortune*, February 3, 2003. Norway has been an exception, prudently investing its oil revenues.

183. **The report looked at 108 countries between 1960 and 1999:** Simeon Djankov, Jose G. Montalvo, and Marta Reynal-Querol, "The Curse of Aid," World Bank (April 2005).

187. **They traditionally made much of their income hauling in fish from the sea, but in the off-season they found alternate work:** Reuven Brenner, *The Force of Finance* (New York: Texere, 2001), p. 52.

187. **From 1963 to 1973, welfare caseloads in New Brunswick more than doubled, and they jumped 85 percent in Nova Scotia:** N. Swan, P. MacRae, and C. Steinberg, "Income Maintenance Programs: Their Effect on Labour Supply and Aggregate Demand in the Maritimes: A Joint Report of the Council of Maritime Premiers and the Economic Council of Canada," Economic Council of Canada (Ottawa, ON, 1976).

187. **"two sets of books . . . (plus another for Stalin when he was alive).":** Michael J. Boskin, "Don't Like the Numbers? Change 'Em," *Wall Street Journal*, January 13, 2010.

188. **Happy Planet Index:** S. Abdallah, S. Thompson, J. Michaelson, N. Marks, N. Steuer, et al., "The Happy Planet Index 2.0," New Economics Foundation (2009).

188. **A study by the OECD asked exactly those questions:** Romina Boarini, Asa Johansson, and Marco Mira d'Ercole, "Alternative Measures of Well-Being," OECD Social, Employment and Migration Working Paper no. 33 (February 17, 2006), p. 30.

189. *60 Minutes* **had a study in hand:** *CBS News, 60 Minutes,* "And the Happiest Place on Earth Is . . .," February 17, 2008.

189. **he was often despondent and repressed:** Jens Andersen, *Hans Christian Andersen: A New Life,* trans. Tiina Nunnally (New York: Overlook Press, 2006).

189. **the birth replacement rate has been negative, according to the government:** Otto Andersen, "Denmark—Official Denmark—Population," Royal Danish Ministry of Foreign Affairs (2002).

190. **the government admits:** Ibid.

190. **reporters did not report finding overwhelming friendliness:** *CBS News, 60 Minutes,* "And the Happiest Place on Earth Is . . ."

190. **Benjamin Radcliff would nod vigorously, for he says:** Benjamin Radcliff, "Politics, Markets, and Life Satisfaction: The Political Economy of Human Happiness," *American Political Science Review* 95, no. 4 (December 2001), p. 941.

190. **Among various studies:** Harris Interactive Poll #55, "Americans Remain More Optimistic and Satisfied with Life Than Europeans," July 20, 2005.

191. **Alice Isen observed doctors diagnosing patient symptoms:** Carlos A. Estrada, Alice M. Isen, and Mark J. Young, "Positive Affect Improves Creative Problem Solving and Influences Reported Source of Practice Satisfaction in Physicians," *Motivation and Emotions* 18, no. 4 (December 1994), pp. 285–99.

196. *Glengarry Glen Ross:* *Glengarry Glen Ross,* written by David Mamet, directed by James Foley (1992).

199. **In 2005, twelve thousand workers were enrolled in the bank, with each costing the company $100,000 to $130,000 annually:** Jeffrey McCracken, "Idle Hands: Detroit's Symbol of Dysfunction," *Wall Street Journal,* March 1, 2006.

199. **His dissertation topic: GM, the UAW, and the city of Flint:** Ibid.

203. **Sony ordered the American workers merely to reassemble television sets:** Sea-Jin Chang and Philip M. Rosenzweig, "A Process Model for MNC Evolution: The Case of Sony Corporation in the United States," Institute for Applied Studies in International Management, Working Paper 95-9 (1995).

204. **golf courses on the other side of the world:** Robertson's two golf courses in New Zealand were named the third and eleventh best in the world in "The Top 25 Golf Courses in the World 2008"; available at www.saveamillionshots.com/stories/the-top-25-golf-courses-world-2008.

205. **He "came to castrate. . . . Animals who mark their territory by urination were subtler than Martin.":** Chris Jaffe, *Evaluating Baseball's Managers* (Jefferson, N.C.: McFarland, 2009).

210. **Julius E. Heuscher published a book called *A Psychiatric Study of Myths and Fairy Tales* (from which Bruno Bettelheim seems to have plagiarized . . .):** See Julius E. Heuscher, *A Psychiatric Study of Myths and Fairy Tales* (Springfield, Ill.: Charles C. Thomas, 1963); Bruno Bettelheim, *The Uses of Enchantment* (New York: Penguin, 1976); Richard Pollak, *The Creation of Dr. B* (New York: Simon & Schuster, 1998), pp. 345–46; Nina Sutton, *Bettelheim* (New York: Knopf, 1995); and Robert Alan Segal, *Theorizing About Myth* (Boston: University of Massachusetts, 1999).

210. **Heuscher points to lessons:** Heuscher, *A Psychiatric Study of Myths and Fairy Tales*, p. 85.

211. **the studies showed:** See Roy F. Baumeister, Jennifer D. Campbell, Joachim I. Krueger, and Kathleen D. Vohs, "Does High Self-Esteem Cause Better Performance, Interpersonal Success, Happiness, or Healthier Lifestyles?" *Psychological Science in the Public Interest* 4, no. 1 (May 2003).

211. **Now most automobile drivers are convinced they are more skillful than the guy in the next lane, and should therefore be allowed to drive faster:** D. Walton and J. Bathurst, "An Exploration of the Perceptions of the Average Driver's Speed Compared to Perceived Driver Safety and Driving Skills," *Accident Analysis and Prevention* 30 (1998), pp. 821–30.

211. **Cloninger has been able to train mice:** Debra A. Gusnard, C. Robert Cloninger, et al., "Persistence and Brain Circuitry," *PNAS* 100, no. 6 (March 18, 2003), pp. 3479–84.

212. **The theory posits:** See, e.g., Krzysztof Nowakowski, "Psychopathy vs. Emotional Intelligence in Penitentiary Recidivists," *Problems of Forensic Sciences* 79, no. 79 (2009), pp. 283–93.

213. **Twenge . . . updated the study with new data in 2009:** See Jean M. Twenge and W. Keith Campbell, *The Narcissism Epidemic: Living in the Age of Entitlement* (New York: Free Press, 2009).

214. **Consider this contrast:** See also Cam Marston, *Motivating the "What's in It for Me?" Workforce* (New York: Wiley, 2007).

214. **Jean Twenge's research points exactly to these differences:** Jean M. Twenge, *Generation Me* (New York: Free Press, 2006), p. 69.

214. **According to a survey for careerbuilder.com:** Ron Alsop, "The 'Trophy Kids' Go to Work," *Wall Street Journal*, October 21, 2008.

214. **A disgruntled young Yale grad, feeling rather entitled, wrote a book:** Anya Kamenetz, *Generation Debt: Why Now Is a Terrible Time to Be Young* (New York: Riverhead, 2002).

216. **the city council passed a law:** ABC News Online, "Council Bans Goldfish Bowls," July 24, 2004.

220. **"Wherever you go, there you are.":** The quotation may have come by way of Confucius.

222. **Here's a real-life example:** Laurie Roberts, "State Rushes in Where Outlaws Dare to Braid," *Arizona Republic*, March 17, 2004. The case created enough publicity that the state legislature eventually adjusted the law to let Ms. Farmer off the hook and free to braid.

223. **most of them showed that it's pretty easy to trick them:** Since the brain's cognitive control system does not fully develop until a person reaches his mid-twenties, experiments on students should have an asterisk next to them if they are intended to create inferences for the adult population.

223. **those with high Social Security numbers bid more:** Lawrence E. Williams and John A. Bargh, "Experiencing Physical Warmth Promotes Interpersonal Warmth," *Science* 322, no. 5901 (October 24, 2008), pp. 606–7; and Daniel Ariely, *Predictably Irrational* (New York: HarperCollins, 2008), pp. 26–28.

223. **Former chef Anthony Bourdain:** Anthony Bourdain, *Kitchen Confidental* (New York: Bloomsbury, 2000).

224. **In 1998 an experimenter sent students into a classroom:**

Thomas Gilovich, Kenneth Savitsky, and Victoria Husted Medvec, "The Spotlight Effect in Social Judgment," *Journal of Personality and Social Psychology* 78, no. 2 (2000), pp. 212–15.

225. **Franklin stated a general principle:** Benjamin Franklin, *The Autobiography of Ben Franklin*, as given in *Benjamin Franklin: Writings*, J. A. Leo Lemay, ed. (New York: Library of America, 1987), p. 1404; and J. Jecker and D. Landy, "Liking a Person as Function of Doing Him a Favor," *Human Relations* 22 (1969), pp. 371–78.

226. **It becomes a "character trait . . . you're going to be fifty dollars short, huh?'":** Chris Rock, *Rock This!* (New York: Hyperion, 1997), pp. 91–92.

227. **People who use cash spend 14 percent less:** See James A. Roberts, "Money Attitudes, Credit Card Use and Compulsive Buying Among American College Students," *Journal of Consumer Affairs* (December 22, 2001).

228. **Only 40 percent of Generation Y . . . pay their bills on time:** National Foundation for Credit Counseling 2010 survey, cited in Christine Dugas, "'Generation Y' Faces Some Steep Financial Hurdles," *USA Today*, April 23–25, 2010, p. A2.

228. **Two parts of the brain are at war:** "Teenage Risk-Taking: Biological and Inevitable?" *Science Daily* 12 (April 2007).

228. **the results can be terribly disappointing:** Though many writers and commentators claim that credit cards spur additional spending among adults, research is not overwhelming. In Jonah Lehrer's *How We Decide*, Carnegie Mellon's George Loewenstein is quoted saying, "The nature of credit cards ensures that your brain is anesthetized against the pain of payment." Yet Loewenstein conducted a recent field study that showed, "surprisingly . . . credit cards do not increase spending." See George Loewenstein and Elif Incekara Hafalir, "The Impact of Credit Cards on Spending," Working Paper, April 13, 2009.

228. **Chris Rock provides some further profound thoughts:** *Chris Rock: Never Scared*, HBO Special, written by Chris Rock, directed by Joel Gallen (2004).

229. **according to his biographer:** James S. Hirsch, *Willie Mays* (New York: Scribner's, 2010), p. 549.

231. **Almost all products have fallen in price:** www.census.gov/
population/socdemo/well-being/2005-tables/tab1.xls; and Mark J. Perry,
"The Rich Are Getting Richer and the Poor Are Getting Richer," Enterprise
Blog, December 1, 2009.

231. **People who give their time or their money to charity are 40
to 45 percent more likely to say they are very happy:** Brooks, *Gross National Happiness*, p. 177.

231. **A study . . . showed a sunnier state of mind in those who volunteered than those who turned down the opportunity:** P. Dulin and
R. Hill, "Relationships Between Altruistic Activity and Positive and Negative Affect Among Low-Income Older Adult Service Providers," *Aging &
Mental Health* 7, no. 4 (2003), pp. 294–99.

232. **compared with other countries:** Charities Aid Foundation,
"International Comparisons of Charitable Giving," CAF Briefing Paper,
November 2006.

232. **The Charities Aid Foundation concluded:** Ibid., p. 2.

233. **A careful study by Jonathan Gruber and Daniel Hungerman
concluded:** Jonathan Gruber and Daniel M. Hungerman, "Faith-based
Charity and Crowd Out During the Great Depression," *Journal of Public
Economics* 91, nos. 5–6 (June 2007), pp. 1043–69. Note that Gruber is not
known as an enemy of government programs and has been a key adviser
to advocates of government-sponsored health care plans.

234. **Charitable giving soared:** Richard B. McKenzie, "Was the Decade of the 1980s a 'Decade of Greed'?" St. Louis: Center for the Study of
American Business, Washington University (July 1991).

235. **You might take a moment to go to the Web site:** ww5
.komen.org/AboutUs/SusanGKomensStory.html.

236. **As Jane Nathanson, a longtime trustee of the Los Angeles
Museum of Contemporary Art, explained:** Jennifer Steinhauer, "Wielding Iron Checkbook to Shape Cultural Los Angeles," *New York Times*, February 8, 2010, p. C5.

236. **The institute revealed:** *ABC News*, "Failing to Serve America's
Heroes on the Home Front," November 9, 2007.

236. *Time* **named the Charity Navigator Web site one of the "coolest" fifty:** "50 Coolest Websites for 2006," *Time*, August 2006.

237. **Thomas Loving (his real name) at the University of Texas, Austin, found:** Timothy J. Loving, Erin E. Crockett, Aubri A. Paxson, "Passionate Love and Relationship Thinkers," *Psychoneuroendocrinology* 34, no. 6 (July 2009), pp. 939–46.

238. **A recent article in *Men's Health* recommended:** Lisa Haney, "Take Her Outside," *Men's Health* (May 2010), p. 117.

238. **A study in the *American Sociological Review* reported:** Janet Kornblum, "Study: 25% of Americans Have No One to Confide In," *USA Today*, June 22, 2006.

240. **Andre Agassi in his remarkable memoir admits:** Andre Agassi, *Open* (New York: Knopf, 2009), p. 139.

243. **As Albert O. Hirschman noted:** Albert O. Hirschman, *The Passions and the Interests* (Princeton: Princeton University Press, 1977).

INDEX

and emotions, 40–41, 46–49,
    49–50, 52–57
and entrepreneurship, 45–46
and evolution, 45, 50
and external stimulus, 57–60
and genetics, 41–42, 65–66
limbic brain, 40–41, 100
mammalian brain, 40–41
neocortical brain, 41, 44
regions of the brain, 40–42
and risk assessment, 228
and Rule of Repeats, 149
and sports, 162–64
and time perception, 42–45
See also neurotransmitters
branding, 160, 229–30
Brave New World (Huxley), 101
Brickman, Marshall, 217–18
Brickman, Philip, 17
Broad, Eli, 236
Brokaw, Tom, 174
Bronson, Po, 211
Bronze Age, 130
Brooks, Arthur, 82, 120
Brooks, David, 180–81
Bryson, Bill, 42
Bublé, Michael, 149
Buchholz Hypothesis, 130
Buddhism, 5–6, 9, 16, 21
Buffett, Warren, 135
Bunco parties, 239
Burroughs, Edgar Rice, 11
Bush, George W., 132
Bushmen culture, 183–84

Cadillac, 199
Cage, John, 77
Cain and Abel, 136
Callas, Maria, 174–75
Calvinists, 36
Campbell, Donald T., 17
Canada, 186
cancer treatment, 235
cannibalism, 107
Cannon, Walter, 172
capitalism, 5–8, 125–26, 226. *See also*
    free market economics
captivity, 99–100
caretaking behavior, 102
cargo cults, 184

Cartagena, Colombia, 181
Carter, Jimmy, 21
Carvey, Dana, 72
Catholic Church, 124
cause and effect, 71
CCK (cholecystokinin), 61
celebrities, 78–79
cerebral cortex, 53
Chaney, Lon, 49–50
Charities Aid Foundation, 232
charity, 35, 57, 135–36, 231–34,
    234–37
Charity Navigator, 236–37
chastity vows, 16
Chavez, Hugo, 181, 187
Chevrolet, 199
children
    and control of their environment,
        69, 71–72
    and education, 209
    and folktales, 210
    one-child policies, 154
    and touch, 240
    and work/play preference, 118–19
chimpanzees, 97–100, 125, 133–34
China, 25, 153–54
choice, 70, 160–61, 172–73
Chopra, Deepak, 96
Chrysler, 197
Churchill, Winston, 86, 125
Cinnabon company, 30
Civil War, 136
Clark, Gregory, 154, 158
Cleaver, Eldridge, 99
Cloninger, C. Robert, 211–12
coal mining, 117
Coase, Ronald, 225
cognitive controller, 228
Cohen, Randy, 153
collective memory, 12
Colon, Panama, 180
colonialism, 154
comedy, 171
commodity pricing, 201
communal societies, 156
communitarianism, 66, 159
companionship, 89
competition
    and brain physiology, 50, 58
    and charity, 100–103, 234–37